HEALTH FOOD COOKBOOK

HEALTH FOOD COOKBOOK

Jackie Burrow & Mary Norwak

Octopus

NOTES

Standard tablespoon and teaspoon measurements are used in all recipes. All spoon measures are level.

Fresh herbs are used unless otherwise stated. If unobtainable substitute a bouquet garni of the equivalent dried herbs, or use dried herbs instead but halve the quantities stated.

Home-made stock should be used whenever possible. Beef, chicken or ham stocks give the best flavor, but for vegetarian diets use vegetable stock or add Brewer's yeast to water.

If compressed yeast is unobtainable substitute active dry yeast and reduce the quantity accordingly.
$1^1/_2$ packages active dry yeast = 1 oz cake compressed yeast.

Ovens should be preheated to the specified temperature.

First published 1979 by
Octopus Books Limited
59 Grosvenor Street,
London W1

© 1979 Octopus Books Limited
ISBN 7064 0937 X

Produced by Mandarin Publishers Limited
22a Westlands Road
Quarry Bay, Hong Kong

Printed in Spain by Artes Graficas Toledo
Depósito legal: TO. 636-1979

CONTENTS

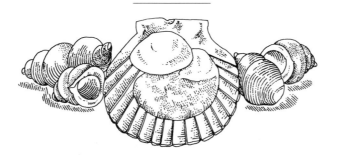

INTRODUCTION

A guide to nutrition and meal planning

Suggest eating health foods to many people and their reaction is one of horror and their comments something like 'It's so dull and unappetizing'. What many of them are doing is confusing eating healthily with a strict, limiting diet.

What we really do when we eat health foods is to ensure that we get a varied, well-balanced diet, essential for our good health. Simply, we eat the *best* foods for us.

In our present-day society, malnutrition is rare – rickets and scurvy are almost things of the past – but we still need good food in order to live. Food provides us with energy to work and keep warm; helps with the growth and repair of the body; and

helps to control the body functions. The foods essential to good health are readily available to us all, but the pace at which we live means that we don't always get the best from them. More and more we rely on pre-packaged convenience foods, which cannot provide all the goodness of their fresh equivalents. Or we prepare fresh foods hastily, thus destroying some of their value.

The aim of this book is to outline the benefits of a healthy eating pattern and to show how relatively quick and easy healthy eating can be. Most of all, we aim to prove – with a selection of tempting recipes – that healthy eating is anything but dull!

Nutrients in food

Food is composed of various nutrients which the body needs in order to keep healthy. There are five types of essential nutrients, each of which plays a special part in maintaining health. To ensure that the body receives these nutrients in the required proportions, it is important to follow a balanced diet.

In the following chart these nutrients are identified and their main sources are listed.

Nutrient	Functions	Deficiency Symptoms	Prime Food Sources	Special Points
CARBO-HYDRATES	Provide the body with energy for work and warmth. May also be converted into body fat.	Reduced stamina and energy.		
Sugar Carbohydrates	These provide a source of quick energy, but most of their prime food sources contribute little else in the way of nutrients and are therefore very fattening.		Sugars (all types), honey, jam, syrup, dried fruit, bananas.	Excessive consumption of sugar promotes tooth decay.
Starch Carbohydrates	In addition to carbo-hydrate, starch foods also contain vegetable protein and useful amounts of minerals and B group vitamins.		Flour, bread, cereals, pasta, rice, potatoes, pulses.	
Cellulose	This carbohydrate cannot be digested by the human body but it adds valuable bulk to the diet and aids bowel movement.	Constipation	Wholegrain cereals, raw vegetables, fruit, bran	A wholefood diet provides plenty of cellulose.
FATS	Provide the body with energy for work and warmth. May also form body fat. Supply fat-soluble vitamins A, D and E.	Reduced energy, bad skin, possible lack of fat-soluble vitamins.	*Butter, *processed cooking fats and margarines, *lard, *suet, *fat in meat, *cream, *milk, *cheese, *egg yolk, soft margarines, vegetable oils, oily fish (herrings, etc.)	Fats provide twice as much energy as carbohydrates. Fats high in saturated fatty acids (denoted*) are con-sidered less preferable from a health viewpoint.
PROTEINS	Provide materials for growth and repair of body tissues. They can also provide energy and can sometimes be converted into fat.	Retarded growth and development, increased susceptibility to disease.		As protein is necessary for growth, it is essential that children and pregnant women obtain an adequate amount.
Animal proteins	These contain all the essential amino acids in satisfactory proportions for human needs.		Meat, fish, eggs, milk, cheese.	
Plant proteins	These are deficient in one or more of the amino acids required by the body.		Cereals, bread, flour, pulses, nuts.	By eating a mixture of these at the same meal, it is possible to obtain an adequate intake of all the essential amino acids.
MINERALS	Provide material for growth and repair of the body, and for control of the body processes.			

Calcium	Required for proper development and growth of bones and teeth; muscle and blood. Especially important for pregnant women and children.	Reduced growth, badly formed teeth, rickets.	Milk, cheese, sardines, bread.	Vitamin D helps the absorption of calcium.
Iron	Essential for blood functioning; it is present in haemoglobin which is necessary for the transport of oxygen in the body.	Fatigue, anaemia.	Liver, kidney, beef, eggs, cocoa powder, dried fruit, green vegetables.	Vitamin C helps the absorption of Iron.
Sodium	Essential for maintaining the normal balance of body fluids.	Muscular cramps.	Salt, bacon, ham, saltwater fish, cheese, bread, butter.	Extra salt is required after strenuous exercise and in hot weather to replace loss in perspiration.
Iodine	For production of thyroid hormones.	Stunted growth in children; goitre in adults.	Saltwater fish, iodized salt, watercress.	
VITAMINS	Regulate the metabolic processes. Important for energy utilization, growth, repair and protection.			
Vitamin A	Protects surface tissues, including hair, nails, skin and eyes. Important for eyesight. Necessary for growth of children.	Infection of eyes, respiratory tract and skin. Poor vision at night. Retarded growth.	Fish liver oils, liver, butter, margarine, cheese, eggs, herrings, sardines, almonds, peanuts.	Can be stored by the body so a daily intake is not absolutely essential.
Carotene	Converted into Vitamin A in the body.	(As Vitamin A)	Carrots, spinach, water-cress, dried apricots, tomatoes, cabbage, peas.	
Vitamin B group	B vitamins – thiamine, riboflavine and nicotinic acid form essential links in the chain of processes by which the body obtains energy from food. The other B group vitamins are also involved in metabolism.	B vitamins are generally found together in the same foods, so a dietry deficiency of one vitamin is unlikely and symptoms would probably reflect a multiple deficiency. Growth of children is checked. General weakening of body: depression, fatigue, inflamed skin, tongue and eyes; nervous disorders.	Yeast extract (Brewer's yeast) wholewheat bread, wheatgerm, cereals, liver, beef, pork, bacon, cheese, fish, pulses.	Cannot be stored by the body so a daily intake is essential. B vitamins are water-soluble and may be lost in cooking liquid.
Vitamin C	Concerned with growth and repair of tissues. Important for body's resistance to infection.	Depression, low resistance to infection, poor skin and slow healing of wounds. Chronic deficiency results in the disease scurvy.	Fresh fruit and vegetables, especially blackcurrants, lemons, oranges, grape-fruit, rose hips, Brussels sprouts, cauliflower, cabbage, parsley, tomatoes, lettuce.	Cannot be stored by the body so a daily intake is essential. Vitamin C dissolves in water and much is lost in cooking. Further losses occur after cutting foods.
Vitamin D	Important for the absorp-tion and laying down of calcium in the bones. Especially important for developing children and expectant mothers.	Poor teeth and bones. Rickets in children.	Cod liver oil, oily fish, liver, eggs, milk, butter, margarine.	Vitamin D is also produced by the action of the sun's rays on the skin. It can be stored by the body.

The Essential Nutrients

Once it is known which essential nutrients are contained in which foods, a balanced diet can be planned, but it is also useful to know a little more about how the nutrients work.

Carbohydrates

Energy can be provided by carbohydrates, fats and proteins. However, proteins are also needed for growth and maintenance of body tissues. It is therefore important, particularly for growing children, to have an adequate intake of carbohydrate to ensure that proteins are used mainly for body building rather than energy.

Sugar carbohydrates (see page 8) provide quick energy: a spoonful of glucose will give you a lift when you're flagging but little else, and if this energy is not burnt up, then they can cause overweight. People who are slimming often try to cut out *all* carbohydrates for this reason. However, this can be detrimental to health because a small intake of carbohydrate is absolutely essential for the correct breakdown of fat stores.

Starch carbohydrates, such as bread and cereal contain other vital nutrients, such as protein and minerals, and are therefore less fattening than sugar carbohydrates. The third kind of carbohydrate is cellulose, which is indigestible to the human body. Cellulose forms the cell walls of fruit and vegetables; it is also found in unrefined cereals and nuts. Although it cannot be digested, it is important as roughage in the diet.

When planning meals, remember that the body needs vitamin B, so that carbohydrates and proteins can be used completely. Also remember to combine carbohydrates and proteins, like cereals with milk, or brown bread with a boiled egg, so that the carbohydrate provides energy while the protein builds and repairs tissue.

Fats

The body uses fats to provide energy and to form body fat for warmth and protection. Fats are a more concentrated energy food than carbohydrate, and anyone who uses a vast amount of energy needs an adequate intake to avoid a very bulky high-carbohydrate diet.

Children need a large amount of energy and, as they only have small stomachs and cannot cope with large quantities of carbohydrates, it is important that they have sufficient fat – in the form of milk, cheese and egg yolks, for example.

Fats are also important because they contain vitamins, particularly A and D. They are digested more slowly than carbohydrates, and do not provide such a quick energy source.

Proteins

Protein is necessary for growth. It is thus particularly important for children to eat enough, as it is necessary for developing bones, muscles, skin and blood. However, adults need it for more or less the same reason – in their case, old tissue breaks down and needs to be replaced.

Proteins are composed of amino acids – there are twenty-two of these commonly found in foods, eight of which are essential for the adult and ten for the growing child. These 'essential amino acids' must be supplied by the foods we eat. Protein from animal sources usually contains all the essential amino acids; vegetable proteins are normally deficient in some essential amino acids. If all animal foods are excluded from the diet, it must be carefully planned to ensure an adequate protein intake.

VALUABLE SOURCES OF VITAMIN C: tomatoes, lemons, tangerines, new potatoes, Brussels sprouts, strawberries, blackcurrants, rose hip syrup, oranges and grapefruit.

Minerals

A variety of minerals are essential to the body, but most of them are required only in minute quantities. The four most important minerals are calcium, iron, iodine and sodium.

Calcium is necessary for bones and teeth; children, who are growing and forming new bones and teeth, require more than adults. An adult body contains about 1 kg (2 lb) calcium, while a baby has only about 25 g (1 oz), so a large amount is accumulated in the growing years. Calcium is also important for muscles and blood functioning. Milk and cheese provide most of the calcium we need: 75 g (3 oz) Cheddar cheese contains as much calcium as 600 ml (1 pint) milk.

Iron is present in the haemoglobin of the blood. The amount of iron found in the body is only enough to make a very small nail, but it is very important; if you don't have enough iron in your food anaemia can develop.

Iodine is needed in a tiny quantity, to help the thyroid gland work properly; this gland controls the rate at which chemical changes take place in the body. If there is not enough iodine in the diet the thyroid gland becomes enlarged. Lack of iodine in children can adversely affect their development.

Sodium or salt is essential for body fluids. It is lost from the body in sweat and must be replaced.

Vitamins

Vitamins are only present in very small amounts in food, but they are vital to the body – it cannot live without any one of them. They help the body to use the other nutrients in food, and protect it from illness. A good mixed diet will provide all the necessary vitamins. However, doctors may recommend that small children and expectant mothers take supplements of vitamins A and D, in particular. Only the correct amount of supplements should be taken, as the body stores excess vitamins A and D and it is possible to accumulate too much, resulting in illness.

Vitamin A is essential for growth; it helps the formation of bones and teeth, keeps skin and eyes healthy, and helps eye sight. It also keeps the throat and breathing passages in good working order. Vitamin A is present in animal foods which are rich in fat, and in some fruit and vegetables in the form of carotene, which is converted into vitamin A in the body. All red, orange and dark green fruits and vegetables contain carotene.

Vitamin D is contained in fat-rich animal foods and is also produced from the action of sunshine on the skin. It works in conjunction with calcium and phosphorus to build up bones and teeth.

Vitamin B group comprises a number of vitamins which are vital for metabolic processes, especially obtaining energy from carbohydrates. They cannot be stored in the body and must be taken every day.

Vitamin C, also known as ascorbic acid, is essential for general health and growth and also helps wounds to heal and broken bones to mend. Found in fruit and vegetables, it is easily destroyed. When plant cells are broken down, either by cutting or cooking, an enzyme is released which destroys vitamin C. Vegetables should therefore be cooked very quickly in a little boiling water, as this destroys the enzyme. Bicarbonate of soda (baking soda) also destroys vitamin C and should therefore never be added to the cooking water.

VALUABLE SOURCES OF IRON: spinach, kidneys, steak, watercress, wholewheat bread, dried apples, dried figs, dried apricots, dates and broccoli.

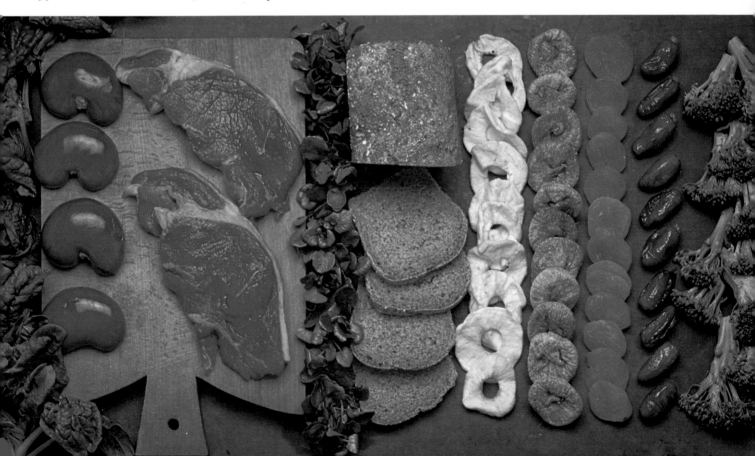

Valuable foods

A balanced healthy diet should contain those foods which are nutritionally most beneficial to us. The range of these 'valuable foods' is enormous and, by basing our diet on a wide selection of them, we obtain the variety necessary to maintain our enjoyment of food – as well as a healthy eating pattern.

Cereals are a rich source of carbohydrate and therefore provide the body with energy. They also contain small amounts of useful vegetable protein and B group vitamins. The main dietary cereals are wheat, maize (corn), barley, oats, rice and rye, and their carbohydrate content ranges from about 66 per cent (oats) to 72 per cent (rye). They store well, are relatively cheap to buy, and can be combined with many other ingredients to give quick and easy meals.

As cereals are mainly carbohydrate, they are more beneficial eaten with a protein food. For example, breakfast cereal with milk provides a good balance of carbohydrate and protein. Furthermore, the protein value of the cereal is greater than if it were eaten on its own because milk supplies the amino acids which are deficient in cereal.

Breakfast cereals often have extra vitamins and minerals added, so even if this is all you eat in the morning – plus fruit for vitamin C – you will still obtain a healthy supply of nutrients.

Calcium, iron and some group B vitamins are added to flour – so bread, too, is good for you: it provides a valuable staple food containing carbohydrate, vegetable protein and fat, as well as the vitamins and minerals added to the flour.

Meat and offal (variety meats) are concentrated sources of protein and a variety of vitamins and minerals. Meat does, however, contain a proportion of fat under the skin and distributed between the muscle fibres.

Pork, ham and bacon are particularly rich in thiamine.

Liver is a particularly valuable food in the diet: 100 g (4 oz) calf's (veal) liver yields 45 per cent of the recommended daily ten times as much as cod.

Liver is a particularly valuable food in the diet: 100 g (4 oz) calf's (veal) liver yields 45 per cent of the recommended daily intake of protein – as well as enough iron, vitamin A and riboflavin for two days. It also contains vitamins C and D. Tongue, sweetbreads and tripe are other excellent sources of protein and are all easily digested; tripe also provides calcium. Heart and kidneys are again prime sources of protein and B group vitamins; kidneys are also a rich source of iron.

All offal (variety meat) is relatively fat-free and thus plays an important part in low-fat diets.

Fish is rich in animal protein, sodium, iodine and nicotinic acid. It is therefore a highly nutritious protein food, and is more tender and easily digested than meat.

Oily fish, such as herring and mackerel, are very popular and useful in the diet, providing a valuable source of protein, unsaturated fat, calcium, iron, vitamin D and the B group vitamins – riboflavin and nicotinic acid. Oil, containing vitamins A and D, is distributed throughout the flesh of these fish while most other varieties of fish only have oil in the liver which is not normally eaten. Cod and halibut liver oil are thus concentrated sources of the oil-soluble vitamins A and D, and are sometimes used as dietry supplements. Canned salmon and sardines are rich sources of protein and vitamin B group; if the bones are eaten too, they are excellent sources of calcium and phosphorus.

Shellfish – such as crabs, lobsters, prawns and shrimps – also provide protein, fat and iodine. Molluscs such as oysters, mussels and scallops, are not of such great food value, though they are useful sources of vitamins and minerals.

Milk is sometimes called the perfect food. It provides sufficient quantities of most of the essential nutrients in an easily digested form. It is therefore particularly valuable for babies, small children and invalids, but it is an excellent food for everybody. Milk does, however, lack iron, and is deficient in vitamin C, so these nutrients must be supplied by other sources.

Cheese retains the valuable constituents of milk and is a valuable source of protein, fat, calcium, vitamin A and riboflavin. Hard cheeses (Cheddar, Gruyère, etc.) are composed of about one-third protein, one-third fat and one-third water. Because of the high fat content, some people find cheese hard to digest but grated cheese is more easily digested and can be combined with a variety of other foods – in salads or cooked dishes.

Eggs are rich in animal protein and egg yolk contains plenty of iron; eggs are also useful sources of vitamins A, D and the B group vitamins. However, they are also a concentrated source of fat and cholesterol, and should be eaten in moderation by those on a low-cholesterol or low-fat diet.

Vegetables play an important part in the diet. Besides adding variety and colour to meals, they provide valuable fibre, minerals and vitamins A and C. They also contain protein and starch.

The nutritional content of vegetables varies considerably. As a rough guide, the green leafy vegetables are high in vitamin C – especially broccoli, kale, Brussels sprouts, peppers, cabbage, cauliflower, spinach and watercress. These vegetables also provide vitamin A in the form of carotene, some B group vitamins, iron, calcium and other minerals.

Root vegetables, especially carrots, are very rich in carotene. Potatoes are, of course, high in starch; although not particularly high in vitamin C, they provide an important source for those who consume large quantities. Potatoes also yield useful amounts of protein, iron and some B group vitamins. Pulses (legumes) are a rich source of vegetable protein, energy and other nutrients and are particularly valuable in a vegetarian diet.

Ideally, vegetables should be eaten absolutely fresh, and raw as often as possible. Nutritive value is normally reduced during storage, preservation, preparation and cooking. Vitamin C and the water-soluble B vitamins are most susceptible to loss.

Fruit is a good source of vitamin C and provides us with valuable roughage; some fruits also contain vitamin A. Rosehips, blackcurrants, redcurrants and strawberries are very rich in vitamin C; oranges, lemons, grapefruit, raspberries, gooseberries and loganberries are good sources; bananas, melon and tangerines only provide a little, while apples, pears and plums are poor sources. Vitamin C is easily lost in cooking, so eat fruit raw whenever possible. Vitamin A is found in small quantities in apricots, tomatoes and peaches.

Dried fruits are a rich source of energy and add flavour to both sweet and savoury dishes. Although the dehydration process destroys practically all vitamin C, most dried fruits are useful sources of other vitamins and minerals. Prunes and dried apricots, for example, are useful sources of carotene; dried figs supply protein and B group vitamins, as well as fibre and energy.

Nuts are highly nutritious. They are a rich source of vegetable protein and energy, and contain useful amounts of B group vitamins, iron and calcium.

Our Daily Needs

Everyone needs adequate protein, vitamins, minerals and energy to keep healthy. The main sources of each nutrient have already been discussed. To make sure that you are obtaining a balanced diet, eat some food from each of the following food groups every day:

Group 1: meat, fish, poultry and eggs*
Group 2: milk, cheese and yogurt*
Group 3: fruit and vegetables
Group 4: bread and cereals
Group 5: fats

* Vegetarians, particularly those who do not eat foods in either groups 1 or 2, should include a variety of vegetable protein foods – pulses (legumes), cereals, nuts etc. – instead.

Avoid sugary foods, such as sweets and cakes, as far as possible, and remember that the foods in groups 1 and 2 are also a source of fats (group 5).

Every person's needs are slightly different and this must be borne in mind when cooking for a family.

Young children

Children up to primary school age are growing fast and need plenty of protein, calcium, iron and vitamins. They also use a great deal of energy, but it is important to avoid supplying this in the form of sugar carbohydrates. Too many sweets, sugary cakes and sweet biscuits are detrimental to teeth – especially when eaten between meals. These foods tend to create a 'sweet tooth' which reduces the appetite for other foods rich in the vital nutrients needed for health and growth. Try to satisfy children's energy requirements with other carbohydrate sources; the chapter on Wholegrain baking provides plenty of healthy alternatives.

To establish good eating habits, avoid giving children snacks between meals as far as possible. If they are hungry, provide fruit, cheese or nuts, rather than sweets or biscuits (cookies).

Milk is not a perfect food for the growing child because it lacks iron, but it is an excellent source of other nutrients – especially protein and calcium. Babies are usually born with a store of iron which will last several months; when this supply is exhausted they need to be fed small amounts of other foods which contain iron, such as egg yolk or puréed spinach. Toddlers who refuse to drink milk on its own may well enjoy a milkshake, prepared with puréed fruit, honey and milk, such as Banana flip (page 29). Small children should be encouraged to eat plenty of fruit and vegetables; a lack of these may lower their resistance to colds and other infections. For children who don't like fresh vegetables, try serving them in a sauce or in wholewheat pancakes (crêpes); for example Broccoli pancakes (crêpes) (page 103).

Teenagers

Many children have very large appetites when they reach adolescence, not surprisingly since their nutrient requirements are high. It is most important that teenagers satisfy their

appetites with well balanced meals. Too many of them consume large quantities of 'empty calorie foods', like sweets and crisps. As a result they develop spotty skins and some have a weight problem. Girls often become figure conscious at this age and develop food fads. Often they cut out breakfast in an attempt to slim, then become so hungry by mid-morning that they resort to mid-morning empty-calorie snacks.

Always try to persuade children to eat breakfast and encourage them to eat plenty of raw fruits, vegetables and high protein foods.

The elderly

Because the elderly are less active, their energy needs are lower than those of younger adults, so they require less of the energy-giving foods – fats and carbohydrates. Older bodies do not digest food as quickly, or absorb nutrients as effectively, so it is particularly important for elderly people to have a carefully balanced diet, which provides enough of the nutrients required to maintain and repair the body tissues, without excess energy. Meals should therefore be based primarily on protein foods, fresh fruit and vegetables. Fish and eggs are more easily digested than meat; cheese, yogurt, milk, liver and kidney are also valuable and can be purchased in small quantities.

Elderly people usually have smaller appetites because they are less active, and are often tempted to nibble at biscuits (cookies) rather than prepare fresh and balanced meals daily. This can result in nutrient deficiencies and must be avoided.

DAILY SUMMER MENU (see page 150): Breakfast – Muesli; Lunch – Baked Crab, Peach yogurt shake; Dinner – Cucumber, lemon and mint soup, Spring beef casserole, Hot berry snow.

Pregnancy

The idea of 'eating for two' during pregnancy is old-fashioned and ill-advised. Stoking up on carbohydrate foods when expecting a baby will only result in excess weight gain; doctors recommend that weight should increase by only 11 kg (24 lb) during the total pregnancy period. A carefully balanced diet is the answer. Pregnant women require extra iron, calcium and vitamin C. Liver, kidney, eggs, milk, cheese, yogurt, fish, fresh vegetables and fruit will supply these extra nutrients.

At work all day

Anyone who goes to work needs a good breakfast; even if it has to be a quick one. A carefully balanced evening meal is also important. Lunchtime can be a problem though, particularly if heavy business meals are regularly eaten or if a meal has to be taken to work. Packed lunches can, however, be as nutritious as other meals, providing the ingredients are chosen carefully (see page 19). When eating out at lunchtime, try to avoid the high energy foods on the menu and don't drink too much alcohol with your meal – as it is also full of 'empty calories'!

Dietary Considerations

Cholesterol, insufficient fibre and excess calorie intake are sometimes termed 'The diseases of the modern Western diet', yet the reasons for the description are frequently misunderstood.

Dietary Fibre

The fibrous part of plant foods, called cellulose, is a starch carbohydrate. It was once thought to be useless to the body because it cannot be digested but it is now accepted that this dietary fibre provides the roughage which is essential to the healthy working of the digestive system. Fibre carries plenty of moisture and cleans the intestine and bowels, thus helping to eliminate waste products of the foods we eat.

Many of today's foods are preserved or processed in such a way that the fibre originally present is lost. For example, all the fibre supplied by the bran in cereal is lost when white flour is refined. It is therefore important to avoid over-refined foods as much as possible. Choose wholewheat bread and flour in preference to refined varieties and eat plenty of fresh fruit and vegetables, particularly the outer leaves and skins.

Cholesterol

This is a fatty substance which is essential to the body. It is present in all body cells and body fluids, including blood. It is a normal constituent of animal tissue, so that all food of animal origin may contain it. The body manufactures all of the cholesterol it requires so a dietary intake is not essential.

Cholesterol-rich foods include egg yolk, dairy produce, brains, liver and kidney. Plants contain no cholesterol and therefore neither do vegetable oils.

Studies indicate that a high blood cholesterol level increases the risk of coronary disease. In view of this, it is wise to know a little about the various types of fat we use in our diet. Fats are composed of fatty acids which may be 'saturated' or 'unsaturated'. Saturated fatty acids markedly raise the blood cholesterol level; these saturated fatty acids form a large proportion of animal fats, such as butter, lard and beef fat.

Unsaturated fatty acids do not raise the blood cholesterol level and highly unsaturated ones, called 'polyunsaturated fatty acids', actually tend to lower the level. Vegetable oils, particularly soy bean, sunflower and cotton seed oil, and vegetable margarine, contain a high proportion of polyunsaturated fatty acids. By using these vegetable fats in preference to animal fats it is possible to lower the blood cholesterol level considerably, which is highly beneficial for health.

If cholesterol intake has to be cut down for health reasons, the total amount of fat eaten – including food prepared from fats, such as ice-cream and pastry – must be cut. Dairy produce and eggs should be restricted, and chicken, veal and fish eaten instead of pork, lamb and beef. Vegetable oils may be used for cooking, and vegetable margarine may be used for baking and spreading.

Vegetable fats provide as many calories as animal fats and should also be cut down if calorie intake is to be restricted.

Calories

The amount of energy provided by the food we eat is measured in calories. Energy is required to maintain the normal processes of the body, such as breathing, heartbeat and circulation. On average, a woman uses 1300 to 1400 calories a day, and a man uses about 1600 to 1800 calories simply staying alive. In addition, about 700 to 1200 calories are needed for everyday activities, such as standing, walking, eating or running.

The energy we obtain from the food we eat should balance the energy used; if it doesn't the surplus calories will be converted into fat and stored in the body.

Starches, sugars and proteins yield 4 calories per gram, while fats – a more concentrated form of energy – supply 9 calories per gram. By using these values the energy content of any food can be calculated from the proportion of nutrients it contains. So-called 'empty' calorie foods, such as sugar, simply provide energy but no other nutrients. The food value table (pages 155-9) provides a comprehensive list of food calorie values – a useful reference for those who are concerned about their weight. By following a diet which provides less calories than needed, surplus fat is used up as energy and you are on the way to a slimmer figure. (See also page 10.)

Vegetarianism

Vegetarianism is frequently associated with food faddism, yet the vegetarian diet can be a perfectly acceptable one. Most people in the Western world who choose to follow a vegetarian diet, do so either because they feel it is ethically wrong to eat flesh, or because they simply find meat unpalatable.

There are two main types of vegetarian diet. The vegan diet excludes all food from animal sources, including dairy produce. Their sources of protein are therefore restricted to cereals, nuts, pulses (legumes) and other vegetables. Lacto-vegetarians will, however, eat milk, cheese and eggs.

A vegetarian diet can supply all the necessary nutrients, but it must be carefully planned to do so. Vegans, in particular, must eat an assortment of vegetable proteins at each meal to ensure that they obtain an adequate supply of all the essential amino acids. Vegetable proteins may be incomplete eaten alone, but they are perfectly capable of supplementing each other's amino acid deficiencies when eaten together. Essential minerals, vitamins and fats can be provided from vegetable sources, but care must be taken that sufficient iron is included in the diet.

PACKED LUNCH: Prawn
(shrimp) quiche (page 50);
Potato and courgette (zucchini)
salad (page 76); wholewheat
bread and fruit.

Planning your Meals

Many people do not bother to plan meals ahead because they feel it is not worth the effort and they don't have time anyway. But planning several meals at a time – ideally, for a week – need only take a few minutes to do and can actually save you time in the long run. If you know what you're going to cook for the following few days, you can shop just once and avoid waste. Most important, you can ensure that all essential nutritional needs are met, and such mineral rich foods as liver and oily fish are included regularly. Planning ahead is likely to provide more interesting and varied meals, as well as more healthy ones.

Three meals a day – breakfast, a light meal and a main meal – should be sufficient for a healthy, balanced diet. A milk drink at bedtime will encourage a good night's sleep.

Too busy to cook

All too frequently there doesn't seem to be a spare minute to cook, or the effort involved hardly seems worthwhile. The answer is often a quick high-calorie snack which may give instant energy and sustain appetite for a while, but, as a habit, it may build up overweight.

If life is always hectic, try to build up a regular meal pattern so that some dishes can be prepared in advance when there is time for cooking. If there's no time to cook vegetables, wholewheat bread and a crunchy vegetable salad are delicious replacements. When an instant snack is inevitable, choose fruit, cheese and wholewheat bread, rather than sweets, crisps (fries) or biscuits (cookies).

Breakfast

So often this first meal of the day is rushed or missed completely. But it is important to start the day with breakfast – to provide the body with sufficient energy to last the morning, and avoid the temptation of a mid-morning snack.

Breakfast need not be a heavy meal, or take long to prepare. Fresh fruit or fruit juice, wholewheat toast, an egg and a drink will provide a well-balanced meal. Cereals are popular, especially with children; accompany them with a hot milk drink – such as cocoa or drinking chocolate which will add valuable iron – and they will have a good start to the day.

Light meal

This may be eaten at midday or in the evening. Include eggs, or cheese – in wholewheat sandwiches or toasted snacks – if they haven't been served at another meal. Wholewheat flans, a cheeseboard, or pancakes (crêpes) with savoury fillings will provide a tasty, nourishing meal. Finish with fresh fruit or yogurt and a refreshing drink. If time is again a problem, a meal-in-a-glass is an excellent quick nourishing snack.

Main meal

Each main meal should contain some foods rich in protein and plenty of fruit and vegetables, as these are rich sources of vitamins and minerals. If serving a first course, keep it simple – clear soup, grapefruit, fruit juice or salad. For the main course, include a wide variety of dishes in your weekly menu – casseroles, grilled (broiled) meat, fish, egg and cheese dishes. Make sure that meat is lean and aim to serve offal (variety meats) once a week. Always serve vegetables or salad – as an accompaniment – if they do not form the basis of the main course. Complete the meal with cheese and fresh fruit as often as possible. Limit rich puddings and cream to special occasions, and avoid over-sweetening desserts.

Single meals

It is not difficult to plan well-balanced meals for a family, but catering for oneself can create problems. Some single people take great pleasure in cooking for themselves, but many find it a chore and rely on convenience foods, pre-packed meals or carbohydrate snacks instead. The occasional snack meal, lacking in nutritional value, rarely does any harm because dietry needs are usually made up later in the day. However, if badly planned meals are eaten regularly, they can become detrimental to health. Even on a shoestring budget, it is still possible to enjoy nutritionally sound meals.

Look at the list of five basic food groups (see page 14) and see which foods can be bought in small portions, and which will store well. In group one, for example, meat may be expensive, or not obtainable in small enough portions, but a single chicken quarter, a portion of liver, kidneys and eggs are all relatively cheap and can be cooked in a variety of appetizing ways. Cheese and yogurt can also be bought in small quantities. Margarine keeps well and can be used for spreading as well as cooking, while a stock of cereals, crispbreads and pulses (legumes) is also useful and can be stored easily. Only fruit and vegetables need to be bought regularly.

Most of the recipes in this book can be prepared in small quantities, or used for several meals. All of the breakfast dishes are easily adapted for single portions and many are suitable for other meals, too. Salads are good for an individual meal – especially if they contain a protein food.

A dessert always makes a meal on your own more appealing, and if you halve the recipes in the fruit and nuts chapter there will be enough for two meals. Try to make a single meal more interesting too, by starting with fruit juice, for example.

Office meals

Canteen meals tend to be stodgy, pub snacks are usually inadequate, and restaurant meals are expensive, so the answer to a workday lunch is often something eaten at a desk. A packed meal can be a nourishing stop-gap between breakfast and the main evening meal. Be sure to eat something at midday, or tiredness ensues and work suffers.

A packed meal doesn't have to be a dull sandwich, nor just a bunch of lettuce leaves. Ideally it should include something from each of the food groups (see page 14). Pack the meal attractively in a polythene (plastic) box to avoid crushing. Use margarine tubs for salads or fruit and take home-made soup in a flask, or buy milk to drink.

Many of the recipes in this book are perfect for packed meals – especially the salads and savoury flans. Finish with fresh fruit and you will have a nourishing, satisfying meal.

School meals

Some children prefer a packed lunch for school, and the same general rules apply as for office meals. Children must have easily-handled food, so sandwiches or bread rolls are ideal, but the filling must be adequate and a good source of protein. Use wholewheat bread sandwiched with eggs, cheese, fish and meat, and avoid sweet fillings like jam or bananas as they are low in protein. Do give plenty of variety during the week so that lunch doesn't become dull and unappetizing. Instead of making sandwiches – for example – provide wholewheat rolls, a hard-boiled (cooked) egg and a wedge of cheese, or fingers of lean cold meat to make a change. Complete the meal with fruit and a yogurt, rather than sweets or chocolate biscuits (cookies).

LIGHT MEAL: Broccoli pancakes (crêpes) (page 103), fruit and cheese.

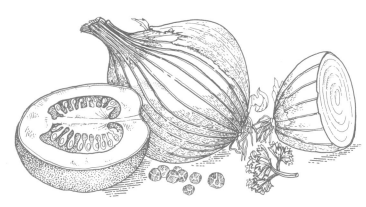

Adding Flavour

One of the problems of changing to a controlled healthy diet is that you may find the food less appetizing at first. When a palate is used to rich sauces and artificial flavours, it is sometimes difficult for it to accept plainly grilled (broiled) meat or fish, simple cakes, or vegetables without butter or creamy dressings, with the same enthusiasm. Careful seasoning and the use of juices, herbs, spices and low-calorie vegetables can, however, make all the difference between a bland diet and one which is tempting but still healthy.

Extracts and pastes

Yeast or meat extracts can be used to flavour gravy or soup, or they may be spread on toast or bread as a base for an egg or cheese topping. If there is a temptation to eat something sweet with a cup of tea or coffee mid-morning or afternoon, try a thin slice of wholewheat toast lightly spread with a savoury extract or anchovy paste instead.

Stock (bouillon) cubes

Stock (bouillon) cubes and powders are available in a variety of flavours to suit most savoury dishes. Home-made stock gives the best flavour, but when none is available a stock (bouillon) cube may be used instead, providing the seasoning is carefully adjusted.

Fruit juices and rinds

Lemon juice is invaluable in the kitchen as it brings out all the natural flavours of the foods with which it is used. A wedge of lemon with fish is a well known accompaniment, but it is also good with veal, chicken and rabbit, and goes well with salads and lightly cooked vegetables. Orange juice is less well-known as an accompaniment, but it may be used for salad dressings and in pork, veal or duck dishes. The sharp juice of Seville oranges is particularly good with fish. Grated orange and lemon rinds also add flavour to dishes as well as providing additional Vitamin C.

Wine, cider and tomato juice

Thick gravy and sauces will not be missed if meat and fish are cooked in a dry wine, dry (hard) cider or tomato juice instead. These give flavour and colour to food, and the alcohol content is negligible as alcohol is driven off during the cooking process. A few drops of dry sherry, stirred in just before serving, will improve a clear soup or gravy.

Sugars and syrups

Refined sugar and syrup sweeten foods but add no particular flavouring. Honey, black treacle (molasses) and natural brown sugars, such as Muscovado and molasses sugar, will add a rich flavour and colour to desserts, cakes and other baked goods.

Vegetables

A few low-calorie vegetables are very useful for adding flavour to savoury dishes. A small quantity of chopped green or red peppers, celery or onions will add colour and texture, while mushrooms or tomatoes make a perfect garnish.

Salt is indispensable in the kitchen for it makes all food more palatable and helps to bring out subtle flavours. Sea salt has the finest flavour; it may be bought in flake form, or finely ground, or it may be freshly ground in a salt mill at the table.

Vanilla is a fragrant pod (bean) which may be used to flavour sugar, milk and desserts. For convenience it is usually bought in its less expensive, and less subtle form – vanilla essence (extract).

Herbs

Fresh, frozen or dried herbs will enhance the flavour of most savoury dishes and some sweet ones. Fresh herbs should preferably be used when available. Dried herbs must be used with discretion as their flavour is less subtle; use half of the recommended quantity of fresh herbs in the recipe. A small selection of the most popular herbs will make a world of difference to simple foods.

Basil has a fairly strong flavour and is delicious with tomatoes, kebabs, fish and seafood. It is also very good sprinkled sparingly on grilled (broiled) meat or fish.

Bay is combined with thyme and parsley in the classic 'bouquet garni', used to flavour all kinds of soups and stews. Bay leaves are also used in marinades, with oily fish, such as mackerel and salmon, and they impart a delicious spicy flavour to milk puddings and egg custards.

Caraway seeds are often used to flavour cakes, but they are delicious in cabbage dishes too.

Chervil looks like rather delicate parsley. It has a refreshing spicy flavour and is good for light soups and egg dishes.

Dill leaves impart a delicious flavour to new potatoes, and to fish. The seeds are used, whole or ground, in lamb stews, soups and in pickled cucumber.

Fennel is sometimes known as 'the fish herb' because its slight flavour of aniseed goes so well with all fish dishes.

Garlic, used with discretion, is a splendid addition to meat and poultry dishes, and to salads. It should be crushed with a little salt to release the full flavour. Garlic powder is available for those who prefer a mild garlic flavour.

Horseradish – grated into cream – is a traditional accompaniment to beef, but it can also be grated and added to beetroot (beet), or coleslaw.

Marjoram has a sweet, slightly spicy flavour which improves stuffings, meat and tomato dishes.

Mint is usually made into a sauce to serve with lamb, but chopped fresh mint is good with new potatoes, peas and vegetable salads, and can also be used in fruit salads.

Oregano is a strongly-flavoured variety of wild marjoram, used extensively in Italian dishes – especially in sauces to serve with pasta.

Parsley is often only used as a garnish, but it can be added generously to many dishes, and it is rich in Vitamin C. Add chopped parsley liberally to soups, sauces and cooked vegetables – especially to broad (lima) beans, peas, potatoes and carrots.

Rosemary has a sweet, pungent flavour. Traditionally used with lamb, it is also good with beef, pork, chicken and white fish.

Sage is a strongly-flavoured herb which goes particularly well with fatty meat, especially pork and duck.

Savory looks like thyme, but gives a more subtle flavour to fish and broad (lima) beans.

Tarragon gives an excellent flavour to chicken, fish and egg dishes. Make tarragon vinegar by steeping a few sprigs in white wine vinegar and use in salad dressing for a subtle flavour.

Thyme is used in bouquet garni and to flavour savoury dishes of all kinds. It has a strong flavour and needs to be used sparingly.

Spices

A hint of spice helps to bring out the flavour in both sweet and savoury dishes. Freshly ground spice has a far better flavour than ready-ground.

Allspice is also known as pimento or Jamaica pepper. It is called allspice because the flavour is like a mixture of cloves, cinnamon and nutmeg. It is not, however, the same as mixed spice.

Cayenne is a hot and stimulating ground pepper.

Cinnamon is a spice from the bark of an evergreen tree.

Ground cinnamon is a favourite flavouring for cakes. Cinnamon sticks gives a subtle flavour to many desserts, savoury dishes and drinks.

Cloves are very pungent and may be used, whole or ground, in sweet and savoury dishes; the flavour goes particularly well with apples.

Curry Powder is a mixture of many spices and varies widely in composition. Many people prefer to grind the different spices freshly and mix them just before use. A pinch of ready-made curry powder will spice up savoury dishes, sauces and salad dressings.

Ginger has a distinctive flavour which is very popular for cakes and biscuits; it is also an important ingredient in curries and Chinese dishes. For a pleasant flavour, sprinkle a little on meat or chicken before grilling (broiling).

Mace is the outer husk of nutmeg and has a similar, though milder flavour. A pinch of mace will help to bring out the flavour of cold meat and poultry dishes.

Nutmeg is used to flavour cakes, desserts and vegetables, as well as hot drinks.

Paprika is made from the fruit of the sweet pepper and has a slightly sweet flavour. It is good in meat and poultry dishes, and its bright red colouring makes it a useful garnish.

Pepper tastes best when freshly ground. Black pepper suits most dishes, but use white pepper in delicate dishes and sauces which will be spoiled by specks of black.

Cooking for Healthy Eating

Having chosen the right foods for a healthy diet, it is just as important to make sure that they are not then ruined by poor preparation and cooking. The most perfect vegetable will be tasteless and of little nutritional value if it is boiled for an hour in a large pan of water; delicate fish will be spoiled if boiled furiously in liquid, or fried in a bath of fat; and crisp, fresh-tasting apples will be unrecognizable if stewed endlessly in sweetened water. For maximum nutrient retention, eat fruit and vegetables raw as often as possible.

It is very easy to become careless about basic cooking methods, and not to bother about the required quantity of cooking liquid, or exact cooking time. To ensure you really do get the optimum value from the dishes in this book, check that you are preparing foods in the best possible way to retain their nutritional value.

Boiling and Simmering

Many foods which are referred to as 'boiled' are best cooked at a temperature below boiling point, termed simmering. Meat, fish and chicken will be tough if boiled fast; the liquid should be brought to boiling point at a steady pace, then the temperature should be lowered so that the liquid only just bubbles – or simmers. Vegetables should be added to boiling water and cooked quickly; always use minimum liquid.

Poaching

This process is similar to simmering, but is even more gentle; the liquid should only just be quivering. This method is used for food of a delicate consistency which would be spoiled by high heat. It is a particularly good way of cooking fish, eggs and fruit so that their texture and shape are retained. The liquid used for poaching can often be used in an accompanying sauce for the finished dish, so that no flavour is lost from the main ingredient.

Stewing

This may take place on top of the cooker in a flameproof casserole or heavy-based saucepan, or in the oven. Meat and vegetables are cooked very gently in just enough liquid to cover them. It is an ideal method for cooking cheaper cuts of meat so that they become really tender. Meat for stewing must have a small quantity of fat otherwise it may become hard and dry during cooking.

For a brown stew, first seal the meat in a little oil; this helps the meat keep its shape and retain all its flavour, as well as lightly colouring the finished casserole. For a white stew, cover the meat with cold water and bring slowly to the boil, then skim off any scum so that the liquid remains clear and the meat is pale. Add vegetables and flavourings when the liquid comes to the boil, then cover and simmer until tender. The latter process is always carried out on top of the cooker.

Braising

This is similar to stewing, but is used for better cuts of meat. The ideal pan to use is an iron casserole so that it can be used on top of the cooker and in the oven. Brown the meat on all sides in a little oil and then remove from the pan. Add a selection of diced vegetables to the pan – onions, carrots, celery, etc. – and cook gently without browning. Place the

meat on top of the vegetables, and add a little liquid – just enough to cover about a quarter of the meat. Cover the pan tightly and simmer for about 45 minutes on top of the cooker, then continue cooking in a moderate oven (170°C/325°F, Gas Mark 3) for about 2 hours. Serve the meat with a gravy made from the pan juices.

Vegetables, such as chicory (endive) and celery hearts, can be braised in a similar way – in a little stock or water, seasoned and flavoured with herbs.

Steaming

This long, slow, thorough method of cooking is especially suitable for vegetables, fish and puddings. The food – cooked in a special steamer over a pan of water and covered with a tight fitting lid – is exposed to and surrounded by concentrated steam. The water in the saucepan must never stop boiling, or cooking ceases, and more boiling water should be added once or twice during cooking.

Roasting

True roasting is carried out in front of an open fire and the meat has to be regularly turned and basted. Today we 'roast' meat in an oven, but this dry all-round heat actually bakes food, and the semblance of a roast is only achieved by basting, which keeps the meat moist and juicy. As the meat is generally surrounded by fat, it is not really suitable for those who wish to avoid animal fats in their diet. The meat can, however, be placed on a rack in the pan so that some of the fat drains away from the meat.

Vegetables such as potatoes, parsnips and onions can be added to the roasting pan to cook in the meat juices. When the meat is cooked, skim the juices and use to make gravy.

Grilling (Broiling)

This is an excellent method of cooking good quality meat, poultry and fish, particularly where fat is to be avoided. When grilling (broiling) red meat – such as steak, lamb chops, liver or kidney – brush lightly with oil and place under a high heat to seal in the juices. Reduce the heat and cook according to taste; if the meat is to be well done, lower the grill (broiler) pan from the heat to prevent it becoming hard and dry. Turn once or twice during cooking, using tongs so that the surface is not pierced and juices released and lost.

White meat – such as veal, chicken or pork – and fish should be grilled (broiled) at a moderate heat throughout. These foods need longer cooking than red meats, and if sealed first, the hard outer surface will prevent heat from reaching the inner meat. Cook them further from the heat, too, to prevent them drying.

The best thickness for grilled meat is about 2.5 cm (1 inch), though fish may obviously be a little thinner. Do not use salt on meat when grilling (broiling) as it tends to harden the meat.

Tomatoes and mushrooms are traditional accompaniments to grilled (broiled) food: place mushrooms on grill (broiler) rack to cook in the meat juices; brush tomatoes lightly with oil and add to the pan when the heat is lowered, or serve raw.

Frying

Frying, as we all know, means cooking food in preheated shallow or deep fat. People who wish to follow a healthy eating pattern should try to avoid fried food, as a certain amount of fat is bound to be absorbed by the food during frying. If you do have to fry food – for example, to brown meat before stewing – then oil is the best frying medium. Heat the oil before adding food, and only fry a little food at a time, as too much will cool the oil and the food will become heavy and greasy; reheat the oil before adding more food. Always drain fried food thoroughly on a wire rack or crumpled kitchen paper towels and serve at once.

The Healthy Way to a Slimmer Figure

Overweight or obesity is simply the result of consuming too much food, the excess being stored as body fat. It is most important to avoid excess weight. Apart from being unattractive and depressing, statistics show that fat people are more likely to suffer from heart disease, circulatory problems, kidney diseases and diabetes. Obesity also aggravates a range of other disorders, such as arthritis, respiratory diseases and back problems.

Extra weight does not, of course, appear overnight; it accumulates over an extended period of eating more food than the body requires. If you are overweight, it does not necessarily mean that you eat a lot but you are eating more than you need. Many factors – such as age, sex, height and the amount of physical activity you do – all affect energy needs, so individual calorie requirements vary considerably. Some people are inclined to put on weight more easily than others simply because they have a low metabolic rate; i.e. they require less energy than most people to maintain basic living processes, such as heartbeat, breathing and circulation. So each person's calorie requirements will be slightly different.

The only way to lose weight is to eat foods which provide less energy than the body needs so that the body will draw on fat reserves for energy. The safest and most effective way to slim is to cut down on energy-rich foods and follow a diet based on fresh wholefoods – rich in the vital nutrients required to keep you healthy. Extra physical activity will also help you to slim – and keep you fit. You could lose weight by disregarding this advice and eating your daily calorie allowance in chocolate, for instance, but you would soon begin to miss some important nutrients and health would inevitably suffer.

Avoid 'crash diets' designed to bring about a rapid weight loss. Followed for a few days they may slim off extra inches for a special occasion but they rarely bring about a permanent weight loss. If crash diets are followed for any length of time they can deprive the body of essential nutrients, resulting in tiredness, irritability and such unpleasant disorders as ketosis.

If you intend to lose a considerable amount of weight, it is always advisable to see a doctor first. For those who want to trim off a little surplus fat – a carefully calorie-controlled diet which includes sufficient quantities of the necessary nutrients will maintain general health.

Calorie Allowances

	Daily calorie needs for weight maintenance	Daily calorie allowance for weight loss
Average Man	2500 to 3500	1400 to 1600
Average Woman	1800 to 2500	1000 to 1200
Active Teenager	2300 to 2800	1400 to 1600

If you stick to the appropriate calorie allowance for weight loss by cutting down on energy-rich foods, your body will draw on fat reserves and you will start to lose weight. About 800 to 1000 calories will be taken from body fat each day, and this should give an average weight loss of 0.5 to 1 kg (1½ to 2lb) each week.

To start with, weight loss is often quite dramatic but then adopts a slower steady rate. The initial quick weight losses are largely fluid losses; subsequent slower losses are generally fat losses.

To check your progress, weigh yourself once or twice a week on the same scales and at roughly the same time of day. After the first week, aim for a gradual weight loss as this is better for health and is more likely to result in a permanently lowered calorie intake.

Planning your slimming diet

Never miss a meal completely – several small meals are better than one large meal each day. When you start dieting, relieve hunger pangs by nibbling small pieces of raw carrot, celery, cucumber, radish and apple. If you have a family to cook for, you can enjoy the dishes in this book, but omit the accompanying potatoes or bread. Don't add extra fat or oil when cooking, leave gravy unthickened, and have fresh fruit instead of a pudding. Eat plenty of citrus fruits, berry fruits, melon, rhubarb, tomatoes, celery, Brussels sprouts, lettuce, cress and cucumber.

Don't try to lose weight by giving up liquids. Water is calorie-free and is needed for normal functioning of the body. Herbal and lemon teas, black coffee, low-calorie fruit juices and low-calorie soft drinks may be taken throughout the day.

Avoid foods which contain starch and sugar. Cut out sweets, jam, sugar in drinks, puddings, cakes, biscuits (cookies), canned fruit, thickened soups and sauces, and pasta. Bread and cereals contain valuable minerals and vitamins and some protein, so eat a moderate amount of them which will also help to reduce your appetite for sweet foods. Avoid fatty foods, such as fried foods, cream, fat, meat, oil and mayonnaise dressings. Use a low-fat spread for bread, glazing vegetables and making sauces; use a liquid or powder sweetener instead of sugar.

If possible, cut out alcoholic drinks completely as they are high in calories. If you have to drink socially – a small glass of dry white wine is the best choice – or have a low calorie tonic water with a slice of lemon and ice cubes if you can manage without alcohol.

To ensure good health, it is advisable to eat the following foods every day: 300 ml (1/2 pint) milk, 25 g (1 oz) cheese, 1 egg, 75 g (3 oz) bread, 1 orange and up to 15 g (1/2 oz) butter. Have at least one portion of liver and oily fish each week, and be sure to have enough iron-rich foods – such as egg, sardines, red meat and leafy green vegetables.

Your main meal of the day should include a high protein food – such as meat, poultry or fish – and the other should contain cheese or eggs, unless of course you are a vegetarian.

Use a calorie chart to check your shopping. Cottage cheese and curd cheese are lower in calories than hard cheeses. Look for labels which say 'low-fat' or 'medium-fat' on dairy products, such as cheeses and yogurt, and use those for the recipes in this book.

Fat is a concentrated source of calories – so always drain excess fat or oil from food. Trim fat from meat and avoid frying – bake, boil, poach, steam, braise or grill (broil) instead. As far as possible, eat vegetables and fruit raw so that none of their nutrients are lost during cooking.

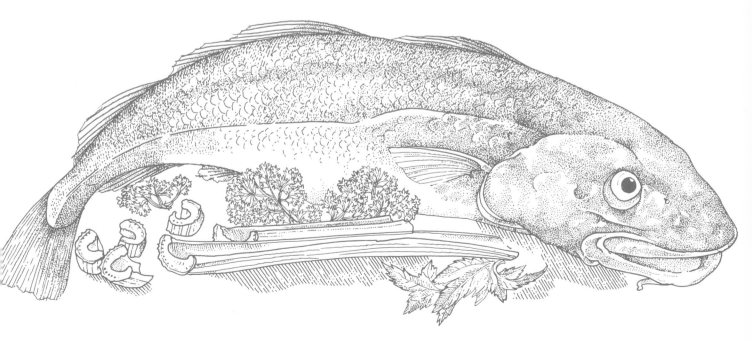

BREAKFASTS

Many nutritionists believe breakfast to be the most important meal of the day, yet a great number of people go without it, including children. Some people cannot face food in the morning, others are trying to slim, and some say they simply haven't the time to prepare and eat a meal at breakfast time.

Breakfast comes at the end of an 8 to 10 hour 'fast'. If it is ignored, the body may not receive any food for a further 4 to 5 hours until the midday meal. Not surprisingly, the body cannot function as effectively if it is deprived of nourishment. The findings of a 10-year research project, known as The Iowa Breakfast Studies, published in 1973, show just how important this first meal of the day is.

121 people took part in the project, including men and women of all ages, and older boys and girls, from a variety of occupations and different social and economic groups. Over a period of weeks they were given different breakfasts and asked to perform a series of physical and mental tests. The same tests were also performed by the subjects when they had eaten no breakfast at all.

The study showed that people were most energetic and mentally alert after eating a breakfast which provided a quarter of their daily recommended intake of protein and energy. They were able to work well, reacted quickly and did not tire easily. When the same people missed breakfast completely, their work output was lower, they were less mentally alert, less energetic and were very hungry by mid-morning. A small breakfast containing less than the recommended intake of calories and protein produced less efficient work and the subjects were hungry by mid

morning; similar results were found if breakfast provided sufficient energy but not enough protein.

So it is important to start the day with a good supply of nutrients for sufficient mental and physical energy to take you through until lunchtime. If you enjoy a cooked breakfast, it is well worth the little extra time required to prepare and cook one. Try a Country grill (broil) (page 35) or Farmhouse scramble (page 32) as a healthy change from traditional fried eggs and bacon.

If however, you haven't the time or appetite for a cooked meal first thing in the morning, necessary nutrients can equally well be obtained from cereals and fruit. Meusli (page 30) can be made in advance and stored ready for use. Served with milk or yogurt, cereals provide valuable protein, B group vitamins and minerals. A little natural brown sugar or honey can be added for sweetening. Top with fresh citrus fruit or serve with a glass of fruit juice and you will obtain a good supply of Vitamin C – which is not only essential in itself, it helps the body to absorb valuable iron from cereals and bread. Wholewheat bread or toast to round off breakfast ensures a good addition of dietry fibre to aid digestion.

If appetite is completely lacking early in the morning, it may be due to a late meal the night before, or it may simply be a bad habit which needs breaking. For a light sustaining start to the day try a Banana flip (page 29) or Breakfast in a glass (page 28) rather than avoiding food altogether. As your body gets used to the idea of breakfast, you will find your appetite will improve and you will be able to increase the quantity and variety of food you consume, so breakfast becomes as enjoyable as any other meal of the day.

Citrus starter (page 28); Farmhouse scramble (page 32); Baked stuffed tomatoes (page 41); Bran bread (page 136)

Citrus Starter

Metric/Imperial	American
2 oranges, peel and pith removed and divided into segments	2 oranges, peel and pith removed and divided into segments
1 grapefruit, peel and pith removed and divided into segments	1 grapefruit, peel and pith removed and divided into segments
25 g / 1 oz seedless raisins	3 tablespoons seedless raisins
25 g / 1 oz walnuts, chopped	1/4 cup chopped walnuts
2 tablespoons clear honey	2 tablespoons clear honey

Put all the ingredients in a bowl and mix well. Cover and leave in the refrigerator overnight.

The next morning, divide equally between 4 individual serving bowls.

Serves 4

Spiced Grapefruit Refresher

This makes an excellent breakfast starter, but may also be served as a first course for a more formal meal.

Metric/Imperial	American
2 grapefruit	2 grapefruit
25 g / 1 oz Muscovado sugar	1 1/2 tablespoons Barbados sugar
pinch of ground ginger	pinch of ground ginger
pinch of ground cinnamon	pinch of ground cinnamon

Cut the grapefruit in half, then separate the segments from the surrounding skin. Mix together the sugar and spices, then sprinkle over the grapefruit.

Cover with plastic cling film, then chill in the refrigerator overnight before serving.

Serves 4

Prune Fluff

This makes a delicious starter for breakfast for those who like fruit but may dislike the idea of prunes.

Metric/Imperial	American
225 g / 8 oz prunes	1 1/3 cups prunes
juice of 1/2 orange	juice of 1/2 orange
40 g / 1 1/2 oz Muscovado sugar	2 tablespoons Barbados sugar
300 ml / 1/2 pint natural yogurt	1 1/4 cups unflavored yogurt

Put the prunes in a bowl, then pour on enough boiling water to just cover. Leave to stand overnight until the prunes are plump and have absorbed the liquid.

The next morning, remove the stones (seeds) and work the flesh in an electric blender with the remaining ingredients for 45 seconds until thoroughly mixed and creamy.

Divide equally between 4 individual serving dishes and serve chilled.

Serves 4

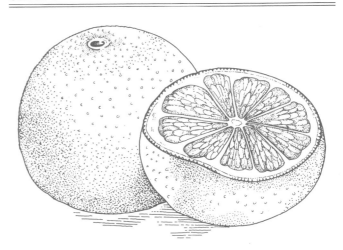

Breakfast in a Glass

This makes a quick breakfast or lunch which is both refreshing and sustaining and is ideal if you are eating alone.

Metric/Imperial	American
300 ml / 1/2 pint orange juice	1 1/4 cups orange juice
1 tablespoon lemon juice	1 tablespoon lemon juice
1 tablespoon clear honey	1 tablespoon clear honey
1 tablespoon wheatgerm	1 tablespoon wheatgerm
1 egg	1 egg

Put all the ingredients in an electric blender and blend for 30 seconds. Pour into a chilled glass and serve immediately.

Serves 1

Banana Flip

This makes a tempting and nourishing breakfast, particularly for children who refuse to eat a cooked meal; it is equally good for a quick light lunch.

Metric/Imperial	American
4 bananas	4 bananas
600 ml / 1 pint milk	2½ cups milk
225 g / 8 oz cottage cheese	1 cup cottage cheese
25 g / 1 oz Muscovado sugar	1½ tablespoons Barbados sugar
pinch of ground cinnamon	pinch of ground cinnamon

Peel the bananas, then cut them into small pieces. Place the chopped bananas and milk in an electric blender. Blend for 30 seconds. Add the cottage cheese and sugar and blend for a further 30 seconds.

Pour into chilled glasses and sprinkle with cinnamon. Serve immediately.

Serves 4

Banana Honey Shake

Metric/Imperial	American
2 bananas	2 bananas
1 tablespoon wheatgerm	1 tablespoon wheatgerm
600 ml / 1 pint milk	2½ cups milk
2 tablespoons clear honey	2 tablespoons clear honey

Peel the bananas, then cut them into small pieces. Work to a purée with the remaining ingredients in an electric blender for 30 seconds.

Pour into chilled glasses and serve immediately.

Serves 2

Morning Starter

Metric/Imperial	American
300 ml / ½ pint orange or grapefruit juice	1¼ cups orange or grapefruit juice
2 tablespoons clear honey	2 tablespoons clear honey

Chill the fruit juice in the refrigerator overnight.

The next morning, put 1 tablespoon honey into each of 2 chilled glasses, pour in the fruit juice, then stir briskly until well mixed.

Serve before muesli, wholewheat toast or a cooked breakfast dish.

Serves 2

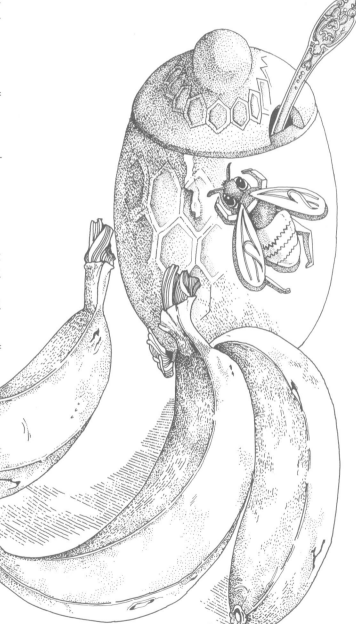

Muesli

For a good muesli base, it is advisable to use a mixture of different grains and seeds. Bran is very dry, wheatgerm has a strong flavour and sesame seeds are very hard, so ingredients should be used sparingly.

Metric/Imperial	American
225 g / 8 oz rolled oats	2¼ cups rolled oats
225 g / 8 oz barley flakes or kernels, sesame and sunflower seeds, bran and wheatgerm, mixed according to taste	2¼ cups barley flakes or kernels, sesame and sunflower seeds, bran and wheatgerm, mixed according to taste
50 g / 2 oz mixed nuts, chopped	½ cup mixed chopped nuts
50 g / 2 oz seedless raisins and coarsely chopped dried fruit (apples, apricots, dates, figs), mixed according to taste	⅓ cup seedless raisins and coarsely chopped dried fruit (apples, apricots, dates, figs), mixed according to taste

Put the oats in a bowl, then stir in the remaining ingredients.

Store in a tin or other airtight container and use as required. Serve with brown sugar or honey and milk, cream or yogurt. Fresh fruit may be added according to season.

Makes 500 g / 1¼lb / 5¼ cups muesli

Swiss Breakfast

Metric/Imperial	American
1 tablespoon wheatgerm	1 tablespoon wheatgerm
1 tablespoon rolled oats	1 tablespoon rolled oats
4 tablespoons water	¼ cup water
1 teaspoon lemon juice	1 teaspoon lemon juice
1 dessert apple	1 dessert apple
1 tablespoon clear honey	1 tablespoon clear honey
2 tablespoons single cream	2 tablespoons light cream
25 g / 1 oz hazelnuts, chopped	¼ cup chopped filberts
TO SERVE:	TO SERVE:
fresh fruit in season (bananas, grapes, peaches, raspberries, strawberries, etc.)	fresh fruit in season (bananas, grapes, peaches, raspberries, strawberries, etc.)

Put the wheatgerm, oats and water in a serving bowl. Cover and leave in the refrigerator overnight.

The next morning, stir in the lemon juice. Do not peel the apple but grate it coarsely, then stir into the oat mixture with the honey and cream. Sprinkle on the nuts and serve immediately, with fresh fruit in season.

Serves 1

ABOVE RIGHT: Granola; Fruit muesli with yogurt
BELOW: Swiss breakfast; Muesli

Fruit Muesli with Yogurt

Metric/Imperial

100 g / 4 oz rolled oats
4 tablespoons wheatgerm
2 tablespoons dried milk
   powder
2 tablespoons clear honey
450 ml / ¾ pint milk
50 g / 2 oz prunes, stoned
   and chopped
50 g / 2 oz stoned dates,
   chopped
25 g / 1 oz seedless raisins
25 g / 1 oz walnuts,
   chopped
1 orange, peel and pith
   removed and divided into
   segments
1 grapefruit, peel and pith
   removed and divided into
   segments
100 g / 4 oz grapes, halved
   and seeded
300 ml / ½ pint natural
   yogurt (optional)

American

1 cup rolled oats
¼ cup wheatgerm
2 tablespoons dried milk
   solids
2 tablespoons clear honey
2 cups milk
⅓ cup prunes, pitted and
   chopped
⅓ cup pitted dates,
   chopped
3 tablespoons seedless
   raisins
¼ cup chopped walnuts
1 orange, peel and pith
   removed and divided into
   segments
1 grapefruit, peel and pith
   removed and divided into
   segments
1 cup grapes, halved and
   seeded
1¼ cups unflavored yogurt
   (optional)

Put the oats in a bowl, add the wheatgerm, milk powder (solids), honey, milk, dried fruit and nuts and stir well to mix. Cover and leave in the refrigerator overnight.

The next morning, divide the muesli equally between 4 individual serving bowls, then arrange the prepared fruit on top. Serve immediately, topped with yogurt, if liked.

Serves 4

Granola

Metric/Imperial

muesli base (see page 30)
100 g / 4 oz desiccated
   coconut
100 g / 4 oz vegetable
   margarine
100 g / 4 oz clear honey

American

muesli base (see page 30)
1⅓ cups shredded coconut
½ cup vegetable margarine
⅓ cup clear honey

Put the muesli base in a bowl, add the coconut and stir well to mix.

Put the margarine and honey in a pan and heat very gently until just melted, stirring occasionally. Pour into the dry mixture and stir well to mix.

Sprinkle the mixture into a roasting pan and bake in a preheated moderately hot oven (190°C / 375°F, Gas Mark 5) for about 20 minutes until golden and crisp. Stir the mmixture once or twice during baking, so that it does not burn on top.

Leave the granola to cool, then store in a tin or other airtight container and use as required. Serve as for muesli base with milk, cream or yogurt and fresh fruit according to season.

Makes about 1 kg / 2 lb / 9 cups granola

Poached Eggs on Wholewheat Toast

Metric/Imperial
300 ml / ½ pint water
pinch of salt
4 eggs
4 slices wholemeal bread
25 g / 1 oz vegetable
  margarine
1 teaspoon yeast extract

American
1¼ cups water
pinch of salt
4 eggs
4 slices wholewheat bread
2 tablespoons vegetable
  margarine
1 teaspoon Brewer's yeast

Put the water and salt in a small pan and bring to the boil. Crack one egg into a cup. Using a spoon, stir the water very quickly to create a 'whirlpool'. Slide the egg into the water, then simmer for 3 minutes until the egg is firmly set.

Toast one slice of bread lightly on both sides, then spread with margarine and a little yeast extract. Remove the egg from the pan with a slotted spoon and place on top of the toast. Serve immediately. Repeat with the remaining eggs and bread.

Serves 4

Farmhouse Scramble

Metric/Imperial
100 g / 4 oz lean bacon
  rashers, derinded and
  chopped
3 eggs
salt
freshly ground white pepper
175 g / 6 oz cottage cheese
4 slices wholemeal bread
25 g / 1 oz vegetable
  margarine
watercress sprigs to garnish

American
½ cup chopped Canadian
  bacon
3 eggs
salt
freshly ground white pepper
¾ cup cottage cheese
4 slices wholewheat bread
2 tablespoons vegetable
  margarine
watercress sprigs to garnish

Put the bacon in a small pan and fry gently until the fat runs, stirring frequently. Fry for a further 4 minutes, then remove from the pan with a slotted spoon and keep hot.

Crack the eggs into a bowl. Add salt and pepper to taste, then whisk with a fork until lightly mixed.

Pour into the pan and cook gently until the eggs begin to coagulate but are not fully set, stirring and lifting constantly. Stir in the cottage cheese and continue cooking until the mixture is just firm.

Meanwhile, toast the bread lightly on both sides, then spread with the margarine. Arrange on warmed, individual serving plates. Stir the bacon into the egg mixture, then pile onto the toast and garnish with watercress. Serve immediately.

Serves 4

Baked Tomato Eggs

Each tomato should be large enough to hold an egg.

Metric/Imperial	American
4 large tomatoes	4 large tomatoes
100 g / 4 oz cooked ham, finely chopped	1/2 cup finely chopped cooked ham
1 teaspoon chopped parsley	1 teaspoon chopped parsley
salt	salt
freshly ground black pepper	freshly ground black pepper
4 eggs	4 eggs

Cut the tops off the tomatoes, then scoop out the pulp and seeds. Work the pulp through a sieve (strainer) to remove the seeds. Put the pulp in a bowl with the ham, parsley and salt and pepper to taste. Stir well.

Divide the mixture equally between the tomatoes, pressing it down well. Stand the tomatoes in a baking dish and crack one egg into each tomato. Sprinkle lightly with salt and pepper.

Bake in a preheated moderately hot oven (190°C / 375°F, Gas Mark 5) for 15 minutes until the eggs are set. Serve immediately.

Serves 4

Scrambled Eggs

Metric/Imperial	American
4 eggs	4 eggs
4 tablespoons single cream	1/4 cup light cream
salt	salt
freshly ground white pepper	freshly ground white pepper
50 g / 2 oz vegetable margarine	1/4 cup vegetable margarine
4 slices wholemeal bread	4 slices wholewheat bread
1 teaspoon snipped chives	1 teaspoon snipped chives
1 teaspoon chopped parsley	1 teaspoon chopped parsley

Crack the eggs into a bowl, add the cream and salt and pepper to taste, then whisk with a fork until lightly mixed.

Melt half the margarine in a small pan. Add the egg mixture and cook gently until the eggs begin to coagulate but are not fully set, stirring and lifting constantly.

Meanwhile, toast the bread lightly on both sides, then spread with the remaining margarine. Arrange on warmed individual serving plates. When the eggs are only just set, but still very creamy, stir in the chives and parsley. Pile onto the toast and serve immediately.

Serves 4

Breakfast Omelette

Vary the filling for this delicious, quick-to-prepare breakfast by adding a little lean chopped ham, or a few chopped walnuts, to the cottage (curd) cheese filling.

Metric/Imperial	American
2 eggs	2 eggs
salt	salt
freshly ground black pepper	freshly ground black pepper
100 g / 4 oz cottage cheese	1/4 lb cottage cheese
1 tablespoon vegetable oil	1 tablespoon vegetable oil

Break the eggs into a bowl. Add salt and pepper to taste and whisk until light and frothy. Stir in half of the cottage cheese and mix well.

Heat the oil in a small omelette pan and pour in the egg mixture. Cook over moderate heat, drawing the edge of the omelette into the centre with a knife, as it becomes firm.

When the omelette is lightly set, spread the remaining cottage cheese over the top and continue to cook gently for 1 minute. Fold the omelette in half and transfer to a hot serving plate. Serve immediately, with wholewheat toast and a glass of orange juice, if liked.

Serves 1

Country Grill (Broil)

Metric/Imperial	American
3 tablespoons oil	3 tablespoons oil
4 slices lambs' liver	4 slices lamb liver
4 lambs' kidneys, skin and cores removed and split lengthways	4 lamb kidneys, skin and cores removed and split lengthways
salt	salt
freshly ground black pepper	freshly ground black pepper
4 tomatoes, halved	4 tomatoes, halved
8 large mushrooms	8 large mushrooms
2 teaspoons chopped parsley to garnish	2 teaspoons chopped parsley to garnish

Remove the rack from the grill (broiler) pan, then line the pan with foil and brush with a little of the oil.

Put the liver in the centre of the pan, then arrange the kidneys around the liver. Brush with a little oil.

Grill (broil) under medium heat for 3 minutes until the liver and kidneys change colour then turn them over carefully and sprinkle with salt and pepper.

Arrange the tomatoes around the kidneys, cut sides uppermost. Put the mushrooms in the pan, caps uppermost.

Sprinkle both the tomatoes and mushrooms lightly with salt and pepper and brush with oil.

Return the pan to the grill (broiler) for a further 5 minutes. Sprinkle with parsley and serve hot.

Serves 4

Wholewheat Crêpes

Metric/Imperial	American
100 g / 4 oz wholemeal self-raising flour	1 cup wholewheat self-rising flour
1 egg, beaten	1 egg, beaten
300 ml / ½ pint milk	1¼ cups milk
4 tablespoons clear honey	¼ cup clear honey
50 g / 2 oz seedless raisins	⅓ cup seedless raisins
pinch of grated nutmeg	pinch of grated nutmeg
oil for frying	oil for frying

Put the flour in a bowl and make a well in the centre. Pour in the egg and milk and beat well to give a smooth batter.

Mix the honey, raisins and nutmeg in a separate bowl.

Heat a little oil in a 20 cm / 8 inch frying pan (skillet). When the oil is hot, quickly pour in enough batter to thinly coat the bottom of the pan, tilting the pan to spread the batter evenly. Cook until the top of the batter is set and the underside is golden brown. Turn and cook the other side.

Spiced grapefruit refresher (page 28); Country grill (broil)

Slide onto a warm plate, cover and keep warm by standing the plate over a pan of hot water. Continue until all the batter has been used up, making 8 crêpes in all.

Spread each crêpe with a spoonful of the honey mixture, then fold to form wedge-shaped parcels. Serve immediately.

Serves 4

Wholewheat crêpes

Poached Haddock and Eggs

Metric/Imperial	American
450 g / 1 lb smoked haddock fillets, cut into 4 pieces	1 lb smoked haddock fillets, cut into 4 pieces
600 ml / 1 pint water	2½ cups water
4 eggs	4 eggs
freshly ground black pepper	freshly ground black pepper
25 g / 1 oz vegetable margarine	2 tablespoons vegetable margarine

Put the fish in a frying pan (skillet) and cover with the water. Bring slowly to the boil, then simmer for about 10 minutes or until the fish is tender but not breaking up. Transfer with a slotted spoon to warmed serving plates and keep hot.

Bring the cooking liquid to the boil. Using a spoon, stir the water very quickly to create a 'whirlpool'. Crack one egg into a cup, then slide it carefully into the water. Repeat with the remaining eggs. Simmer for 3 minutes until each egg is firmly set.

Meanwhile, sprinkle the fish with pepper to taste and put a little margarine on each piece. Keep hot.

Remove the eggs from the pan with a slotted spoon and place one on each piece of fish. Serve immediately.

Serves 4

DAIRY FOODS

With their versatility and high nutrient content, dairy foods play an important part in our diet. No single food can supply all nutrients in the required quantities but milk is the most complete of all foods, and it is easily digested. 600ml (1 pint) of milk supplies our daily calcium requirement, while the protein content is equivalent to that of 3 large eggs or 75 g (3 oz) liver, beef or white fish.

Cheese contains most of the nutrients in milk and is a particularly good source of protein and calcium. Most varieties, including both hard cheeses (Cheddar, Gruyère, etc.) and soft cheeses (Brie, Camembert, etc.) have a fairly high fat content because they are manufactured from whole milk. Cottage cheese is prepared from skimmed milk and therefore has a low fat content. It is easily digested and is very satisfying, which is a great asset in a slimming diet. Eaten in a quickly prepared salad or added to cooked dishes, it provides bulk, flavour and nutrients, but few calories.

Yogurt is another milk product, once considered only as a health food, but now a very enjoyable item in everyday meals. Over the years, some fantastic claims have been made for yogurt and what it can do, from increasing the life-span to curing any number of internal disorders. It is, in fact, a most wholesome food – high in protein, low in fat and rich in calcium. Home-made yogurt, prepared from whole milk, contains all the food value of milk. Commercially manufactured varieties usually have most of the fat removed and extra protein and vitamins added. Yogurt is almost three times as digestible as milk and makes an excellent light meal.

While all of these milk-based foods are very good to eat just as they are, they can equally well be used in cooking. Cottage cheese goes well with both vegetable and fruit salads, and can also be made into delicious cheesecakes and a variety of puddings. Its rather bland flavour can be used to advantage in fish dishes where it will enhance, rather than disguise, the delicate flavour of fish.

Yogurt is almost a miracle ingredient in the kitchen. It can be used in soups and sauces; blended into savoury mousses and salad dressings; whisked into nourishing meal-in-a-glass drinks; used as a topping for baked fish or meat dishes; used to baste kebabs or marinade poultry. It can also provide a valuable thickening agent for savoury sauces – thus avoiding the need to use flour – and can similarly be used to thicken custards. In a variety of desserts, including ices, soufflés and fruit fools, yogurt can be used as a refreshing and less fattening alternative to cream.

Of the dairy foods, the egg is the most versatile of all. Eggs are a high-quality protein food; they also supply substantial amounts of vitamins A and D and riboflavin, and egg yolk is an excellent source of iron. They do however contain a high proportion of fat and cholesterol, particularly the yolk, and should be eaten with caution by those who are cutting down on their intake of animal fats. In addition to all this goodness, an egg only contains about 80 calories, so it is a perfect food for those who are watching their weight.

Eggs can of course be cooked quickly and served in a variety of guises as a meal or snack. They are easily digested and provide goodness without bulk – a particular advantage for children and anyone with a reduced appetite through illness. When eggs are cooked, the protein 'sets' or coagulates. This property enables eggs to be used for binding dry ingredients together, thickening sauces and setting custards. An extra egg may be added to a rice pudding, or whisked into a soup or sauce, or blended into a nourishing drink.

Cucumber, Lemon and Mint Soup

Metric/Imperial	American
1 tablespoon oil	1 tablespoon oil
1 small onion, peeled and finely chopped	1 small onion, peeled and finely chopped
½ cucumber, peeled and cut into 5 mm / ¼ inch cubes	½ cucumber, peeled and cut into ¼ inch cubes
450 ml / ¾ pint natural yogurt	2 cups unflavored yogurt
300 ml / ½ pint chicken stock	1¼ cups chicken stock
finely grated rind and juice of 1 lemon	finely grated rind and juice of 1 lemon
2 tablespoons chopped mint	2 tablespoons chopped mint
salt	salt
freshly ground black pepper	freshly ground black pepper
mint sprigs to garnish	mint sprigs to garnish

Yogurt dip (page 40); Cucumber, lemon and mint soup; Slimmer's watercress soup; Summer tomato soup; Greek vegetable soup

Heat the oil in a pan, add the onion and fry gently for 3 minutes. Add the cucumber and fry for a further 5 minutes. Transfer to a bowl and leave to cool.

Stir in the yogurt and stock, then the lemon rind and juice, mint and salt and pepper to taste.

Chill in the refrigerator for 1 hour. Pour into 4 individual chilled bowls, garnish with mint sprigs and serve chilled.

Serves 4

Slimmer's Watercress Soup

Metric/Imperial	American
2 bunches watercress, trimmed	2 bunches watercress, trimmed
1 tablespoon oil	1 tablespoon oil
1 small onion, peeled and finely chopped	1 small onion, peeled and finely chopped
600 ml / 1 pint chicken stock	2½ cups chicken stock
2 egg yolks	2 egg yolks
150 ml / ¼ pint natural yogurt	⅔ cup unflavored yogurt
salt	salt
freshly ground white pepper	freshly ground white pepper

Remove 16 leaves from the watercress and reserve for the garnish. Chop the remaining watercress and stems.

Heat the oil in a pan, add the onion and fry gently until soft and golden. Add the watercress and the stock and bring to the boil. Lower the heat, cover and simmer for 20 minutes.

Rub the soup through a sieve (strainer), or work to a purée in an electric blender. Put the egg yolks in a bowl and whisk in the yogurt. Stir in 4 tablespoons / ¼ cup of the purée and mix well.

Pour the remaining purée into the rinsed-out pan. Add the yogurt mixture, stirring constantly, then heat through gently without boiling. Taste for seasoning.

Pour into 4 individual bowls and garnish with the reserved watercress leaves. This soup may also be served chilled.

Serves 4

Summer Tomato Soup

Metric/Imperial	American
600 ml / 1 pint tomato juice	2½ cups tomato juice
600 ml / 1 pint natural yogurt	2½ cups unflavored yogurt
finely grated rind and juice of 1 lemon	finely grated rind and juice of 1 lemon
½ cucumber, peeled and cut into 5 mm / ¼ inch cubes	½ cucumber, peeled and cut into ¼ inch cubes
salt	salt
freshly ground black pepper	freshly ground black pepper
TO GARNISH:	TO GARNISH:
4 slices lemon	4 slices lemon
2 teaspoons snipped chives	2 teaspoons snipped chives

Put the tomato juice in a bowl, add the yogurt and mix well. Stir in the lemon rind and juice, then the cucumber and salt and pepper to taste.

Chill in the refrigerator for 1 hour. Pour into 4 individual bowls. Garnish with lemon slices and chives. Serve chilled.

Serves 4

Greek Vegetable Soup

Choose vegetables according to season. Peas, sweetcorn kernels, beans and chopped carrots make a good summer selection. In winter, diced root vegetables may be used, or frozen ones.

Metric/Imperial	American
450 ml / ¾ pint beef stock	2 cups beef stock
100 g / 4 oz mixed vegetables, chopped	¾ cup mixed vegetables, chopped
1 egg yolk	1 egg yolk
300 ml / ½ pint natural yogurt	1¼ cups unflavored yogurt
salt	salt
freshly ground black pepper	freshly ground black pepper
1 tablespoon chopped mint leaves	1 tablespoon chopped mint leaves
finely grated rind of 1 lemon	finely grated rind of 1 lemon

Put the stock in a pan and bring to the boil. Add the vegetables, then lower the heat, cover and simmer for 10 minutes or until just tender.

Meanwhile, put the egg yolk in a bowl and whisk in the yogurt. Stir in 6 tablespoons of the hot liquid and mix well.

Add to the soup in the pan, stirring constantly, then heat through gently without boiling. Season with salt and pepper to taste.

Pour into 4 individual serving bowls, garnish with chopped mint and lemon rind and serve hot.

Serves 4

Borshch

Metric/Imperial	American
2 tablespoons oil	2 tablespoons oil
2 onions, peeled and finely chopped	2 onions, peeled and finely chopped
3 raw beetroot, peeled and roughly chopped	3 raw beets, peeled and roughly chopped
175 g / 6 oz cabbage, finely shredded	2 cups finely shredded cabbage
750 ml / 1¼ pints beef stock	3 cups beef stock
2 tablespoons vinegar	2 tablespoons vinegar
¼ teaspoon salt	¼ teaspoon salt
freshly ground black pepper	freshly ground black pepper
4 tablespoons natural yogurt to serve	¼ cup unflavored yogurt to serve

Heat the oil in a large pan, add the onions and fry gently until soft and golden. Add the remaining ingredients, except the yogurt, and bring to the boil. Lower the heat, cover and simmer for 1 hour.

Rub the soup through a sieve (strainer), or work to a purée in an electric blender. Pour the purée into the rinsed-out pan and reheat gently, adding a little stock or water if the soup is too thick.

Pour into 4 individual bowls, swirl 1 tablespoonful yogurt in the centre of each bowl and serve hot.

Serves 4

Yogurt Dip

Metric/Imperial	American
150 ml / ¼ pint natural yogurt	⅔ cup unflavored yogurt
225 g / 8 oz cottage cheese	1 cup cottage cheese
1 tablespoon grated onion	1 tablespoon grated onion
6 pickled gherkins, very finely chopped	6 small sweet dill pickles, very finely chopped
3 celery sticks	3 celery stalks
3 carrots	3 carrots
½ cucumber	½ cucumber
1 tablespoon sea salt	1 tablespoon coarse salt
600 ml / 1 pint iced water	2½ cups ice water

Put the yogurt, cottage cheese, onion and gherkins (dill pickles) in a bowl and stir well to mix. Chill in the refrigerator for 1 hour.

Meanwhile, cut each celery stick (stalk) into 4 lengths. Peel the carrots and split each one lengthwise into quarters. Cut the cucumber in half, then cut each half lengthwise into 4 pieces.

Put the celery, carrots and cucumber in a bowl, sprinkle with the salt, then pour on the iced water. Chill in the refrigerator for 1 hour.

Put the yogurt dip in a serving bowl and stand the bowl on a large plate. Drain the vegetables and arrange on the plate around the dip.

Serves 4 to 6

Cottage Cheese Mousse

Metric/Imperial	American
450 g / 1 lb cottage cheese, sieved	2 cups cottage cheese, sieved
150 ml / ¼ pint natural yogurt	⅔ cup unflavored yogurt
squeeze of lemon juice	squeeze of lemon juice
1 tablespoon tomato purée	1 tablespoon tomato paste
salt	salt
freshly ground black pepper	freshly ground black pepper
100 g / 4 oz peeled shrimps	½ cup shelled shrimp
TO GARNISH:	TO GARNISH:
½ teaspoon paprika	½ teaspoon paprika
1 teaspoon snipped chives	1 teaspoon snipped chives

Put the cottage cheese and yogurt in a bowl and mix together, using a fork. Add the lemon juice and tomato purée (paste) and season well with salt and pepper. Stir well.

Divide the mixture equally between 4 individual ramekins, pressing down well. Top each ramekin with shrimps, then chill in the refrigerator for 1 hour.

Sprinkle with paprika and chives before serving.

Serves 4

Egg Mousse

Metric/Imperial	American
4 hard-boiled eggs, shelled	4 hard-cooked eggs, shelled
1 teaspoon Worcestershire sauce	1 teaspoon Worcestershire sauce
dash of Tabasco sauce	dash of Tabasco sauce
pinch of paprika	pinch of paprika
salt	salt
freshly ground white pepper	freshly ground white pepper
2 teaspoons gelatine	2 teaspoons gelatin
2 tablespoons water	2 tablespons water
150 ml / 1/4 pint natural yogurt	2/3 cup unflavored yogurt
225 g / 8 oz peeled prawns	1 cup shelled shrimp

Cut the eggs in half lengthwise, then remove the yolks and work them through a sieve (strainer) into a bowl. Add the Worcestershire sauce, Tabasco, paprika and salt and pepper to taste. Mix well. Chop the egg whites finely. Place the gelatine and water in a cup over a pan of hot water and stir until dissolved. Whisk the yogurt into the egg yolk mixture with the gelatine, then fold in the chopped egg whites.

Pour the mixture into a 15 cm / 6 inch straight-sided serving dish, then chill in the refrigerator for 2 hours.

Pile the prawns (shrimp) in the centre of the mousse just before serving. Serve with a crisp green salad.

Serves 4

Baked Stuffed Tomatoes

Metric/Imperial	American
4 large tomatoes	4 large tomatoes
1 small onion, peeled and grated	1 small onion, peeled and grated
1 tablespoon chopped parsley	1 tablespoon chopped parsley
175 g / 6 oz cream cheese	3/4 cup cream cheese
100 g / 4 oz lean cooked ham, chopped	1/2 cup chopped lean cooked ham
salt	salt
freshly ground black pepper	freshly ground black pepper
2 tablespoons water	2 tablespoons water

Cut the tops off the tomatoes and reserve for lids. Scoop out the insides of the tomatoes, then work the pulp through a sieve (strainer) to remove the pips (seeds).

Put the tomato pulp in a bowl. Add the onion, parsley, cream cheese and ham and mix well. Add salt and pepper to taste.

Spoon the mixture into the hollowed-out tomatoes and place the lids on top. Stand the tomatoes in a baking dish, then pour in the water. Bake in a preheated hot oven (220°C / 425°F, Gas Mark 7) for 15 minutes.

Serve hot or cold.

Serves 4

Cottage Bake

Metric/Imperial	American
1 tablespoon oil	1 tablespoon oil
1 small onion, peeled and finely chopped	1 small onion, peeled and finely chopped
100 g / 4 oz mushrooms, sliced	1 cup sliced mushrooms
225 g / 8 oz cottage cheese	1 cup cottage cheese
2 eggs	2 eggs
50 g / 2 oz cooked ham, chopped	1/4 cup chopped cooked ham
2 tablespoons chopped mixed fresh herbs	2 tablespoons chopped mixed fresh herbs
salt	salt
freshly ground black pepper	freshly ground black pepper
chopped parsley to garnish	chopped parsley to garnish

Heat the oil in a pan, add the onion and fry gently until soft and golden. Add the mushrooms and fry for a further 3 minutes.

Meanwhile, put the cottage cheese and eggs in a bowl and beat together with a fork. Stir in the ham, then the cooked onions and mushrooms. Add the herbs and salt and pepper to taste.

Spoon the mixture into a lightly oiled baking dish, then bake in a preheated moderately hot oven (200°C / 400°F, Gas Mark 6) for 20 minutes. Sprinkle with chopped parsley and serve hot.

Serves 4

Oriental Salad

Metric/Imperial	American
450 g / 1 lb cottage cheese	2 cups cottage cheese
3 tablespoons double cream, lightly whipped	3 tablespoons heavy cream, lightly whipped
225 g / 8 oz cooked chicken, diced	1 cup diced cooked chicken
1 orange, peeled, divided into segments and skinned	1 orange, peeled, divided into segments and skinned
25 g / 1 oz stem ginger, finely chopped	3 tablespoons finely chopped preserved ginger
1 small lettuce	1 small head of lettuce
1 bunch watercress	1 bunch watercress
12 black grapes, halved and pipped, to garnish	12 purple grapes, halved and seeded, to garnish

Put the cottage cheese, cream and chicken in a bowl and fold gently to mix. Stir in the orange segments and ginger.

Arrange a bed of lettuce and watercress on 4 individual plates. Spoon the cheese mixture on the centre of each plate. Garnish with the grapes before serving.

Serves 4 to 6

Smoked haddock and yogurt mousse;
Fish roe stuffed eggs

Oriental salad

Fish Roe Stuffed Eggs

Metric/Imperial	American
8 hard-boiled eggs, shelled	8 hard-cooked eggs, shelled
150 ml / ¼ pint natural yogurt	⅔ cup unflavored yogurt
juice of 1 lemon	juice of 1 lemon
100 g / 4 oz lumpfish roe	½ cup fish roe
salt	salt
freshly ground black pepper	freshly ground black pepper

Cut the eggs in half lengthwise, then remove the yolks. Put the yolks in a bowl with the yogurt and lemon juice and mash well together. Work in the fish roe, then add salt and pepper to taste.

Pile the mixture into the egg whites and serve on a bed of lettuce.

Serves 4

Smoked Haddock and Yogurt Mousse

Metric/Imperial	American
225 g / 8 oz smoked haddock fillets	½ lb smoked haddock fillets
300 ml / ½ pint natural yogurt	1¼ cups unflavored yogurt
2 hard-boiled eggs, shelled	2 hard-cooked eggs, shelled
finely grated rind of ½ lemon	finely grated rind of ½ lemon
2 teaspoons lemon juice	2 teaspoons lemon juice
2 teaspoons gelatine	2 teaspoons gelatin
2 tablespoons water	2 tablespoons water
salt	salt
freshly ground white pepper	freshly ground white pepper
paprika to garnish	paprika to garnish

Poach the haddock in water to cover for 10 minutes. Drain well, then remove the skin and any bones and flake the flesh finely into a bowl. Add the yogurt and mix gently together. Chop 1 egg finely and add to the fish mixture with the lemon rind.

Put the lemon juice, gelatine and water in a small cup. Stand the cup in a pan of hot water and stir well until the gelatine becomes syrupy. Remove from the heat and cool for 2 minutes.

Stir the gelatine into the fish mixture, add salt and pepper to taste, then divide the mixture equally between 4 individual ramekins. Chill in the refrigerator for 1 hour.

Slice the remaining egg and use to decorate each ramekin, then sprinkle with paprika to garnish.

Serves 4

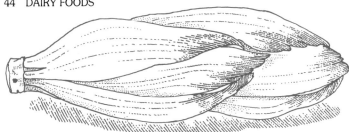

Chicory (Belgian Endive) and Ham in Yogurt Sauce

Metric/Imperial	American
2 heads chicory	2 heads Belgian endive
4 thin slices cooked ham	4 thin slices cooked ham
150 ml / ¼ pint natural yogurt	⅔ cup unflavored yogurt
4 tablespoons milk	¼ cup milk
1 egg yolk	1 egg yolk
salt	salt
freshly ground black pepper	freshly ground black pepper
2 teaspoons grated Parmesan cheese	2 teaspoons grated Parmesan cheese
chopped parsley to garnish	chopped parsley to garnish

Put the chicory (Belgian endive) in a bowl and cover with boiling water. Leave to stand for 3 minutes, then drain very thoroughly.

Split each head in half lengthwise to make 4 pieces, then roll a slice of ham around each piece. Place the pieces side by side in a shallow baking dish.

Put the yogurt, milk and egg yolk in a bowl and whisk with a fork until well mixed. Add salt and pepper to taste. Pour the sauce over the ham, then sprinkle with the cheese. Bake in a preheated moderate oven (180°C / 350°F, Gas Mark 4) for 25 minutes. Serve hot, garnished with parsley.

Serves 4

Cottage Cheese Cocottes

Metric/Imperial	American
2 eggs	2 eggs
1 large slice wholemeal bread, crusts removed	1 large slice wholewheat bread, crusts removed
3 tablespoons hot milk	3 tablespoons hot milk
100 g / 4 oz shelled prawns or shrimps	¼ lb shelled shrimp
225 g / 8 oz cottage cheese	½ lb cottage cheese
1 teaspoon made mustard	1 teaspoon made mustard
salt	salt
freshly ground black pepper	freshly ground black pepper
1 small green pepper, cored, seeded and sliced into rings	1 small green pepper, cored, seeded and sliced into rings

Break the eggs into a bowl and whisk with a fork until frothy. Place the bread in an electric blender and grind coarsely.

Fold the breadcrumbs, milk, prawns or shrimps and cottage (curd) cheese into the beaten eggs. Stir in the mustard and season with salt and pepper to taste.

Grease individual ovenproof ramekin dishes and divide the mixture evenly between them. Top each one with a green pepper ring.

Stand the dishes in a roasting pan, containing about 2.5 cm / 1 inch water and bake in a preheated moderately hot oven (190°C / 375°F, Gas Mark 5) for 35 minutes. Serve hot, with peas or beans and baked tomatoes, if liked.

Serves 4

Cottage Pears

Metric/Imperial	American
4 ripe dessert pears	4 ripe dessert pears
juice of ½ lemon	juice of ½ lemon
225 g / 8 oz cottage cheese	1 cup cottage cheese
25 g / 1 oz walnuts, chopped	¼ cup chopped walnuts
salt	salt
freshly ground black pepper	freshly ground black pepper
2 celery sticks, cut into 2.5 cm / 1 inch slices	2 celery stalks, cut into 1 inch slices
1 carrot, peeled and coarsely grated	1 carrot, peeled and coarsley grated
1 bunch watercress, stems removed and leaves roughly chopped	1 bunch watercress, stems removed and leaves roughly chopped

Cut the pears in half lengthwise but do not peel them. Remove the cores, then brush the pears immediately with the lemon juice to prevent discoloration.

Put the cottage cheese and walnuts in a bowl, stir well, then add salt and pepper to taste. Fill the pears with the cheese mixture.

Mix together the celery, carrot and watercress, then arrange on individual plates. Place the pear halves on top. Serve immediately.

Serves 4 or 8

NOTE: Allow 1 pear half per person for a starter, 2 for a main course.

Baked Yogurt Custard

Metric/Imperial	American
300 ml / ½ pint natural yogurt	1¼ cups unflavored yogurt
few drops of vanilla essence	few drops of vanilla extract
few drops of liquid glucose	few drops of liquid glucose
2 eggs, beaten	2 eggs, beaten
150 ml / ¼ pint milk	⅔ cup milk
¼ teaspoon grated nutmeg	¼ teaspoon grated nutmeg

Put the yogurt, vanilla and glucose in a bowl and mix well. Add the eggs and milk and beat well to an even colour. Pour into a baking dish and sprinkle with the nutmeg.

Stand the dish in a roasting pan and pour in enough water to come 2.5 cm / 1 inch up the sides of the pan. Bake in a preheated moderate oven (160°C / 325°F, Gas Mark 3) for 40 minutes.

Serve hot or cold with fresh or stewed fruit.

Serves 4

Yogurt and Orange Jelly

Metric/Imperial	American
15 g / ½ oz gelatine	2 envelopes gelatin
1 tablespoon water	1 tablespoon water
300 ml / ½ pint orange juice	1¼ cups orange juice
150 ml / ¼ pint natural yogurt	⅔ cup unflavored yogurt

Put the gelatine and water in a small cup. Stand the cup in a pan of hot water and stir well until the gelatine becomes syrupy. Remove from the heat and cool for 2 minutes.

Put the orange juice and yogurt in a separate bowl, pour in the gelatine, then mix thoroughly.

Pour into a chilled 600 ml / 1 pint / 2½ cup mould. Leave to set, then chill in the refrigerator for 2 hours before serving.

Serves 4

Slimmer's Coeur à la Crème

Metric/Imperial	American
2 teaspoons gelatine	2 teaspoons gelatin
2 tablespoons water	2 tablespoons water
350 g / 12 oz cottage cheese, sieved	1½ cups cottage cheese, sieved
150 ml / ¼ pint natural yogurt	⅔ cup unflavored yogurt
juice of ½ lemon	juice of ½ lemon
salt	salt
freshly ground black pepper	freshly ground black pepper

Put the gelatine and water in a small cup. Stand the cup in a pan of hot water and stir well until the gelatine becomes syrupy. Remove from the heat and cool for 2 minutes.

Put the cottage cheese, yogurt and lemon juice in a bowl and mix well. Add the gelatine and salt and pepper to taste; mix thoroughly.

Spoon the mixture into 4 individual ramekins, then chill in the refrigerator for 4 hours. Turn out and serve with fresh fruit in season.

Serves 4

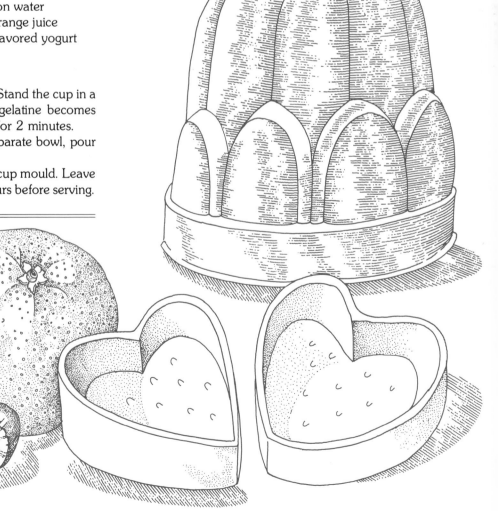

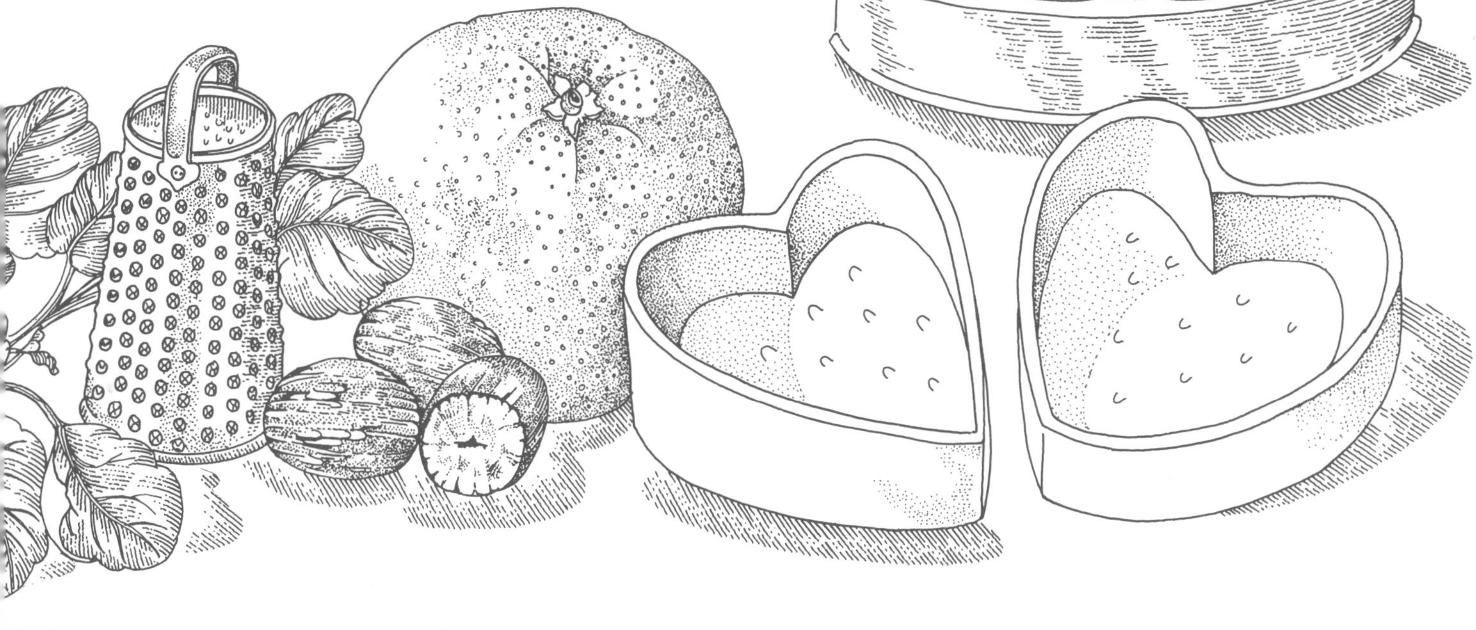

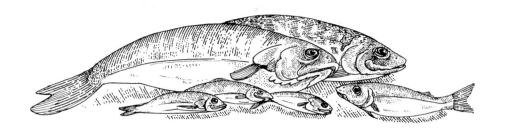

FISH & SHELLFISH

Freshly caught fish is wholesome, delicious and highly nutritious. It has a high protein content – 15 to 20 per cent, depending on the type of fish – and the protein is of good quality because it contains all of the essential amino-acids. It is also easily digested and is therefore particularly valuable for children, old people and anyone whose appetite is reduced through illness.

The fat contained in fish, unlike fat in meat, is highly unsaturated – a healthy advantage over meat. It is also a useful source of vitamins A and D. The amount of fat in different fish varies enormously. Oily fish, such as herring, mackerel and salmon, contain from 10 to 18 per cent. However white fish, such as cod, plaice (flounder) and sole, contain less than 2 per cent fat and can therefore play an important role in slimming diets – providing a valuable source of protein, vitamins and minerals, with comparatively few calories.

Unfortunately fish has one drawback – it is the most perishable of all fresh foods. Before buying fish, always check carefully to ensure it is absolutely fresh: choose fish with a moist, shiny skin, firm flesh, bright eyes and – most important – no sign of an odour. Although fresh fish can be stored in the refrigerator for a day or two, it is best eaten as soon as possible after purchase.

Care should be taken to avoid overcooking fish, which spoils the flavour and texture. After cooking, fish should be just tender, with creamy, firm flesh. Grilling (broiling) and poaching are the simplest ways to cook fish in order to retain its full flavour. Only a little flavouring is necessary – salt, freshly ground black pepper and a sprinkling of lemon juice. Poaching should be carried out in the minimum quantity of liquid; use a mixture of dry white wine and water, add a bouquet garni and simmer very gently until just tender.

Another delicious way to serve whole fish or fillets is to coat them with wholewheat breadcrumbs and then to quickly grill (broil) or fry in a little vegetable oil. A tasty way of cooking oily fish, such as mackerel, is to bake them, stuffed with onion slices, garlic cloves, herbs, lemon juice and seasoning.

Fish is very versatile and, with the addition of vegetables and herbs, can quickly be turned into a range of delicious dishes – soups, casseroles, pies, mousses and pâtés; it is also excellent served cold in salads.

Both fish and shellfish are ideal to serve as a first course for a three-course meal – providing a tasty, nourishing appetizer which is not so filling that it will detract from the main course. Unless you intend to serve a cold fish salad the following day, only cook as much fish as you intend to serve, because it does not reheat successfully.

Some people – men in particular – do not believe that fish can provide a substantial meal unless it is cooked in batter and eaten with plenty of chips! This is simply not true. Served with wholesome accompaniments – such as wholewheat bread, brown rice, or pulses (legumes) – and tasty vegetables – like mushrooms, tomatoes and spinach – fish becomes a substantial, satisfying meal.

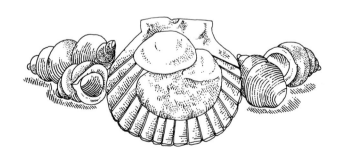

Spiced fish casserole (page 56); Sailor's mussels (page 48);
Baked trout (page 52)

Fish Chowder

Metric/Imperial	American
750 g / 1½ lb cod or haddock fillets	1½ lb cod or haddock fillets
1.75 litres / 3 pints water	7½ cups water
freshly ground black pepper	freshly ground black pepper
1 onion, peeled and sliced	1 onion, peeled and sliced
2 potatoes, peeled and sliced	2 potatoes, peeled and sliced
3 tomatoes, sliced	3 tomatoes, sliced
2 teaspoons yeast extract	2 teaspoons Brewer's yeast
1 teaspoon chopped thyme	1 teaspoon chopped thyme
2 teaspoons chopped parsley	2 teaspoons chopped parsley
2 teaspoons tomato purée	2 teaspoons tomato paste
salt	salt
2 teaspoons Worcestershire sauce	2 teaspoons Worcestershire sauce
juice of 1 lemon	juice of 1 lemon

Put the fish in a pan with the water and a pinch of pepper. Bring to the boil, then lower the heat and poach gently for 15 minutes or until the fish is tender. Drain off the water and reserve. Cut the fish into 2.5 cm / 1 inch cubes, discarding the skin and any bones.

Put the fish and the reserved water in the rinsed-out pan with the remaining ingredients, except the Worcestershire sauce and lemon juice. Bring to the boil, then lower the heat, cover and simmer for 45 minutes.

Stir in the Worcestershire sauce and lemon juice, then serve very hot with wholewheat bread or crackers.

Serves 4

Soft Roes on Toast

Metric/Imperial	American
450 g / 1 lb soft roes, washed	1 lb soft roes, washed
salt	salt
2 tablespoons mushroom ketchup	4 tablespoons minced cooked mushrooms
1 tablespoon Worcestershire sauce	1 tablespoon Worcestershire sauce
½ teaspoon anchovy essence (optional)	freshly ground black pepper
freshly ground black pepper	4 slices wholewheat bread
4 slices wholemeal bread	juice of 1 lemon
juice of 1 lemon	pinch of cayenne pepper
pinch of cayenne pepper	

Poach the roes in salted water to cover for 15 minutes, then drain very thoroughly.

Mix together the mushroom ketchup (mushrooms), Worcestershire sauce and anchovy essence if using. Add salt and pepper to taste, then add the roes and mix well.

Toast the bread lightly on both sides. Pile the roes on the toast and grill (broil) under medium heat for 3 minutes.

Arrange on individual warmed serving plates, then sprinkle with the lemon juice and cayenne pepper. Serve hot.

Serves 4

Sailors' Mussels

Metric/Imperial	American
48 mussels	48 mussels or clams
6 shallots, peeled and chopped	6 shallots, peeled and chopped
300 ml / ½ pint dry cider	1¼ cups hard cider
2 teaspoons flour	2 teaspoons flour
15 g / ½ oz vegetable margarine	1 tablespoon vegetable margarine
2 tablespoons chopped parsley	2 tablespoons chopped parsley
salt	salt
freshly ground black pepper	freshly ground black pepper

Wash the mussels (or clams) and scrub them very thoroughly. Discard any which are open. Put them in a heavy pan with the shallots and cider. Cover and cook over high heat for 5 minutes until all the mussels (or clams) have opened; discard any which are still closed.

Lift out the mussels (or clams) and discard the top shell from each one. Divide them equally between 4 individual soup bowls and keep hot.

Work the flour and margarine together to form a ball. Drop the ball into the cooking liquid and simmer until the sauce has thickened slightly, stirring constantly. Stir in the parsley, then add salt and pepper to taste. Pour the sauce over the mussels and serve immediately.

Serves 4

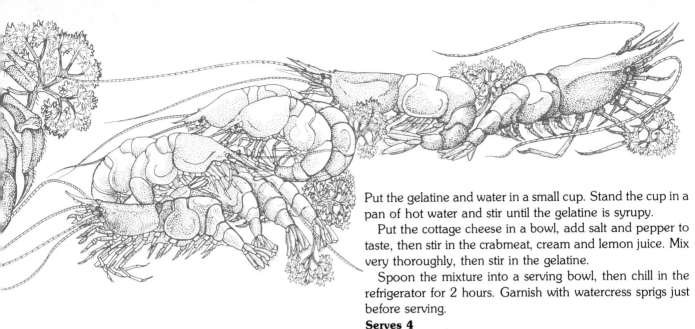

Put the gelatine and water in a small cup. Stand the cup in a pan of hot water and stir until the gelatine is syrupy.

Put the cottage cheese in a bowl, add salt and pepper to taste, then stir in the crabmeat, cream and lemon juice. Mix very thoroughly, then stir in the gelatine.

Spoon the mixture into a serving bowl, then chill in the refrigerator for 2 hours. Garnish with watercress sprigs just before serving.

Serves 4

Prawn (Shrimp), Apple and Celery Cocktail

Metric/Imperial	American
1 lettuce, shredded	1 head of lettuce, shredded
salt	salt
2 celery sticks, finely chopped	2 celery stalks, finely chopped
1 dessert apple, peeled, cored and chopped	1 dessert apple, peeled, cored and chopped
225 g / 8 oz peeled prawns	1 cup shelled shrimp
juice of 1 lemon	juice of 1 lemon
freshly ground black pepper	freshly ground black pepper
pinch of paprika to garnish	pinch of paprika to garnish

Divide the lettuce equally between 4 glasses and sprinkle lightly with salt. Put the remaining ingredients, except the paprika, in a bowl and mix well.

Divide the mixture equally between the glasses, sprinkle with paprika and serve chilled.

Serves 4

Crab and Cottage Cheese Mousse

Metric/Imperial	American
15 g / ½ oz gelatine	2 envelopes gelatin
150 ml / ¼ pint water	²/₃ cup water
450 g / 1 lb cottage cheese, sieved	2 cups cottage cheese, sieved
salt	salt
freshly ground black pepper	freshly ground black pepper
225 g / 8 oz crabmeat	1 cup crabmeat
3 tablespoons single cream	3 tablespoons light cream
2 teaspoons lemon juice	2 teaspoons lemon juice
watercress sprigs to garnish	watercress sprigs to garnish

Baked Crab

The crabmeat may be fresh, canned or frozen provided it is thawed. The dish is best made with a mixture of about one-third dark meat and two-thirds white meat.

Metric/Imperial	American
2 tablespoons oil	2 tablespoons oil
1 onion, peeled and finely chopped	1 onion, peeled and finely chopped
1 garlic clove, peeled and crushed	1 garlic clove, peeled and crushed
2 green peppers, cored, seeded and finely chopped	2 green peppers, cored, seeded and finely chopped
2 tomatoes, skinned, seeded and chopped	2 tomatoes, skinned, seeded and chopped
2 tablespoons chopped parsley	2 tablespoons chopped parsley
450 g / 1 lb crabmeat	2 cups crabmeat
salt	salt
freshly ground white pepper	freshly ground white pepper
2 eggs, lightly beaten	2 eggs, lightly beaten
2 tablespoons wholemeal breadcrumbs	2 tablespoons wholewheat breadcrumbs

Heat the oil in a pan, add the onion and fry gently for 5 minutes until soft and golden, stirring occasionally. Add the garlic, green peppers, tomatoes and parsley and continue cooking gently for 15 minutes, stirring occasionally.

Add the crabmeat to the pan with salt and pepper to taste. Then add the eggs and cook until just set, stirring constantly.

Spread the crab mixture in a greased shallow baking dish and sprinkle the breadcrumbs on top. Bake in a preheated moderately hot oven (190°C / 375°F, Gas Mark 5) for 10 minutes or until the crumbs are crisp and brown. Serve hot.

Serves 4

Prawn (Shrimp) Quiches

Metric/Imperial

wholewheat pastry made
    with 225 g / 8 oz flour
    (see page 145)
25 g / 1 oz vegetable
    margarine
1 small onion, peeled and
    chopped
2 eggs, beaten
100 g / 4 oz cottage cheese,
    sieved
2 tablespoons single cream
2 teaspoons chopped
    parsley
salt
freshly ground white pepper
100 g / 4 oz peeled prawns
chopped parsley to garnish

American

wholewheat dough made
    with 2 cups flour (see
    page 145)
2 tablespoons vegetable
    margarine
1 small onion, peeled and
    chopped
2 eggs, beaten
½ cup cottage cheese,
    sieved
2 tablespoons light cream
2 teaspoons chopped
    parsley
salt
freshly ground white pepper
½ cup shelled shrimp
chopped parsley to garnish

Roll out the pastry dough on a lightly floured surface and use to line 4 individual quiche dishes. Prick the bases lightly with a fork, cover with kitchen foil, then weigh down with baking beans or rice.

Bake in a preheated moderately hot oven (200°C / 400°F, Gas Mark 6) for 10 minutes, then remove the beans or rice and the foil.

Meanwhile, melt the margarine in a pan, add the onion and fry gently for 3 minutes, stirring occasionally.

Put the eggs, cottage cheese, cream, parsley and salt and pepper to taste in a bowl and beat well to mix. Stir in the onion and prawns (shrimp). Divide the mixture equally between the flan cases.

Bake in a preheated moderate oven (180°C / 350°F, Gas Mark 4) for 20 minutes. Garnish with parsley and serve hot.
Serves 4

RIGHT: Spiced herrings; Swedish pickled shrimp
BELOW: Prawn (shrimp) quiches

Swedish Pickled Shrimp

Metric/Imperial	**American**
450 g / 1 lb peeled shrimps	2 cups shelled shrimp
6 black peppercorns, crushed	6 black peppercorns, crushed
½ teaspoon chopped thyme	½ teaspoon chopped thyme
1 bay leaf	1 bay leaf
150 ml / ¼ pint tarragon vinegar	⅔ cup tarragon vinegar
1 lettuce	1 head of lettuce
dill leaves to garnish	dill leaves to garnish

The shrimps may be fresh, or thawed frozen ones which have been well drained.

Put the shrimps in a bowl and sprinkle with the crushed peppercorns and the thyme. Put the bay leaf on top and pour on the vinegar. Chill in the refrigerator for 2 hours.

Arrange a bed of lettuce leaves in 4 individual serving bowls. Drain the shrimps and arrange a mound of them on each bed of lettuce. Sprinkle with dill leaves. Serve with thinly sliced brown bread or crispbread, and butter.

Serves 4

Spiced Herrings

Metric/Imperial	**American**
4 herrings	4 herrings
2 onions, peeled and chopped	2 onions, peeled and chopped
2 tablespoons whole pickling spice	2 tablespoons whole pickling spice
salt	salt
freshly ground black pepper	freshly ground black pepper
450 ml / ¾ pint dry cider	2 cups hard cider

Split the fish down the back, open out and clean. Reserve the roes. Wash the herrings well and dry them on kitchen paper towels. Mash the roes with a fork and mix with one quarter of the onion. Stuff the fish with this mixture and arrange them head to tail in a baking dish.

Sprinkle the remaining onion, the pickling spice and salt and pepper to taste, over the fish. Pour on the cider. Cover and bake in a preheated moderate oven (160°C / 325°F, Gas Mark 3) for 1¼ hours. Leave the fish to cool in the cooking liquid, then chill in the refrigerator overnight. Serve cold with salad.

Serves 4

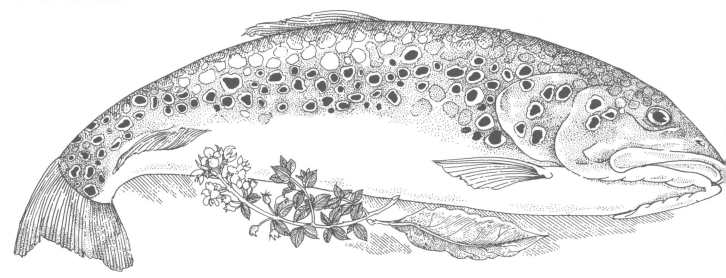

Trout in Yogurt Sauce

Metric/Imperial	American
150 ml / ¼ pint wine vinegar	⅔ cup wine vinegar
150 ml / ¼ pint water	⅔ cup water
1 small onion, peeled and sliced	1 small onion, peeled and sliced
1 bay leaf	1 bay leaf
1 parsley sprig	1 parsley sprig
1 thyme sprig	1 thyme sprig
salt	salt
freshly ground white pepper	freshly ground white pepper
4 × 225 g / 8 oz trout, cleaned, washed and dried	4 × ½ lb trout, cleaned, washed and dried
SAUCE:	SAUCE:
150 ml / ¼ pint natural yogurt	⅔ cup unflavored yogurt
3 tablespoons grated horseradish	3 tablespoons grated horseradish
juice of ½ lemon	juice of ½ lemon
1 tablespoon tarragon vinegar	1 tablespoon tarragon vinegar
1 teaspoon snipped chives	1 teaspoon snipped chives
pinch of cayenne pepper	pinch of cayenne pepper

Put the vinegar, water, onion, bay leaf, parsley and thyme in a small pan with salt and pepper to taste. Bring to the boil, then lower the heat and simmer for 30 minutes.

Put the trout in a separate pan, then strain the vinegar liquid over the trout. Simmer very gently for 20 minutes, then drain well and place on a warmed serving dish. Keep hot.

To make the sauce: put all the ingredients in a heatproof bowl and stand over a pan of gently simmering water. Stir until the sauce is thick and creamy, then pour over the fish and serve immediately. This dish can alternatively be served cold.

Serves 4

Baked Trout

Metric/Imperial	American
2 tablespoons oil	2 tablespoons oil
2 garlic cloves, peeled and crushed	2 garlic cloves, peeled and crushed
2 onions, peeled and finely chopped	2 onions, peeled and finely chopped
100 g / 4 oz mushrooms, chopped	1 cup chopped mushrooms
2 tablespoons capers	2 tablespoons capers
2 tablespoons wholemeal flour	2 tablespoons wholewheat flour
25 g / 1 oz ground almonds	¼ cup ground almonds
4 × 225 g / 8 oz trout, cleaned, washed and dried	4 × ½ lb trout, cleaned, washed and dried
2 tablespoons chopped parsley	2 tablespoons chopped parsley
pinch of chopped marjoram	pinch of chopped marjoram
1 teaspoon salt	1 teaspoon salt
½ teaspoon freshly ground black pepper	½ teaspoon freshly ground black pepper
150 ml / ¼ pint chicken stock	⅔ cup chicken stock
toasted flaked almonds to garnish	toasted sliced almonds to garnish

Heat the oil in a large, shallow flameproof casserole or heavy-based pan. Add the garlic and onions and fry gently for 5 minutes until the onions are soft and golden, stirring occasionally. Stir in the mushrooms, capers, flour and ground almonds and fry gently for a further 3 minutes.

Put the trout on top of the onion mixture, then sprinkle with the parlsey, marjoram, salt and pepper. Pour on the stock.

Bake in a preheated moderately hot oven (200°C / 400°F, Gas Mark 6) for 25 minutes, basting twice. Sprinkle with almonds and serve immediately.

Serves 4

Summer Fish Salad

Metric/Imperial	American
450 g / 1 lb haddock or cod fillets	1 lb haddock or cod fillets
1 onion, peeled	1 onion, peeled
450 ml / ³/₄ pint water	2 cups water
1 teaspoon salt	1 teaspoon salt
4 tablespoons mayonnaise	¹/₄ cup mayonnaise
1 teaspoon chopped parsley	1 teaspoon chopped parsley
1 teaspoon grated onion	1 teaspoon grated onion
1 teaspoon Worcestershire sauce	1 teaspoon Worcestershire sauce
¹/₄ teaspoon freshly ground black pepper	¹/₄ teaspoon freshly ground black pepper
2 celery sticks, finely chopped	2 celery stalks, finely chopped
1 dessert apple, peeled, cored and diced	1 dessert apple, peeled, cored and diced
¹/₂ cucumber, peeled and diced	¹/₂ cucumber, peeled and diced
TO GARNISH:	TO GARNISH:
1 lettuce, shredded	1 head of lettuce, shredded
1 hard-boiled egg, shelled and finely chopped	1 hard-cooked egg, shelled and finely chopped

Put the fish in a pan with the onion, water and salt. Bring to the boil, then lower the heat and poach gently for 25 minutes or until the fish is tender. Drain off the water, then flake the fish into a serving bowl, discarding the skin and any bones. Leave the fish to cool.

Mix together the mayonnaise, parsley, onion, Worcestershire sauce and pepper. Add the celery, apple, cucumber and mayonnaise mixture to the fish and fold gently to mix.

Arrange a border of shredded lettuce around the edge of the bowl and sprinkle the chopped egg in the middle.

Serves 4

Cod Kebabs

Metric/Imperial	American
500 g / 1 lb cod fillet, skinned and cut into 5 cm / 2 inch squares	1 lb cod fillet, skinned and cut in 2 inch squares
salt	salt
freshly ground black pepper	freshly ground black pepper
2 tablespoons lemon juice	2 tablespoons lemon juice
4 tablespoons corn oil	4 tablespoons corn oil
1 teaspoon chopped parsley	1 teaspoon chopped parsley
1 teaspoon chopped marjoram (optional)	1 teaspoon chopped marjoram (optional)
1 garlic clove, peeled and crushed	1 garlic clove, peeled and crushed
4 lean rashers bacon, derinded	4 lean bacon slices, derinded
1 green pepper, cored, seeded and sliced	1 green pepper, cored, seeded and sliced
4 small tomatoes	4 small tomatoes

Place the fish in a shallow dish and sprinkle liberally with salt and pepper. Mix together the lemon juice, oil, parsley, marjoram and garlic and pour over the fish. Cover and leave to marinate in a cool place for about 4 hours.

Cut the bacon and green pepper into 5 cm / 2 inch squares. Drain the fish, reserving the marinade. Thread alternate pieces of fish, bacon and green pepper onto 4 kebab skewers. Press the pieces together firmly and place a whole tomato on one end of each skewer.

Place on a grill (broiler) rack and baste with the marinade. Cook under a preheated moderate grill (broiler) for 8 to 10 minutes until the fish is tender and the green pepper is softened. Turn the skewers and brush with the oil mixture frequently during cooking.

Serve the kebabs hot, with a crisp green salad and brown rice or wholewheat bread.

Serves 4

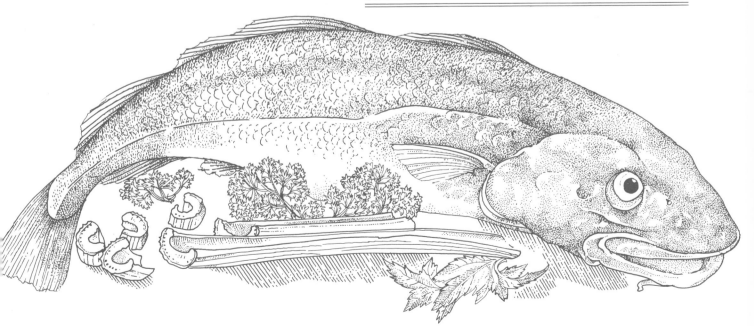

Seafood Salad with Dill

Metric/Imperial	American
450 g / 1 lb smoked haddock fillets	1 lb smoked haddock fillets
600 ml / 1 pint water	2½ cups water
1 bay leaf	1 bay leaf
1 small onion, peeled and sliced	1 small onion, peeled and sliced
1 small carrot, peeled and sliced	1 small carrot, peeled and sliced
4 black peppercorns	4 black peppercorns
225 g / 8 oz peeled prawns	1 cup shelled shrimp
120 ml / 4 fl oz oil	½ cup oil
3 tablespoons wine vinegar	3 tablespoons wine vinegar
freshly ground black pepper	freshly ground black pepper
1 lettuce	1 head of lettuce
1 bunch watercress, trimmed	1 bunch watercress, trimmed
1 tablespoon chopped parsley	1 tablespoon chopped parsley
2 tablespoons chopped dill	2 tablespoons chopped dill

Put the fish in a pan with the water, bay leaf, onion, carrot and peppercorns. Bring to the boil, then lower the heat and poach gently for 15 minutes or until the fish is tender. Drain off the water, then flake the fish into a bowl, discarding the skin and any bones.

Add the prawns (shrimp) to the haddock. Mix together the oil, vinegar and black pepper and pour over the fish. Chill in the refrigerator for 2 hours.

Arrange a bed of lettuce leaves in a serving bowl, then arrange the watercress on top. Drain the fish, place in the centre of the bowl and sprinkle generously with parsley and dill.

Serves 4

Seafood Curry

Metric/Imperial	American
25 g / 1 oz vegetable margarine	2 tablespoons vegetable margarine
1 small onion, peeled and chopped	1 small onion, peeled and chopped
1 teaspoon curry powder	1 teaspoon curry powder
2 teaspoons flour	2 teaspoons flour
150 ml / ¼ pint natural yogurt	⅔ cup unflavored yogurt
1 small dessert apple, cored and chopped	1 small dessert apple, cored and chopped
225 g / 8 oz peeled prawns	1 cup shelled shrimp
2 tomatoes, skinned, seeded and chopped	2 tomatoes, skinned, seeded and chopped
salt	salt
freshly ground black pepper	freshly ground black pepper
lemon wedges to garnish	lemon wedges to garnish

Melt the margarine in a pan, add the onion and fry gently for 3 minutes until soft and golden, stirring occasionally. Stir in the curry powder and flour and cook for 2 minutes.

Remove from the heat and stir in the yogurt, apple and prawns (shrimp). Return to the heat and cook gently for 5 minutes.

Add the tomatoes to the pan and continue cooking for 3 minutes. Add salt and pepper to taste. Garnish with lemon wedges and serve hot, with brown rice.

Serves 4

ABOVE: Seafood curry
RIGHT: Seafood salad with dill; Smoked haddock flan

Smoked Haddock Flan

Metric/Imperial

wholewheat pastry made with 175 g / 6 oz flour (see page 145)
225 g / 8 oz smoked haddock fillets
150 ml / ¼ pint water
juice of 1 lemon
25 g / 1 oz vegetable margarine
1 small onion, peeled and chopped
50 g / 2 oz button mushrooms, sliced
2 eggs, beaten
3 tablespoons single cream
100 g / 4 oz cottage cheese
1 tablespoon chopped parsley
salt
freshly ground white pepper
25 g / 1 oz grated Parmesan cheese
parsley sprig to garnish

American

wholewheat dough made with 1½ cups flour (see page 145)
½ lb smoked haddock fillets
⅔ cup water
juice of 1 lemon
2 tablespoons vegetable margarine
1 small onion, peeled and chopped
½ cup sliced button mushrooms
2 eggs, beaten
3 tablespoons light cream
½ cup cottage cheese
1 tablespoon chopped parsley
salt
freshly ground white pepper
¼ cup grated Parmesan cheese
parsley sprig to garnish

Roll out the pastry dough on a lightly floured surface and use to line a 20 cm / 8 inch flan ring placed on a baking sheet. Prick the base lightly with a fork, cover with foil, then weigh down with baking beans or rice.

Bake blind in a preheated moderately hot oven (200°C / 400°F, Gas Mark 6) for 15 minutes, then remove the beans or rice and the foil.

Meanwhile, put the fish in a pan with the water and half the lemon juice and poach gently for 15 minutes until the fish is tender. Drain off the water, then flake the fish into a bowl, discarding the skin and any bones.

Melt the margarine in a pan, add the onion and mushrooms and fry gently for 3 minutes, stirring occasionally. Add to the fish, mix well, then spread the mixture in the flan case.

Put the eggs, cream, cottage cheese, parsley, remaining lemon juice and salt and pepper to taste in a bowl. Beat well, then pour over the fish. Sprinkle with the Parmesan cheese.

Bake in a preheated moderately hot oven (190° / 375°F, Gas Mark 5) for 40 minutes. Garnish with the parsley sprig and serve hot.

Serves 4

Spiced Fish Casserole

Metric/Imperial	American
3 large tomatoes, skinned and sliced	3 large tomatoes, skinned and sliced
2 celery sticks, finely chopped	2 celery stalks, finely chopped
1 garlic clove, peeled and crushed	1 garlic clove, peeled and crushed
50 g / 2 oz mushrooms, sliced	½ cup sliced mushrooms
salt	salt
freshly ground black pepper	freshly ground black pepper
pinch of grated nutmeg	pinch of grated nutmeg
1 teaspoon chopped parsley	1 teaspoon chopped parsley
1 teaspoon chopped basil	1 teaspoon chopped basil
1 bay leaf	1 bay leaf
1 onion, peeled and sliced	1 onion, peeled and sliced
1 carrot, peeled and sliced	1 carrot, peeled and sliced
750 g / 1½ lb cod fillets	1½ lb cod fillets
3 tablespoons wine vinegar	3 tablespoons wine vinegar
150 ml / ¼ pint water	⅔ cup water

Arrange half the tomato slices in a baking dish and cover with the celery, garlic and mushrooms. Season well with salt and pepper, then sprinkle with the nutmeg and parsley. Add the basil and the bay leaf and top with the onion and carrot.

Arrange the fish on top of this mixture, then cover with the remaining tomato slices. Pour on the vinegar and water. Cover and bake in a preheated moderate oven (180°C / 350°F, Gas Mark 4) for 40 minutes. Serve hot.

Serves 4

Smoked Haddock and Cheese Bake

Metric/Imperial	American
450 g / 1 lb smoked haddock fillets	1 lb smoked haddock fillets
25 g / 1 oz grated Parmesan cheese	¼ cup grated Parmesan cheese
salt	salt
freshly ground white pepper	freshly ground white pepper
150 ml / ¼ pint natural yogurt	⅔ cup unflavored yogurt
300 ml / ½ pint milk	1¼ cups milk
2 eggs, beaten	2 eggs, beaten
1 tablespoon chopped parsley	1 tablespoon chopped parsley

Put the fish in a pan with enough water to just cover. Bring to the boil, then lower the heat and poach gently for 15 minutes or until the fish is tender. Drain off the water, then place the fish in a baking dish.

Sprinkle the cheese and salt and pepper to taste over the fish. Put the remaining ingredients in a bowl, mix well, then pour over the fish.

Stand the dish in a roasting pan and pour in enough water to come 2.5 cm / 1 inch up the sides of the pan. Bake in a preheated moderate oven (180°C / 350°F, Gas Mark 4) for 40 minutes. Serve hot.

Serves 4

Swedish Baked Fish

Metric/Imperial
4 halibut fillets
1 onion, peeled and sliced
4 tablespoons chopped
  parsley
450 ml / ¾ pint tomato
  juice
salt
freshly ground black pepper

American
4 halibut fillets
1 onion, peeled and sliced
¼ cup chopped parsley
2 cups tomato juice
salt
freshly ground black pepper

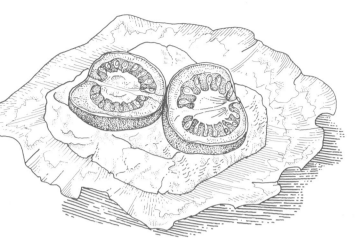

Put the fish in a greased baking dish. Arrange the onion slices on top and sprinkle with half the parsley. Pour on the tomato juice, season well with salt and pepper, then cover with foil.

Bake in a preheated moderately hot oven (200°C / 400°F, Gas Mark 6) for 30 minutes. Sprinkle with the remaining parsley and serve hot.

Serves 4

Work the mixture through a sieve (strainer), taste and adjust seasoning, then pour over the fish. Bake in a preheated moderate oven (180°C / 350°F, Gas Mark 4) for 45 minutes or until the fish is cooked. Serve hot.

Serves 4

Haddock in Tomato Sauce

Metric/Imperial
450 g / 1 lb haddock fillets
1 teaspoon salt
½ teaspoon freshly ground
  black pepper
1 tablespoon oil
1 onion, peeled and finely
  chopped
1 green pepper, cored,
  seeded and finely
  chopped
2 celery sticks, finely
  chopped
1 garlic clove, peeled and
  crushed
1 teaspoon chilli powder
1 bay leaf
1 tablespoon
  Worcestershire saucee
1 × 500 g / 1 lb can
  tomatoes

American
1 lb haddock fillets
1 teaspoon salt
½ teaspoon freshly ground
  black pepper
1 tablespoon oil
1 onion, peeled and finely
  chopped
1 green pepper, cored,
  seeded and finely
  chopped
2 celery stalks, finely
  chopped
1 garlic clove, peeled and
  crushed
1 teaspoon chili powder
1 bay leaf
1 tablespoon
  Worcestershire sauce
1 lb can tomatoes

Cut the fish into 4 pieces, then place in a lightly oiled shallow baking dish. Sprinkle with the salt and pepper then chill in the refrigerator for 30 minutes.

Meanwhile, heat the oil in a pan. Add the onion, green pepper, celery and garlic and fry gently for 5 minutes, stirring occasionally. Add the remaining ingredients and continue cooking gently for 10 minutes, stirring well.

Fish in a Packet

Metric/Imperial
450 g / 1 lb cod fillets
2 tablespoons oil
2 tablespoons lemon juice
salt
freshly ground black pepper
2 tomatoes, sliced
4 fennel sprigs

American
1 lb cod fillets
2 tablespoons oil
2 tablespoons lemon juice
salt
freshly ground black pepper
2 tomatoes, sliced
4 fennel sprigs

Cut the fish into 4 pieces. Cut out four 30 cm / 12 inch squares of foil and brush them liberally with oil. Place one piece of fish on each square of foil, then sprinkle with the remaining oil, the lemon juice and salt and pepper to taste. Place 2 tomato slices on each piece of fish, then top each with a fennel sprig.

Fold the foil around each fish to form a parcel, then place the parcels on a baking sheet. Bake in a preheated moderate oven (180°C / 350°F, Gas Mark 4) for 30 minutes.

Unwrap each parcel carefully, lift the fish out onto warmed serving plates, pour over the cooking juices and serve hot.

Serves 4

MEAT & POULTRY

Some people believe that meat and poultry can have no part in a healthy diet, but this is far from true. Meat and poultry are good sources of high-quality protein, iron and B group vitamins. Unfortunately, they also contain a relatively high proportion of saturated fats, as well as a moderate amount of cholesterol.

Man has, of course, evolved as a flesh-eater, and while a number of people prefer not to eat meat for humanitarian or aesthetic reasons, the fact remains that most of us are accustomed to eating meat and consider it to be an essential part of our meals. Both meat and non-meat diets can be healthy. Vegetarians must make sure that they balance their intake of protein foods to obtain sufficient quantities of all of the essential amino-acids. Meat-eaters should try to moderate the amount they consume in order to restrict intake of saturated fats.

Different types of meat vary in their nutrient composition. Offal (variety meats), especially liver and kidney, contain less fat and are therefore particularly valuable for those on slimming diets – providing rich sources of protein, iron, vitamin A and B group vitamins with comparatively few calories. Liver and kidney also have the advantage of being relatively cheap. Many people do not like the strong flavour of liver or kidney, but combined with other ingredients in pâtés, soups and casseroles – for example – their flavour is less distinct and acceptable to most.

The amount of fat varies considerably from one kind of meat to another and also depends on the cut. Pork and ham contain more fat than lamb or beef. Some meat fat is visible and can be trimmed off, but even apparently lean meat has fat distributed throughout the tissue. Grilling (broiling) and roasting are preferred methods of cooking for less lean cuts of meat, because they enable a certain amount of fat to drain away.

Always use as little fat as possible when cooking meat. Minced (ground) beef will brown effectively in its own fat and bacon can be cooked in a frying pan (skillet) without additional fat.

Like carcass meat, chicken is an excellent source of protein. It is also extremely versatile and can be cooked in numerous different ways. Nowadays chickens are mass produced; they are normally fed antibiotics and hormones to aid growth and feed efficiency. Most people agree that there is a consequent lack of flavour, but there is no significant difference between the nutrient composition of broiler chickens and free-range hens. For maximum flavour it is well worth trying to obtain a free-range bird when serving roast poultry.

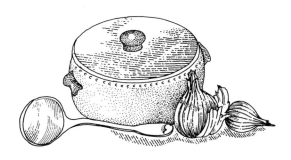

Chicken and olive bake (page 60); Chicken bake with yogurt topping (page 61); Chicken and vegetable fricassée (page 60)

Chicken and Vegetable Fricassée

Metric/Imperial	American
4 chicken portions	4 chicken portions
3 onions, peeled and finely chopped	3 onions, peeled and finely chopped
1 garlic clove, peeled and crushed	1 garlic clove, peeled and crushed
2 celery sticks, thinly sliced	2 celery stalks, thinly sliced
2 carrots, peeled and thinly sliced	2 carrots, peeled and thinly sliced
1 bay leaf	1 bay leaf
150 ml / ¼ pint chicken stock	⅔ cup chicken stock
1 teaspoon chopped thyme	1 teaspoon chopped thyme
1 teaspoon paprika	1 teaspoon paprika
salt	salt
freshly ground black pepper	freshly ground black pepper
chopped parsley to garnish	chopped parsley to garnish

Take a piece of fat from the chicken and rub over the base of a heavy pan. Put in the chicken and cook gently over very low heat until golden on all sides. Add the onions and garlic and continue cooking gently for 3 minutes, stirring occasionally.

Add the remaining ingredients, except the parsley, then cover and cook over low heat for 1¼ hours or until the chicken is tender. Taste and adjust the seasoning. Sprinkle with parsley and serve hot.

Serves 4

Chicken Liver Skewers

Metric/Imperial	American
16 mushrooms	16 mushrooms
4 lean bacon rashers, derinded	4 Canadian bacon slices, derinded
225 g / 8 oz chicken livers	½ lb chicken livers
salt	salt
freshly ground black pepper	freshly ground black pepper
few drops of Tabasco sauce	few drops of Tabasco sauce
1 tablespoon oil	1 tablespoon oil

Wipe the mushrooms but do not wash or peel them. Cut each bacon slice into 3 pieces. Cut each chicken liver in half.

Take 4 kebab skewers, thread 1 mushroom on each. Alternate bacon, chicken livers and mushrooms on each skewer, finishing with a mushroom. Sprinkle with salt, pepper and Tabasco sauce, then brush with oil.

Grill (broil) under medium heat for 6 minutes, turning the skewers frequently until the bacon and livers are completely cooked. Serve hot with salad.

Serves 4

Chicken and Olive Bake

Metric/Imperial	American
4 chicken portions	4 chicken portions
5 tablespoons cider vinegar	⅓ cup cider vinegar
4 tomatoes, skinned and chopped	4 tomatoes, skinned and chopped
2 green peppers, cored, seeded and chopped	2 green peppers, cored, seeded and chopped
2 onions, peeled and chopped	2 onions, peeled and chopped
1 small garlic clove, peeled and crushed	1 small garlic clove, peeled and crushed
1 teaspoon chopped marjoram	1 teaspoon chopped marjoram
salt	salt
freshly ground black pepper	freshly ground black pepper
1 tablespoon olive oil	1 tablespoon olive oil
2 tablespoons tomato purée	2 tablespoons tomato paste
75 g / 3 oz stuffed olives	½ cup stuffed olives
chopped thyme to garnish	chopped thyme to garnish

Put the chicken in a shallow dish. Mix together the vinegar, tomatoes, peppers, onions, garlic, marjoram and salt and pepper to taste. Pour over the chicken. Leave to marinate for 2 hours, turning the chicken once.

Heat the oil in a deep frying pan (skillet). Drain the chicken, reserving the marinade. Add the chicken to the pan and fry until browned on all sides. Stir in the reserved marinade with the tomato purée (paste) and the olives. Cover and simmer over low heat for 1 hour. Taste and adjust seasoning, sprinkle with thyme and serve hot.

Serves 4

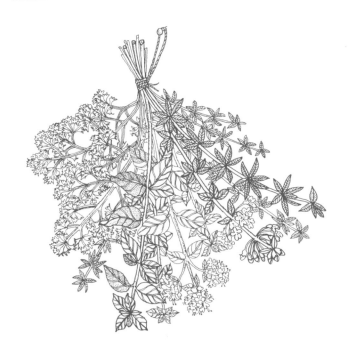

Herbed Chicken

Metric/Imperial	American
1 × 1.75 kg / 4 lb roasting chicken	1 × 4 lb roasting chicken
1 tablespoon oil	1 tablespoon oil
3 tablespoons lemon juice	3 tablespoons lemon juice
salt	salt
freshly ground black pepper	freshly ground black pepper
1 × 500 g / 1 lb can tomatoes	1 × 1 lb can tomatoes
1 teaspoon chopped marjoram	1 teaspoon chopped marjoram
1 teaspoon chopped parsley	1 teaspoon chopped parsley
1 teaspoon snipped chives	1 teaspoon snipped chives
1 teaspoon chopped thyme	1 teaspoon chopped thyme

Put the chicken in a roasting pan, brush with the oil and lemon juice, then sprinkle with salt and pepper.

Roast in a preheated moderately hot oven (190°C / 375°F, Gas Mark 5) for 45 minutes.

Mix together the tomatoes, herbs, and salt and pepper to taste, then pour over the chicken. Reduce the oven temperature to moderate (180°C / 350°F, Gas Mark 4) and continue roasting for 45 minutes, basting the chicken frequently with the tomato mixture. Serve hot with seasonal vegetables or a salad.

Serves 4 to 6

Chicken Bake with Yogurt Topping

Metric/Imperial	American
15 g / ½ oz vegetable margarine	1 tablespoon vegetable margarine
1 small onion, peeled and finely chopped	1 small onion, peeled and finely chopped
2 celery sticks, finely chopped	2 celery stalks, finely chopped
100 g / 4 oz button mushrooms	1 cup button mushrooms
350 g / 12 oz cooked chicken, finely chopped	1½ cups finely chopped cooked chicken
1 tablespoon chopped parsley	1 tablespoon chopped parsley
salt	salt
freshly ground white pepper	freshly ground white pepper
TOPPING:	TOPPING:
300 ml / ½ pint natural yogurt	1¼ cups unflavored yogurt
2 egg yolks	2 egg yolks
1 teaspoon prepared mustard	1 teaspoon prepared mustard

Melt the margarine in a pan. Add the onion, celery and mushrooms and fry gently for 5 minutes, stirring frequently. Add the chicken, parsley and salt and pepper to taste, then transfer the mixture to a casserole and press down firmly.

To make the topping: put the yogurt in a bowl with the egg yolks, mustard and salt and pepper to taste. Mix well, then pour over the chicken.

Bake in a preheated moderately hot oven (190°C / 375°F, Gas Mark 5) for 25 minutes. Serve hot.

Serves 4

Lemon Chops

Metric/Imperial	American
4 lamb chops	4 lamb chops
2 tablespoons corn oil	2 tablespoons corn oil
grated rind of 1 lemon	grated rind of 1 lemon
2 tablespoons lemon juice	2 tablespoons lemon juice
2 teaspoons Muscovado sugar	2 teaspoons Muscovado sugar
1 teaspoon ground ginger	1 teaspoon ground ginger
salt	salt
freshly ground black pepper	freshly ground black pepper
parsley sprigs to garnish	parsley sprigs to garnish

Put the chops into a shallow dish. Mix together the oil, lemon rind and juice, sugar and ginger and pour over the chops. Cover and leave to marinate in a cool place for 3 hours, turning the chops occasionally.

Transfer the chops to a grill (broiler) rack and brush with the marinade. Cook under a preheated grill (broiler) for 15 minutes, turning the chops 2 or 3 times and basting them frequently.

Garnish with parsley sprigs and serve immediately accompanied by brown rice and a crisp green salad or vegetables.

Serves 4

Lamb Provençal

Metric/Imperial	American
500 g / 1 lb lean boned leg of lamb	1 lb lean boneless leg of lamb
2 tablespoons vegetable oil	2 tablespoons vegetable oil
1 large onion, sliced	1 large onion, sliced
1 garlic clove, crushed	1 garlic clove, crushed
1 × 500 g / 1 lb can tomatoes	1 lb can tomatoes
1 tablespoon tomato purée	1 tablespoon tomato paste
150 ml / ¼ pint dry white wine	⅔ cup dry white wine
1 rosemary sprig	1 rosemary sprig
1 thyme sprig	1 thyme sprig
1 bay leaf	1 bay leaf
salt	salt
freshly ground black pepper	freshly ground black pepper
100 g / 4 oz mushrooms, sliced	1 cup sliced mushrooms
1 green pepper, cored, seeded and sliced	1 green pepper, cored, seeded and sliced
chopped parsley to garnish	chopped parsley to garnish

Trim any excess fat from the lamb and cut into 2.5 cm / 1 inch cubes. Heat the oil in a flameproof casserole or heavy

based pan. Add the onion and garlic and sauté until golden.

Add the lamb cubes and cook, stirring frequently, for 5 minutes or until evenly browned. Stir in the tomatoes and their juice, tomato purée (paste) and wine. Add the rosemary, thyme, bay leaf and salt and pepper to taste. Stir well, then cover and simmer for 45 minutes.

Add the sliced mushrooms and green pepper to the casserole. Check the seasoning, cover and continue simmering for a further 20 minutes.

Discard the herbs. Sprinkle with chopped parsley and serve with brown rice.

Serves 4

Lamb Skewers

Metric/Imperial	**American**
450 g / 1 lb boned leg or shoulder of lamb, trimmed of fat and cut into cubes	1 lb boned leg or shoulder of lamb, trimmed of fat and cut into cubes
3 small onions, peeled	3 small onions, peeled
1 garlic clove, peeled and crushed	1 garlic clove, peeled and crushed
1 teaspoon salt	1 teaspoon salt
1 teaspoon ground ginger	1 teaspoon ground ginger
few drops of Tabasco sauce	few drops of Tabasco sauce
¹/₂ teaspoon ground turmeric	¹/₂ teaspoon ground turmeric
pinch of ground coriander	pinch of ground coriander
juice of 1 large lemon	juice of 1 large lemon
1 large green pepper, cored, seeded and cut into 2.5 cm / 1 inch squares	1 large green pepper, cored, seeded and cut into 1 inch squares
8 mushrooms	8 mushrooms
4 small tomatoes	4 small tomatoes
1 tablespoon oil	1 tablespoon oil
chopped mixed herbs to garnish	chopped mixed herbs to garnish

Put the lamb in a shallow dish. Grate 1 onion, then mix with the garlic, salt, ginger, Tabasco, turmeric, coriander and lemon juice and pour over the lamb. Leave to marinate for 2 hours, stirring frequently.

Cut the remaining onions into quarters. Thread 4 kebab skewers with the lamb cubes, onion quarters, green pepper and mushrooms, alternating the ingredients until they are all used up. Thread a tomato at the end of each skewer, then brush the meat and vegetables with the oil.

Grill (broil) under high heat for 12 minutes, turning the skewers frequently until the meat is cooked through and no longer pink. Sprinkle with herbs and serve hot on a bed of rice.

Serves 4

LEFT: Lamb provençal
ABOVE: Lemon chops; Lamb skewers

Lamb in Mint Jelly

Metric/Imperial	American
450 g / 1 lb cooked lamb, thinly sliced	1 lb cooked lamb, thinly sliced
1 packet aspic jelly powder, to set 600 ml / 1 pint liquid	4 teaspoons unflavored gelatin, to set 2½ cups clear chicken stock
salt	salt
freshly ground white pepper	freshly ground white pepper
2 tablespoons dry sherry	2 tablespoons dry sherry
2 tablespoons chopped mint	2 tablespoons chopped mint

Arrange the lamb slices on a flat serving dish. If using aspic, make up according to packet directions. (If using gelatin, dissolve in a little of the stock, then add the remainder.) Leave in a cool place until the liquid is thick and syrupy. Add salt and pepper to taste and stir in the sherry and mint.

Spoon over the lamb slices very carefully so that the meat is evenly covered. Chill in the refrigerator for 2 hours until set. Serve with salad.

Serves 4

Lamb and Vegetable Casserole

Metric/Imperial	American
750 g / 1½ lb boned leg or shoulder of lamb, trimmed of fat and cut into cubes	1½ lb boned leg or shoulder of lamb, trimmed of fat and cut into cubes
2 onions, peeled and chopped	2 onions, peeled and chopped
1 garlic clove, peeled and crushed	1 garlic clove, peeled and crushed
2 carrots, peeled and sliced	2 carrots, peeled and sliced
2 green peppers, cored, seeded and chopped	2 green peppers, cored, seeded and chopped
300 ml / ½ pint tomato juice	1¼ cups tomato juice
salt	salt
freshly ground black pepper	freshly ground black pepper
2 potatoes, peeled and diced	2 potatoes, peeled and diced
225 g / 8 oz French beans, diced	1 cup diced green beans

Take a piece of fat from the lamb and rub over the base of a heavy pan. Add the lamb and cook gently until the meat is browned on all sides.

Add the onions and garlic and continue cooking gently for 5 minutes, stirring occasionally. Add the carrots, peppers, tomato juice and salt and pepper to taste, then cover and simmer for 1 hour.

Add the potatoes and beans to the pan, cover and continue simmering for 30 minutes. Taste and adjust the seasoning, then serve hot with a seasonal green vegetable.

Serves 4

Grilled (Broiled) Liver with Herbs

Metric/Imperial	American
25 g / 1 oz vegetabble margarine, melted	2 tablespoons vegetable margarine, melted
450 g / 1 lb lamb's liver, sliced	1 lb lamb's liver, sliced
1 tablespoon lemon juice	1 tablespoon lemon juice
salt	salt
freshly ground black peppper	freshly ground black pepper
2 teaspoons chopped parsley	2 teaspoons chopped parsley
2 teaspoons chopped thyme	2 teaspoons chopped thyme
2 teaspoons snipped chives	2 teaspoons snipped chives

Brush the grill (broiler) pan with a little of the margarine. Arrange the liver in the pan and brush with the remaining margarine. Grill (broil) under medium heat for 3 minutes on each side; allow 4 minutes on each side if well-done liver is preferred.

Arrange on a warmed serving plate, pour over the lemon juice, then season with salt and pepper to taste. Sprinkle with the herbs and serve immediately.

Serves 4

Italian Supper

Metric/Imperial	American
450 g / 1 lb lamb's liver, thinly sliced	1 lb lamb's liver, thinly sliced
2 tablespoons wholemeal flour	2 tablespoons wholewheat flour
salt	salt
freshly ground black pepper	freshly ground black pepper
1 tablespoon oil	1 tablespoon oil
1 tablespoon vegetable margarine	1 tablespoon vegetable margarine
2 large onions, peeled and sliced	2 large onions, peeled and sliced
150 ml / ¼ pint beef stock	⅔ cup beef stock
2 tablespoons tomato purée	2 tablespoons tomato paste
1 garlic clove, peeled and crushed	1 garlic clove, peeled and crushed
2 teaspoons chopped basil	2 teaspoons chopped basil
150 ml / ¼ pint single cream	⅔ cup light cream
chopped parsley to garnish	chopped parsley to garnish

Coat the liver in the flour, seasoned with salt and pepper. Heat the oil and margarine in a pan. Add the liver and fry gently for 2 minutes on each side. Remove the liver from the pan and keep hot.

Add the onions to the pan and fry gently for 5 minutes until soft and golden. Stir in the stock, tomato purée (paste), garlic and basil. Bring to the boil, then lower the heat and return the liver to the pan. Cover and simmer for 25 minutes.

Remove the liver from the pan, arrange on a warmed serving dish and keep warm.

Stir the cream into the sauce in the pan and heat through gently without boiling. Taste and adjust the seasoning of the sauce, then pour over the liver. Sprinkle with parsley and serve hot.

Serves 4

Baked Liver in Yogurt Sauce

Metric/Imperial	American
25 g / 1 oz vegetable margarine	2 tablespoons vegetable margarine
450 g / 1 lb lamb's liver, thinly sliced	1 lb lamb's liver, thinly sliced
300 ml / ½ pint natural yogurt	1¼ cups unflavored yogurt
2 teaspoons chopped mixed herbs	2 teaspoons chopped mixed herbs
salt	salt
freshly ground white pepper	freshly ground white pepper
pinch of paprika to garnish	pinch of paprika to garnish

Melt the margarine in a flameproof casserole. Add the liver and fry gently until browned on both sides. Drain off any excess fat.

Mix the yogurt with the herbs and salt and pepper to taste, then pour over the liver and bring to the boil.

Cover the casserole, transfer to a preheated moderate oven (160°C / 325°F, Gas Mark 3) and cook for 25 minutes.

Taste and adjust the seasoning, then sprinkle with paprika and serve hot.

Serves 4

Beef Olives

Metric/Imperial	American
750 g / 1½ lb rump steak	1½ lb top rump
2 tablespoons corn oil	2 tablespoons corn oil
1 onion, peeled and chopped	1 onion, peeled and chopped
2 cloves garlic, peeled and crushed	2 cloves garlic, peeled and crushed
50 g / 2 oz mushrooms, chopped	½ cup chopped mushrooms
1 tablespoon chopped parsley	1 tablespoon chopped parsley
1 teaspoon chopped thyme	1 teaspoon chopped thyme
1 large slice wholemeal bread, crusts removed	1 large slice wholewheat bread, crusts removed
salt	salt
freshly ground black pepper	freshly ground black pepper
150 ml / ¼ pint beef stock	⅔ cup beef stock
150 ml / ¼ pint dry red wine	⅔ cup dry red wine
parsley sprigs to garnish	parsley sprigs to garnish

Cut the beef into 4 thin slices. Place between sheets of greaseproof (waxed) paper and beat to flatten. Trim each slice.

Herb Pâté

Metric/Imperial	American
450 g / 1 lb pig's liver, coarsely minced	2 cups coarsely ground pork liver
100 g / 4 oz lean bacon, derinded and coarsely minced	½ cup coarsely ground Canadian bacon
2 garlic cloves, peeled and crushed	2 garlic cloves, peeled and crushed
1 egg, beaten	1 egg, beaten
3 tablespoons beef stock	3 tablespoons beef stock
1 teaspoon chopped parsley	1 teaspoon chopped parsley
1 teaspoon chopped thyme	1 teaspoon chopped thyme
1 teaspoon snipped chives	1 teaspoon snipped chives
salt	salt
freshly ground black pepper	freshly ground black pepper

Heat 1 tablespoon oil in a saucepan and sauté the onion and garlic until softened. Add the mushrooms and herbs and fry, stirring frequently, for 2 minutes.

Place the bread in an electric blender and grind coarsely. Remove the vegetable mixture from the heat and stir in the breadcrumbs. Add salt and pepper to taste and mix well.

Divide the stuffing between the beef slices and spread evenly. Roll up and secure with string. Heat the remaining oil in a flameproof casserole and fry the beef rolls, turning, until evenly browned.

Pour in the stock and wine. Cover and cook in a pre-heated moderate oven (160°C / 325°F, Gas Mark 3) for 1½ hours. Serve hot, garnished with parsley sprigs.

Serves 4

Put all the ingredients in a bowl and mix well. Press the mixture into a small casserole, then cover with a lid or foil. Stand the casserole in a roasting pan, then pour in enough water to come 2.5 cm / 1 inch up the sides of the pan.

Bake in a preheated moderate oven (180°C / 350°F, Gas Mark 4) for 1½ hours.

Cover the pâté with clean foil, put a heavy weight on top, then leave in the refrigerator for 24 hours. Serve with toast or salad.

Serves 4

Kidney and mushroom supper; Beef olives; Herb pâté

Kidney and Mushroom Supper

Metric/Imperial	American
25 g / 1 oz vegetable margarine	2 tablespoons vegetable margarine
1 large onion, peeled and finely chopped	1 large onion, peeled and finely chopped
1 garlic clove, peeled and crushed	1 garlic clove, peeled and crushed
1 carrot, peeled and grated	1 carrot, peeled and grated
100 g / 4 oz button mushrooms	1 cup mushrooms
8 lambs' kidneys, skinned, cores removed and cut in half lengthways	8 lambs' kidneys, skinned, cores removed and cut in half lengthways
2 tablespoons wholemeal flour	2 tablespoons wholewheat flour
2 teaspoons tomato purée	2 teaspoons tomato paste
150 ml / ¼ pint dry red wine	⅔ cup dry red wine
300 ml / ½ pint beef stock	1¼ cups beef stock
salt	salt
freshly ground black pepper	freshly ground black pepper
chopped parsley to garnish	chopped parsley to garnish

Melt the margarine in a heavy pan. Add the onion, garlic, carrot and mushrooms and cook gently for 5 minutes, stirring occasionally.

Add the kidneys and cook gently for a further 5 minutes, turning frequently, until browned on all sides. Remove the kidneys and mushrooms from the pan with a slotted spoon and transfer to a casserole.

Add the flour to the onion mixture and stir well to mix. Add the tomato purée (paste), wine and stock then simmer for 5 minutes, stirring frequently. Add salt and pepper to taste, then pour over the kidneys.

Cover and cook in a preheated moderate oven (180°C / 350°F, Gas Mark 4) for 20 minutes. Taste and adjust the seasoning, sprinkle with parsley and serve hot.

Serves 4

Devilled Kidneys on Toast

Metric/Imperial	American
1 tablespoon mushroom ketchup or 2 tablespoons finely chopped mushrooms	2 tablespoons minced mushrooms
juice of 1 lemon	juice of 1 lemon
1 tablespoon Worcestershire sauce	1 tablespoon Worcestershire sauce
150 ml / ¼ pint water	⅔ cup water
1 teaspoon mustard powder	1 teaspoon mustard powder
salt	salt
freshly ground black pepper	freshly ground black pepper
8 lambs' kidneys, skinned, cores removed and split in half lengthways	8 lambs' kidneys, skinned, cores removed and split in half lengthways
4 slices wholemeal bread	4 slices wholewheat bread
chopped parsley to garnish	chopped parsley to garnish

Mix together the mushroom ketchup or mushrooms, lemon juice, Worcestershire sauce, water, mustard and salt and pepper to taste.

Grill (broil) the kidneys under medium heat for 3 minutes on the cut sides. Pour the devilled mixture into the grill (broiler) pan, then turn the kidneys and grill (broil) the other sides for 2 minutes. Baste and turn the kidneys, then grill (broil) for a further 2 minutes.

Meanwhile, toast the bread lightly on both sides. Arrange on warmed individual serving plates, then place 2 kidneys on each slice of toast. Pour the sauce over the kidneys, garnish with chopped parsley and serve immediately.

Serves 4

Spring Beef Casserole

Metric/Imperial	American
750 g / 1½ lb chuck steak, trimmed of fat and cut into cubes	1½ lb chuck steak, trimmed of fat and cut into cubes
300 ml / ½ pint dry red wine	1¼ cups dry red wine
1 garlic clove, peeled and crushed	1 garlic clove, peeled and crushed
2 cloves	2 cloves
1 bay leaf	1 bay leaf
1 teaspoon salt	1 teaspoon salt
¼ teaspoon freshly ground black pepper	¼ teaspoon freshly ground black pepper
1 lean bacon rasher, derinded and diced	2 tablespoons diced Canadian bacon
2 celery sticks, chopped	2 celery stalks, chopped
3 parsley sprigs	3 parsley sprigs
150 ml / ¼ pint beef stock	⅔ cup beef stock
6 small pickling onions, peeled	6 baby onions, peeled
4 carrots, peeled and sliced	4 carrots, peeled and sliced
12 button mushrooms	12 button mushrooms
100 g / 4 oz peas	¾ cup peas
chopped parsley to garnish	chopped parsley to garnish

Put the beef in a shallow dish. Mix together the wine, garlic, cloves, bay leaf, salt and pepper and pour over the beef. Leave to marinate for 2 hours, stirring frequently.

Put the bacon in a heavy pan and heat gently until the fat begins to run. Drain the meat, reserving the marinade. Add the meat to the bacon and fry briskly until browned on all sides.

Transfer the beef and bacon to a casserole. Pour in the reserved marinade, then add the celery, parsley sprigs and stock. Cover and cook in a preheated moderate oven (160°C / 325°F, Gas Mark 3) for 1 hour.

Add the onions and carrots. Cover and continue cooking for 30 minutes or until the beef is tender. Add the mushrooms and peas and cook for a further 30 minutes. Remove the bay leaf and parsley sprigs. Taste and adjust the seasoning, then sprinkle with chopped parsley and serve hot.

Serves 4

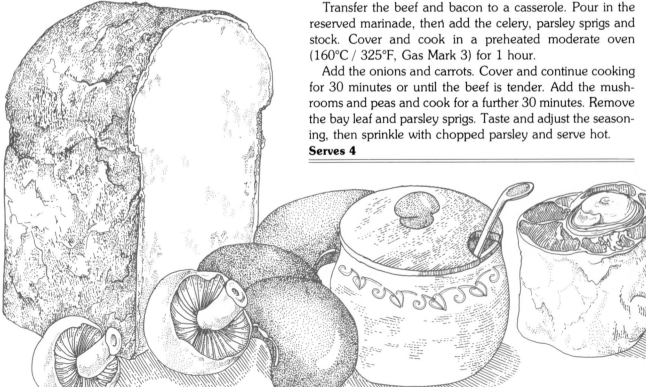

Oxtail and Kidney Casserole

Metric/Imperial	American
25 g / 1 oz vegetable margarine	2 tablespoons vegetable margarine
1 oxtail, trimmed of excess fat and cut into pieces	1 oxtail, trimmed of excess fat and cut into pieces
100 g / 4 oz ox kidney, skinned, core removed and chopped	½ cup skinned and chopped beef kidney
1 large onion, peeled and sliced	1 large onion, peeled and sliced
450 g / 1 lb carrots, peeled and sliced	3 cups peeled and sliced carrots
1 large potato, peeled and grated	1 large potato, peeled and grated
1 garlic clove, peeled and crushed	1 garlic clove, peeled and crushed
2 teaspoons paprika	2 teaspoons paprika
1 teaspoon caraway seeds	1 teaspoon caraway seeds
1 tablespoon tomato purée	1 tablespoon tomato paste
salt	salt
freshly ground black pepper	freshly ground black pepper
600 ml / 1 pint beef stock	2½ cups beef stock

Melt the margarine in a heavy pan. Add the oxtail and fry briskly until browned on all sides. Lower the heat, add the kidney, onion, carrots, potato and garlic and cook gently until the vegetables are lightly coloured, stirring frequently.

Drain off any excess fat, then stir in the remaining ingredients. Bring to the boil, then lower the heat, cover and simmer for 3½ hours or until the oxtail is tender. Taste and adjust the seasoning.

Serve hot with plain boiled potatoes, brown rice or wholewheat bread.

Serves 4

Meat-Stuffed Marrow (Squash)

Metric/Imperial	American
1 medium marrow	1 medium summer squash
450 g / 1 lb minced beef	2 cups ground beef
1 onion, peeled and finely chopped	1 onion, peeled and finely chopped
1 egg, beaten	1 egg, beaten
1 teaspoon chopped parsley	1 teaspoon chopped parsley
1 teaspoon chopped thyme	1 teaspoon chopped thyme
1 tablespoon tomato purée	1 tablespoon tomato paste
½ teaspoon Worcestershire sauce	½ teaspoon Worcestershire sauce
300 ml / ½ pint beef stock	1¼ cups beef stock
salt	salt
freshly ground black pepper	freshly ground black pepper
25 g / 1 oz grated Parmesan cheese	¼ cup grated Parmesan cheese

Peel the marrow (squash) and cut in half lengthways. Scoop out the seeds and pith with a spoon and discard.

Put the beef in a bowl with the remaining ingredients, except the Parmesan cheese. Mix well, then use to fill the marrow (squash) halves.

Put the stuffed marrows (squash) in a baking dish and cover with foil. Bake in a preheated moderate oven (180°C / 350°F, Gas Mark 4) for 1 hour. Remove the foil, sprinkle the cheese over the meat filling then bake for a further 30 minutes. Serve hot.

Serves 4

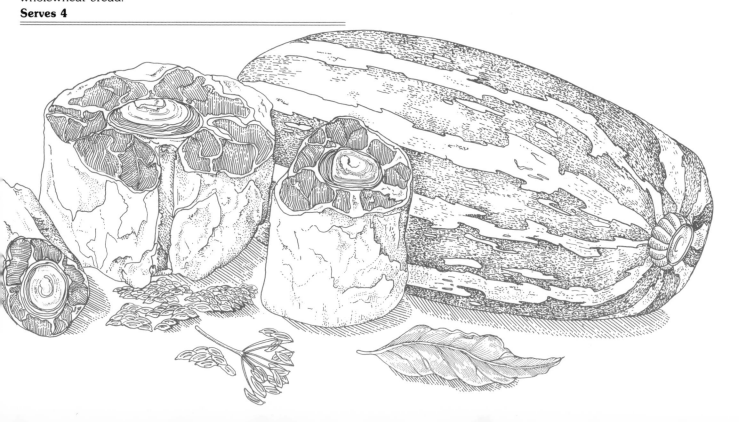

Grilled (Broiled) Sweetbreads

Metric/Imperial	American
2 pairs sweetbreads	2 pairs sweetbreads
1 tablespoon vinegar	1 tablespoon vinegar
600 ml / 1 pint water	2½ cups water
1 teaspoon salt	1 teaspoon salt
40 g / 1½ oz vegetable margarine, melted	3 tablespoons vegetable margarine, melted
25 g / 1 oz wholemeal breadcrumbs	½ cup wholewheat breadcrumbs
lemon wedges to garnish	lemon wedges to garnish

Wash the sweetbreads, put them in a bowl and cover with cold water. Leave to stand for 20 minutes, then drain off the water.

Put the sweetbreads in a pan with the vinegar, water and salt. Bring to the boil, then lower the heat, cover and simmer for 20 minutes.

Drain thoroughly, then transfer to a bowl. Cover with cold water and leave to stand again for 20 minutes. Drain the sweetbreads thoroughly, then pat dry with kitchen paper towels. Remove the membranes and split the sweetbreads in half lengthways.

Brush the grill (broiler) pan with a little of the margarine. Brush the sweetbreads with a little more of the margarine, then roll in the breadcrumbs.

Place the sweetbreads in the pan and coat with the remaining margarine. Grill (broil) under high heat for 3 minutes on each side. Serve with lemon wedges.

Serves 4

Baked Tongue

Metric/Imperial	American
1 ×1.75 kg / 4 lb pickled ox tongue	1 × 4 lb pickled ox tongue
3 onions, peeled and sliced	3 onions, peeled and sliced
2 cloves	2 cloves
1 bay leaf	1 bay leaf
1 ×500 g / 1 lb can tomatoes	1 × 1 lb can tomatoes
freshly ground black pepper	freshly ground black pepper

Put the tongue in a large pan, then add enough cold water to just cover. Bring to the boil, then drain off the water. Cover with fresh cold water and bring to the boil again. Lower the heat, cover and simmer for 2 hours. Drain and reserve 300 ml / ½ pint / 1¼ cups cooking liquid.

Discard the skin, fat and bones and place the tongue in a casserole. Add the remaining ingredients and the reserved cooking liquid.

Bake in a preheated moderate oven (180°C / 350°F, Gas Mark 4) for 1 hour, basting twice.

To serve: do not roll the tongue, but carve across the grain in thick slices and arrange on a flat serving dish. Remove the cloves and bay leaf from the casserole, taste and adjust the seasoning of the sauce, then pour over the tongue and serve hot. The tongue can also be served cold with a selection of salads.

Serves 4

Baked tongue; Grilled (broiled) sweetbreads; Roast veal with orange

Roast Veal with Orange

Metric/Imperial
1 × 1.75 kg / 4 lb leg of
    veal
2 garlic cloves, peeled and
    quartered lengthways
salt
freshly ground black pepper
1 rosemary sprig
300 ml / ½ pint water
finely grated rind of
    1 orange
juice of 2 oranges
1 orange, peeled and sliced,
    to garnish

American
1 × 4 lb leg of veal
2 garlic cloves, peeled and
    quartered lengthways
salt
freshly ground black pepper
1 rosemary sprig
1¼ cups water
finely grated rind of
    1 orange
juice of 2 oranges
1 orange, peeled and sliced,
    to garnish

Make 8 small slits in the surface of the veal with a sharp, pointed knife. Insert the garlic quarters into the slits. Place the meat in a roasting pan, sprinkle with salt and pepper, then place the rosemary on top.

Pour the water around the meat, then roast in a preheated hot oven (220°C / 425°F, Gas Mark 7) for 15 minutes. Lower the heat to moderate (180°C / 350°F, Gas Mark 4) and continue roasting for 1¼ hours.

Sprinkle the orange rind over the meat, then stir the orange juice into the pan juices. Continue cooking for 30 minutes, basting once.

To serve the veal, carve into slices and arrange on a warmed serving dish. Taste and adjust the seasoning of the gravy, then pour a little gravy over the veal and garnish with orange slices. Serve the remaining gravy in a sauceboat. The meat can also be served cold with a selection of salads.
Serves 4

SALADS

Salads are a perfect example of a healthfood because they can comprise such a wide variety of wholesome foods – the essence of a healthy diet. Salads are also very versatile as they can be served as a light vegetable accompaniment to a meal, a starter, main course or as a meal on their own.

Salads have always had a healthy image, although often in the sense that if something is boring and unappetizing it must be good for you, but with a little imagination salads can be a long way from the traditional lettuce leaves, cucumber and tomato.

Salads are especially good for you if the vegetable ingredients are raw, as raw food provides more roughage and none of the nutrients are lost during cooking. Raw vegetables also add a fresh taste and texture to a salad. This is particularly true of root vegetables such as carrots and celeriac; cauliflower, fennel and peppers are also good. One of the most delicious raw vegetables in a salad is the mushroom – especially if marinated in a tasty dressing beforehand. Other vegetables, although they can be eaten raw, are more appetizing if they are very lightly cooked – courgettes (zucchini), leeks, beans and peas, for example. Simply blanch them in boiling water and remove when they are still crisp and slightly crunchy, then rinse in cold water.

Always leave the skins on salad ingredients if possible, especially tomatoes, cucumbers, mushrooms, potatoes and carrots. Not only do they look more attractive, but the nutrients are more concentrated just beneath the skin and they also provide valuable roughage.

The most common salad ingredient is lettuce, but there are many other varieties of leaves which can be substituted and usually have a stronger, more interesting flavour; for example, endive, chicory, spinach, cabbage, Chinese cabbage (bok choy), celtuce and watercress. Many of these are available in winter when lettuce is unavailable, too expensive or of poor quality. Fresh herbs are also a useful addition to salads, especially parsley, thyme, chives and mint.

Salad leaves must be really fresh and crisp and, to retain their vitamin C, should be prepared just before serving. If you have to prepare them in advance, the best way to keep them crisp is to wash and dry them, then store in a covered container or polythene (plastic) bag in the bottom of the refrigerator. Always tear salad leaves with your hands – cutting them breaks the cells and releases an enzyme which then destroys the vitamin C.

Many people do not think of having salads in the winter, but there are lots of ingredients available to make them interesting. Shredded red or white cabbage is always good as a base for a winter salad. Root vegetables, such as carrots, celeriac and beetroot (beet) can be shredded or grated into a salad. Cauliflower florets, celery, fennel, onions and peppers all add to a colourful, tasty salad. And have you ever tried thinly sliced Brussels sprouts?

A wide variety of fruits can also be added to salads to delicious account – oranges, apples, pears, peaches, grapes, bananas, even strawberries, as well as dried fruits. Nuts, sesame and sunflower seeds, bean sprouts, olives and pickled vegetables, cheese and crisply cooked bacon – the possibilities are numerous and the results all tasty and attractive.

More substantial salads can be made using pasta, rice, potatoes and pulses (legumes), all of which must be cooked and cooled before adding to a salad. For main course salads and some starters, add cooked meat, fish, eggs and cheese.

A dressing either makes or breaks a salad, both from a flavour and health point of view – many dressings are too rich and undo all the goodness that the salad is doing. The most common dressing is vinaigrette. For health purposes, use a polyunsaturated oil for vinaigrettes such as sunflower or corn, although a little olive oil can be substituted to give a better flavour if liked. The proportion of vinegar to oil is a matter of taste, but for a healthy dressing use as little oil as possible. Many flavourings can be added to the basic dressing, such as lemon or orange rind and juice, herbs, garlic, mustard and seasoning.

A much simpler and healthier dressing can be made by adding flavourings to fresh lemon, orange or tomato juice. For a creamy dressing that isn't rich, add herbs and seasoning to yogurt. Avoid using cream, soured cream and bottled manufactured dressings.

Delicate salad leaves must be dressed just before serving to prevent them from wilting, but some firmer foods often improve if they are marinated in the dressing for a few hours or even overnight.

Minted Melon and Strawberry Cocktail

If obtainable, ogen melons make an attractive variation. Cut them in half, discard the seeds and scoop out the flesh in balls. Serve the salad in the melon shells.

Metric/Imperial	American
1 small ripe honeydew or cantaloupe melon	1 small ripe honeydew or cantaloupe melon
100 g / 4 oz strawberries, hulled and sliced	1 cup hulled and sliced strawberries
5 cm / 2 inch piece cucumber, sliced and quartered	2 inch piece cucumber, sliced and quartered
finely grated rind and juice of 1 large orange	finely grated rind and juice of 1 large orange
2 tablespoons chopped mint	2 tablespoons chopped mint
15 g / 1/2 oz split blanched pistachio nuts or toasted almonds	2 tablespoons split blanched pistachio nuts or toasted almonds
1/2 small lettuce, shredded	1/2 small head of lettuce, shredded
4-6 mint sprigs to garnish	4-6 mint sprigs to garnish

Cut the melon into quarters, then remove the seeds and skin. Cut the flesh into 1 cm / 1/2 inch cubes or scoop into balls. Place in a bowl with the strawberries and cucumber.

Mix the orange rind and juice with the mint and nuts, then pour onto the salad. Fold gently to mix.

Divide the lettuce equally between 4 to 6 individual serv-ing dishes or glasses. Spoon the salad on top, pouring in any orange juice from the bowl. Serve chilled, garnished with sprigs of mint.

Serves 4 to 6

Avocado, Grapefruit and Sesame Salad

Metric/Imperial	American
2 large avocado pears	2 large avocado pears
juice of 1 small lemon	juice of 1 small lemon
2 grapefruit, peel and pith removed and divided into segments	2 grapefruit, peel and pith removed and divided into segments
1 tablespoon chopped mint	1 tablespoon chopped mint
1 small lettuce	1 small head of lettuce
2 tablespoons sesame seeds	2 tablespoons sesame seeds
mint sprigs to garnish	mint sprigs to garnish

Peel the avocados, cut in half lengthways, then remove the stones (seeds). Slice the pulp, place in a bowl, then sprinkle with the lemon juice. Fold in the grapefruit and mint.

Arrange the lettuce leaves in individual serving bowls. Divide the salad between them, then sprinkle with the sesame seeds. Garnish with mint sprigs and serve immediately.

Serves 4

ABOVE: Minted melon and strawberry cocktail
RIGHT: Stuffed tomato salad; Marinated mushrooms with prawns (shrimp); Avocado, grapefruit and sesame salad

Stuffed Tomato Salad

Metric/Imperial	American
4 large or 6 medium tomatoes	4 large or 6 medium tomatoes
1 dessert apple	1 dessert apple
finely grated rind of 1 orange	finely grated rind of 1 orange
juice of ½ orange	juice of ½ orange
225 g / 8 oz cottage cheese	1 cup cottage cheese
2 tablespoons sultanas	2 tablespoons seedless white raisins
2 tablespoons chopped walnuts	2 tablespoons chopped walnuts
1 tablespoon snipped chives or finely chopped spring onions	1 tablespoon snipped chives or finely chopped scallions
salt	salt
freshly ground black pepper	freshly ground black pepper
1 small lettuce	1 small head of lettuce

Cut the tops off the tomatoes and set aside. Scoop out the centres of the tomatoes, then turn them upside down and leave to drain.

Meanwhile, chop the apple and discard the core. Put the apple in a bowl, sprinkle with the orange rind and juice, then add the remaining ingredients, except the lettuce. Fold gently to mix.

Divide the mixture equally between the tomato cups. Arrange the lettuce leaves on individual serving plates. Place a tomato on each plate and top with the reserved lids. Serve cold, accompanied by crusty wholewheat bread, or serve with Brown rice salad (see page 83).

Serves 4 to 6

Marinated Mushrooms with Prawns (Shrimp)

Metric/Imperial	American
2 shallots or spring onions, trimmed and sliced	2 shallots or scallions, trimmed and sliced
1 garlic clove, peeled and crushed (optional)	1 garlic clove, peeled and crushed (optional)
finely grated rind and juice of 1 lemon	finely grated rind and juice of 1 lemon
5 tablespoons oil	⅓ cup oil
2 tablespoons thyme leaves	2 tablespoons thyme leaves
2 tablespoons chopped parsley	2 tablespoons chopped parsley
salt	salt
freshly ground black pepper	freshly ground black pepper
225 g / 8 oz mushrooms, sliced	2 cups sliced mushrooms
100 g / 4 oz peeled prawns	½ cup shelled shrimp
pinch of paprika	pinch of paprika
TO GARNISH:	TO GARNISH:
4 lemon slices	4 lemon slices
4 unshelled prawns	4 unshelled shrimp

Put the shallots or spring onions (scallions) in a bowl with the garlic if using, the lemon rind and juice, oil, herbs and salt and pepper to taste. Beat well to mix.

Add the mushrooms and toss in the dressing until thoroughly coated. Cover and leave to marinate for 2 hours.

Divide the mushrooms between 4 individual serving plates. Top with the prawns (shrimp) and sprinkle with paprika. Garnish each with a lemon slice and a prawn (shrimp).

Serves 4

Danish Herring Salad

Metric/Imperial	American
225 g / 8 oz beetroot, cooked and diced	1 1/3 cups cooked and diced beets
2 dessert apples, cored and thinly sliced	2 dessert apples, cored and thinly sliced
1 onion, peeled and thinly sliced	1 onion, peeled and thinly sliced
finely grated rind and juice of 1/2 lemon	finely grated rind and juice of 1 lemon
150 ml / 1/4 pint natural yogurt	2/3 cup unflavored yogurt
salt	salt
freshly ground white pepper	freshly ground white pepper
4 pickled herrings or rollmops	4 pickled herrings
parsley sprigs to garnish	parsley sprigs to garnish

Put the beetroot (beets), apples and onion in a bowl. Stir the lemon rind and juice into the yogurt, then add salt and pepper to taste.

Add the yogurt to the beetroot (beet) mixture and stir well until the salad is pale pink in colour. Spoon into a shallow serving dish, arrange the herrings or rollmops on top, then garnish with parsley sprigs. Serve cold.

Serves 4

Mexican Bean Salad

Metric/Imperial	American
225 g / 8 oz dried red kidney beans	3/4 cup dried red kidney beans
900 ml / 1 1/2 pints water	3 3/4 cups water
1 small cauliflower, divided into florets	1 small cauliflower, divided into florets
1 small green pepper, cored, seeded and cut into strips	1 small green pepper, cored, seeded and cut into strips
2 celery sticks, sliced	2 celery stalks, sliced
1 tablespoon grated onion	1 tablespoon grated onion
2 tablespoons chopped parsley	2 tablespoons chopped parsley
Tabasco sauce to taste	Tabasco sauce to taste
150 ml / 1/4 pint vinaigrette dressing (see page 80)	2/3 cup French dressing (see page 80)

Put the beans in a bowl, pour on the water and leave to soak overnight. Alternatively, pour on boiling water and leave to soak for at least 2 hours.

Transfer the beans and soaking water to a pan and bring to the boil. Lower the heat, and simmer for about 1 1/2 hours until the beans are tender. Drain and leave to cool.

Put the beans in a bowl, then add the vegetables and parsley and stir well.

Add Tabasco to taste to the vinaigrette dressing – it should be quite hot. Mix well, then pour over the salad. Leave to marinate for a few hours until the flavour of the dressing penetrates the salad ingredients. Serve cold.

Serves 4

Potato and Courgette (Zucchini) Salad

Metric/Imperial	American
450 g / 1 lb new potatoes, scrubbed	1 lb new potatoes, scrubbed
salt	salt
225 g / 8 oz courgettes, sliced	1 1/2 cups sliced zucchini
4 tablespoons oil	1/4 cup oil
finely grated rind and juice of 1 small orange	finely grated rind and juice of 1 small orange
1 tablespoon wine vinegar	1 tablespoon wine vinegar
1 tablespoon chopped parsley	1 tablespoon chopped parsley
1 tablespoon snipped chives or finely chopped spring onions	1 tablespoon snipped chives or finely chopped scallions
freshly ground black pepper	freshly ground black pepper
TO GARNISH:	TO GARNISH:
50 g / 2 oz bacon, crisply grilled and crumbled, or chopped parsley and snipped chives	3 bacon slices, crisply broiled and crumbled, or chopped parsley and snipped chives

Cook the potatoes in boiling salted water until they are just tender but not broken up. Remove from the water and leave to drain. Add the courgettes (zucchini) to the boiling water, simmer for about 3 minutes until just tender, then drain.

Put the oil in a bowl with the orange rind and juice, vinegar, parsley and chives or spring onions (scallions). Add salt and pepper to taste and beat well.

Cut the larger potatoes into halves or quarters and leave the small ones whole. Put the potatoes and courgettes (zucchini) in a salad bowl, pour on the orange dressing and toss lightly to mix. The potatoes will absorb the flavour better if they are still warm.

Sprinkle the bacon or herbs over the salad just before serving. Serve cold.

Serves 4

Tomato Ring Salad

This is a perfect way to use tomatoes that are too soft for an ordinary salad.

Metric/Imperial	American
750 g / 1½ lb tomatoes, roughly chopped	3 cups roughly chopped tomatoes
1 onion, peeled and chopped	1 onion, peeled and chopped
150 ml / ¼ pint stock or water	⅔ cup stock or water
finely grated rind and juice of 1 orange or lemon	finely grated rind and juice of 1 orange or lemon
1 small bunch herbs (basil, oregano, parsley, mint, as available)	1 small bunch herbs (basil, oregano, parsley, mint, as available)
1 bay leaf	1 bay leaf
1 garlic clove, peeled and crushed (optional)	1 garlic clove, peeled and crushed (optional)
salt	salt
freshly ground black pepper	freshly ground black pepper
25 g / ½ oz gelatine	2 envelopes gelatin
2 tablespoons water	2 tablespoons water
1 teaspoon Worcestershire sauce	1 teaspoon Worcestershire sauce
TO GARNISH:	TO GARNISH:
1 bunch watercress, or 1 box mustard and cress	1 bunch watercress, or 1 box mustard and cress
4 hard-boiled eggs, shelled and cut into wedges	4 hard-cooked eggs, shelled and cut into wedges

Put the tomatoes and onion in a pan. Pour in the stock or water then add the orange or lemon rind and juice, herbs, garlic if using and salt and pepper to taste.

Bring to the boil, then lower the heat, cover and simmer for 20 minutes until the tomatoes are reduced to a pulp. Rub through a sieve (strainer) to make a purée.

Spriinkle the gelatine over the water in a small cup. Stand the cup in a pan of hot water and stir until the gelatine has dissolved. Stir the gelatine into the purée, then add the Worcestershire sauce and salt and pepper to taste.

Pour into a 600-900 ml / 1-1½ pint / 2½-3¾ cup ring mould, then chill in the refrigerator until set.

Unmould just before serving and garnish with the cress and egg slices.

Serves 4

Christmas Salad

This winter salad of vegetables, dried fruit and nuts makes an excellent healthy meal at Christmas time.

Metric/Imperial	American
175 g / 6 oz red or white cabbage, shredded	2¼ cups shredded red or white cabbage
2 large carrots, peeled and grated	2 large carrots, peeled and grated
2 dessert apples, cored and chopped	2 dessert apples, cored and chopped
2 celery sticks, chopped	2 celery stalks, chopped
100 g / 4 oz dates, stoned and chopped	½ cup pitted and chopped dates
50 g / 2 oz sultanas	⅓ cup seedless white raisins
100 g / 4 oz shelled nuts (Brazils, walnuts, almonds, hazelnuts), chopped if large	1 cup shelled nuts (Brazils, walnuts, almonds, filberts), chopped if large
2 tangerines or oranges, peel and pith removed and divided into segments	2 tangerines or oranges, peel and pith removed and divided into segments
100 g / 4 oz Stilton cheese, diced	⅔ cup diced Stilton cheese
150 ml / ¼ pint salad dressing (yogurt, fruit juice or vinaigrette – see page 80)	⅔ cup salad dressing (yogurt, fruit juice or French dressing – see page 80)
salt	salt
freshly ground black pepper	freshly ground black pepper

Put all the ingredients in a bowl, toss well to mix, then taste and adjust the seasoning. Serve cold.

If not to be used immediately, store in an airtight container in the refrigerator. The salad will keep fresh for several days.

Serves 4 as a main course, 8 as an accompaniment to cold meats

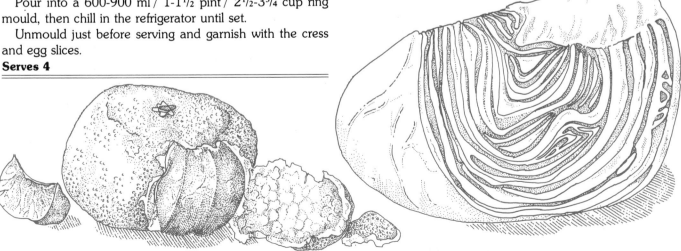

Pasta and Fish Salad

*This salad may be made with any shape of pasta –
noodles, spaghetti, shells, etc.*

Metric/Imperial	American
225 g / 8 oz spinach pasta	½ lb spinach pasta
salt	salt
100 g / 4 oz cooked shelled mussels	½ cup cooked shelled mussels or clams
100 g / 4 oz peeled prawns, cooked	½ cup shelled shrimp, cooked
1 × 50 g / 2 oz can anchovies, drained	1 × 2 oz can anchovies, drained
50 g / 2 oz button mushrooms, sliced	½ cup sliced button mushrooms
2 tomatoes, cut into wedges	2 tomatoes, cut into wedges
150 ml / ¼ pint vinaigrette dressing (see page 80)	⅔ cup French dressing (see page 80)
TO GARNISH:	TO GARNISH:
2 tablespoons chopped parsley	2 tablespoons chopped parsley
2 tablespoons grated Parmesan cheese	2 tablespoons grated Parmesan cheese

Cook the pasta in plenty of boiling salted water for 10 to 15
minutes until 'al dente'. Drain in a colander and rinse under
cold running water. Drain thoroughly.

Put the cooked pasta in a bowl, then add the fish, mush-
rooms and tomatoes. Pour on the dressing and mix gently.
Sprinkle with parsley and Parmesan just before serving.
Serves 4

Chicken Salad Véronique

Metric/Imperial	American
1 × 1.5 kg / 3 lb chicken, with giblets	1 × 3 lb chicken, with giblets
300 ml / ½ pint water	1¼ cups water
1 small onion, peeled and chopped	1 small onion, peeled and chopped
finely grated rind and juice of ½ lemon	finely grated rind and juice of ½ lemon
1 slice fresh root ginger, peeled and chopped	1 slice fresh ginger root, peeled and chopped
few thyme or parsley sprigs	few thyme or parsley sprigs
1 bay leaf	1 bay leaf
salt	salt
freshly ground white pepper	freshly ground white pepper
150 ml / ¼ pint natural yogurt	⅔ cup unflavored yogurt
1 head curly endive, separated into leaves	1 head chicory, separated into leaves
100 g / 4 oz green grapes, halved and seeded	1 cup halved and seeded white grapes
50 g / 2 oz flaked almonds	½ cup flaked almonds

Put the chicken in a large pan with the giblets and the water. Add the onion, lemon rind and juice, ginger, herbs and salt and pepper to taste. Bring to the boil, then lower the heat, cover and simmer for 45 minutes or until tender.

Remove the chicken from the cooking liquid, discard the skin and bones and cut the chicken flesh into neat pieces.

Boil the cooking liquid rapidly until reduced to 150 ml / ¼ pint / ⅔ cup. Strain, leave to cool, then skim off the fat. Stir into the yogurt, add salt and pepper to taste and mix well.

Arrange the endive (chicory) on a serving dish. Top with the chicken and grapes. Pour over the yogurt sauce and scatter the almonds over the top. Serve cold.
Serves 4 to 6

Beef and Orange Salad

Metric/Imperial	American
450 g / 1 lb lean beef (boned sirloin or topside, rump or fillet steak)	1 lb lean beef (boned sirloin or top round, rump or filet steak)
finely grated rind and juice of 1 large orange	finely grated rind and juice of 1 large orange
1 tablespoon wine vinegar	1 tablespoon wine vinegar
1 bay leaf	1 bay leaf
salt	salt
freshly ground black pepper	freshly ground black pepper
200 ml / ⅓ pint water or stock	¾ cup stock or water
100 g / 4 oz mushrooms, sliced	1 cup sliced mushrooms
1 lettuce	1 head of lettuce
1 large carrot, peeled and grated	1 large carrot, peeled and grated
50 g / 2 oz bean sprouts	1 cup bean sprouts

Put the beef in a pan with the orange rind and juice, vinegar, bay leaf and salt and pepper to taste. Pour on the water or stock and bring to the boil.

Lower the heat, cover and simmer for 5 minutes for rare beef, 10 minutes for well done beef. Add the mushrooms and simmer for a further 2 minutes.

Remove the beef and mushrooms from the pan and leave to cool. Boil the cooking liquid until reduced to 150 ml / ¼ pint / ⅔ cup. Leave to cool, then taste and adjust the seasoning.

Cut the beef into strips, then place in a bowl with the mushrooms. Pour over the reduced cooking liquid and leave to marinate for at least 1 hour, turning occasionally.

Arrange the lettuce leaves on a serving dish. Pile the beef mixture in the centre, then strain over the marinade.

Mix together the carrot and bean sprouts and arrange around the beef. Serve cold.
Serves 4

Pasta and fish salad; Beef and orange salad; Tomato ring salad; Chicken salad véronique

Cheese and Bread Salad

This is a good way to use up stale bread – simply soak cubes of bread in vinaigrette dressing and combine with the other ingredients for a delicious salad.

Metric/Imperial	**American**
150 ml / ¼ pint vinaigrette dressing (see opposite)	⅔ cup French dressing (see opposite)
2 slices or crusts wholemeal bread, diced	2 slices or crusts wholewheat bread, diced
100 g / 4 oz Cheddar or Edam cheese, diced	½ cup diced Cheddar or Edam cheese
100 g / 4 oz Mozzarella cheese, diced	½ cup diced Mozzarella cheese
4 tomatoes, sliced	4 tomatoes, sliced
10 cm / 4 inch piece cucumber sliced	4 inch piece cucumber, sliced
1 × 50 g / 2 oz can anchovy fillets, drained (optional)	1 × 2 oz can anchovy fillets, drained (optional)
8 olives, halved and stoned	8 olives, halved and pitted
1 lettuce	1 head of lettuce

Pour the dressing into a bowl. Add the bread and toss to coat thoroughly. Add the remaining ingredients, except the lettuce, and fold gently to mix.

Line a serving dish or bowl with lettuce leaves, then pile the salad in the centre. Pour over anny remaining dressing. Serve cold.

Serves 4

Lemon Yogurt Dressing

Yogurt flavoured with lemon and herbs makes a refreshing oil-free salad dressing.

Metric/Imperial	**American**
150 mll / ¼ pint natural yogurt	⅔ cup unflavored yogurt
finely grated rind and juice of ½ lemon	finely grated rind and juice of ½ lemon
1 tablespoon chopped parsley	1 tablespoon chopped parsley
1 tablespoon snipped chives	1 tablespoon snipped chives
1 tablespoon chopped thyme, mint, watercress or sorrel	1 tablespoon chopped thyme, mint, watercress or sorrel
salt	salt
freshly ground white pepper	freshly ground white pepper

Put all the ingredients in a bowl and beat well. Taste and adjust the seasoning, then pour over the salad just before serving.

Makes 150 ml / ¼ pint / ⅔ cup dressing

Vinaigrette (French) Dressing

Use a polyunsaturated oil such as corn, sunflower or safflower. For a stronger flavour, substitute a small quantity of this with olive oil.

Metric/Imperial	**American**
150 ml / ¼ pint oil	⅔ cup oil
5 tablespoons vinegar or lemon juice	⅓ cup vinegar or lemon juice
1 garlic clove, peeled (optional)	1 clove garlic, peeled (optional)
1 sprig herbs (optional)	1 sprig herbs (optional)
mustardd	mustard
salt	salt
freshly ground black pepper	freshly ground black pepper

Put all the ingredients in a screw-topped jar, adding mustard, salt and pepper to taste. Shake well.

Store in the refrigerator and use as required, adding dressing just before serving when possible.

Makes approximately 150 ml / ¼ pint / ⅔ cup dressing

Piquant Tomato Dressing

This tangy tomato juice dressing is a good alternative to vinaigrette when a strong-flavoured dressing is called for.

Metric/Imperial	American
6 tablespoons tomato juice	6 tablespoons tomato juice
2 tablespoons lemon juice	2 tablespoons lemon juice
1-2 teaspoons Worcestershire sauce	1-2 teaspoons Worcestershire sauce
1 tablespoon chopped herbs (parsley, chives or mint)	1 tablespoon chopped herbs (parsley, chives or mint)
salt	salt
freshly ground black pepper	freshly ground black pepper

Put all the ingredients in a bowl and beat well. Taste and adjust the seasoning, then pour over the salad just before serving.

Makes approximately 120 ml / 4 fl oz / ¹/₂ cup dressing

Minted Fruit Juice Dressing

Freshly-squeezed orange or grapefruit juice makes an excellent salad dressing for slimmers, as it does not need the addition of oil. However, an equal quantity of oil may be added if liked.

Metric/Imperial	American
150 ml / ¹/₄ pint fresh orange or grapefruit juice	²/₃ cup fresh orange or grapefruit juice
1-2 teaspoons chopped mint	1-2 teaspoons chopped mint
salt	salt
freshly ground black pepper	freshly ground black pepper

Put all the ingredients in a bowl and beat well. Taste and adjust the seasoning, then pour over the salad just before serving.

Makes 150 ml / ¹/₄ pint / ²/₃ cup dressing

Ginger Yogurt Salad Dressing

Metric/Imperial	American
150 ml / ¹/₄ pint natural yogurt	²/₃ cup unflavored yogurt
25 g / 1 oz stem ginger, finely chopped	3 tablespoons finely chopped preserved ginger
¹/₄ teaspoon ground ginger	¹/₄ teaspoon ground ginger

Put all the ingredients in a bowl and beat with a fork until well mixed. Chill in the refrigerator for 1 hour.

Serve with a cucumber salad, citrus fruit salad or melon balls.

Serves 4

Cucumber and Tomato Raita

This Indian salad in a yogurt and mint dressing is very refreshing. It is especially good when served with hot, spicy foods.

Metric/Imperial
1 small or ½ large
    cucumber, sliced
½ teaspoon salt
4 tomatoes, thinly sliced
300 ml / ½ pint natural
    yogurt
2 tablespoons chopped
    mint
freshly ground white pepper
mint sprig to garnish

American
1 small or ½ large
    cucumber, sliced
½ teaspoon salt
4 tomatoes, thinly sliced
1¼ cups unflavored yogurt
2 tablespoons chopped
    mint
freshly ground white pepper
mint sprig to garnish

Put the cucumber in a sieve (strainer), sprinkle with the salt and leave to drain for 30 minutes to extract the water.

Arrange the cucumber and tomatoes in a serving dish. Mix the yogurt with the chopped mint and pepper to taste, then pour over the salad. Garnish with mint. Serve chilled.

Serves 4

Italian Salad

Metric/Imperial
½ head curly endive,
    separated into leaves
1 head chicory, sliced into
    rings
1 bulb fennel, sliced into
    rings
1 small head radiccio,
    separated into leaves
    (optional)
8 radishes, sliced if large
4 tablespoons vinaigrette
    dressing (see page 80)
salt
freshly ground black pepper

American
½ head chicory, separated
    into leaves
1 head Belgian endive,
    sliced into rings
1 bulb fennel, sliced into
    rings
1 small head red chicory,
    separated into leaves
    (optional)
8 radishes, sliced if large
¼ cup French dressing (see
    page 80)
salt
freshly ground black pepper

Put all the ingrediennts in a salad bowl, toss well, then taste and adjust the seasoning. Serve cold.

Serves 4

RIGHT: Orange and watercress salad; Brown rice salad
BELOW: Cucumber and tomato raita; Italian salad

Brown Rice Salad

Metric/Imperial	American
100 g / 4 oz brown rice	¹/₂ cup brown rice
salt	salt
100 g / 4 oz shelled peas or sliced beans	³/₄ cup shelled peas, or ¹/₂ cup sliced green beans
100 g / 4 oz sweetcorn kernels	³/₄ cup kernel corn
150 ml / ¹/₄ pint vinaigrette dressing (see page 80)	²/₃ cup French dressing (see page 80)
1 red pepper, cored, seeded and diced	1 red pepper, cored, seeded and diced
50 g / 2 oz salted peanuts	¹/₂ cup salted peanuts
1 small onion, peeled and grated	1 small onion, peeled and grated
freshly ground black pepper	freshly ground black pepper

Cook the rice in boiling salted water for 30 minutes or until tender. Add the peas or beans and corn and simmer for a further few minutes until just tender. Drain thoroughly.

Transfer to a bowl and add half of the dressing while the rice and vegetables are still hot. Toss well to mix, then leave to cool.

Add the remaining ingredients and dressing and mix well. Taste and adjust the seasoning just before serving. Serve cold.

Serves 4

Orange and Watercress Salad

This is an excellent salad to serve with duck.

Metric/Imperial	American
1 large bunch watercress, trimmed	1 large bunch watercress, trimmed
3 oranges, peel and pith removed and thinly sliced into rounds	3 oranges, peel and pith removed and thinly sliced into rounds
1 onion, peeled and thinly sliced into rings	1 onion, peeled and thinly sliced into rings
1 small green pepper, cored, seeded and thinly sliced into rings	1 small green pepper, cored, seeded and thinly sliced into rings
6 tablespoons vinaigrette dressing (see page 80)	6 tablespoons French dressing (see page 80)
black olives to garnish	ripe olives to garnish

Put the watercress in a salad bowl. Arrange the orange slices on top with the onion and pepper rings. Pour on the dressing and garnish with the olives. Serve cold.

Serves 4

VEGETABLES

Our food would certainly be dull without the abundance of vegetables available. They add colour, texture and flavour to the diet, and provide us with roughage, minerals and vitamins.

Most vegetables contain only a small amount of protein, but pulses (legumes) are an exception, being rich in protein, vitamins and minerals. Vegetable protein is not as complete as animal protein because it lacks a few of the essential amino-acids, and strict vegetarians who do not include any dairy foods in their diet must have a very carefully balanced diet to ensure good health. Also, pulses (legumes) have to be reconstituted with water, which dilutes the nutrients.

Soya beans have a particularly high protein content and are often used in vegetarian diets in place of meat. A cheap source of protein, they have always been used extensively in the Far East where they are manufactured into a wide range of health foods. Because of their high protein content, soya beans are often processed to simulate meat, but it seems more appropriate to use them in the many traditional bean recipes available from all over the world – or substitute them for some or all of the meat in such recipes as moussaka, curry or stews. Pulses (legumes) do not contain any vitamin C or A and therefore must be used with, and not instead of, fresh vegetables.

Raw vegetables are the healthiest because no loss of minerals, vitamins or roughage can occur during cooking. However, to most of us a diet of raw vegetables would prove unacceptable so we must prepare and cook them so as to retain as much of the goodness as possible.

When preparing vegetables, throw away as little as possible. So often the tastiest and most nutritious parts are trimmed away, usually because we have been taught that it is not 'nice and proper' to serve them. The most obvious example of this is peeling potatoes and other root vegetables. The nutrients are usually most concentrated just below the skin and peeling removes a high proportion of the goodness. Instead they should be well washed.

Many other vegetables are also often trimmed unnecessarily. For example, don't trim the green parts of leeks as they are sweeter and more delicious than the rest – just remove the roots and damaged tops. Most of the green leaves surrounding a cauliflower can be used too, providing a contrast in colour as well as being economical. The stalks from green leaves, such as spinach, can be chopped up and cooked with the leaves or kept whole and cooked separately and served as a starter, like asparagus. The stems and skins of mushrooms contain most of the flavour, so don't trim them away – just wash thoroughly and trim the tops of the stalks if necessary. Don't skin tomatoes unless they are to be cooked in a casserole or soup. Very young peas and beans can be eaten in their pods, particularly mange-tout (snow peas) and broad (lima) beans – just top and tail and cook like green beans.

Vegetables should be cooked in as little fast boiling water as possible until they are only just tender and still retain their crispness and bright colour. Apart from being much better for you, they are more appetizing and much tastier cooked this way. Always add the vegetables to boiling water – this destroys the enzyme present which destroys vitamin C. Also cover the pan so that they will cook more quickly, allowing the vegetables at the top to cook in the steam. An even better way is to steam them over boiling water so that they don't come into contact with the water. *Never* add bicarbonate of soda (baking soda); although it helps vegetables to retain a good colour, it destroys vitamin C.

Use the water in which vegetables are cooked for sauces, soups, stews, etc. Alternatively, reduce the cooking water by boiling to concentrate the flavour and use it as a glaze for the vegetables. Serve vegetables as soon as possible after cooking, as keeping them also reduces vitamin C content.

Another good way of cooking vegetables is stir-frying in the Chinese style. The vegetables are cooked quickly in a little oil over a high heat, stirring all the time until they are just tender and still crisp. This is ideal for cooking a mixture of vegetables together – start with those that take longest to cook, then add the remaining vegetables in stages, ending with those that just need heating through.

Vegetables are incredibly versatile and, with a little imagination, can be prepared and cooked in many different ways to produce delicious soups, mousses, soufflés, quiches, pâtés, casseroles, pies, pasta and rice dishes, or simply enjoyed – raw or cooked – on their own.

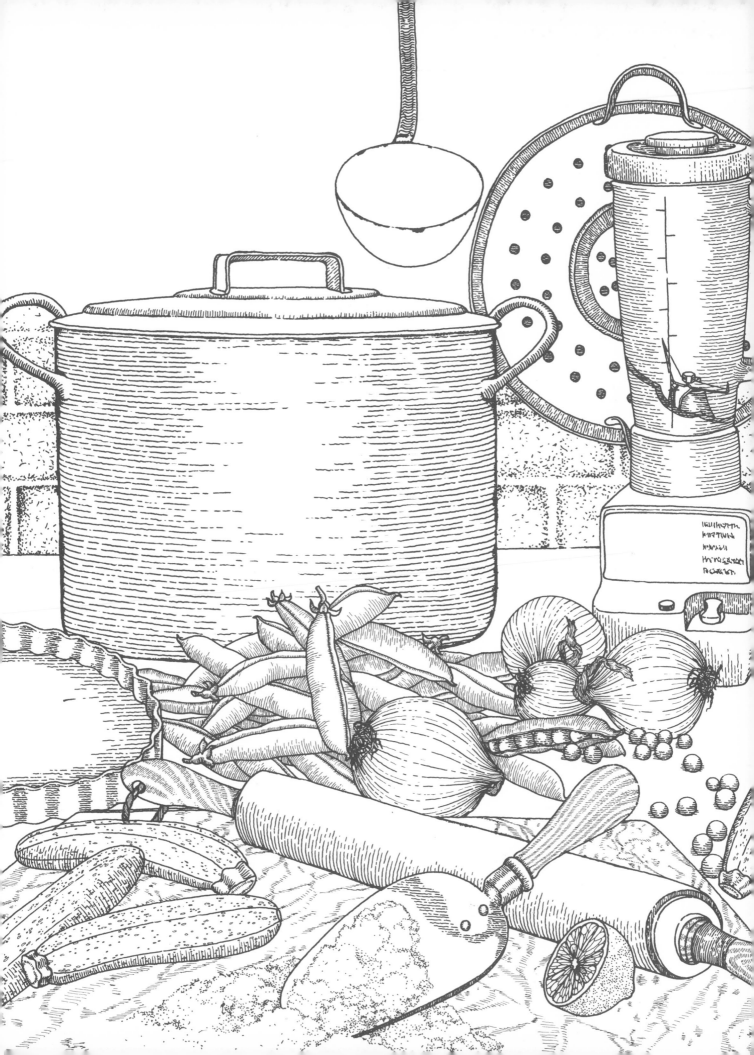

Beetroot (Beet) and Orange Soup

Metric/Imperial
450 g / 1 lb raw beetroot, peeled and diced
1 large onion, peeled and chopped
finely grated rind and juice of 3 oranges
1 bay leaf
1.2 litres / 2 pints stock
salt
freshly ground black pepper
150 ml / ¼ pint natural yogurt
1 orange, sliced, to garnish

American
2⅔ cups peeled and diced raw beets
1 large onion, peeled and chopped
finely grated rind and juice of 3 oranges
1 bay leaf
5 cups stock
salt
freshly ground black pepper
⅔ cup unflavored yogurt
1 orange, sliced, to garnish

Put the beetroot (beets) in a pan with the onion, orange rind and juice, bay leaf, stock and salt and pepper to taste.

Bring to the boil, then lower the heat, cover and simmer for 1 hour until the beetroot (beet) is tender.

Work the soup to a purée through a sieve (strainer) or in an electric blender. Return to the rinsed-out pan, then bring to the boil, stirring occasionally.

Taste and adjust seasoning, stir in the yogurt and serve hot or chilled, garnished with orange slices.

Serves 4 to 6

Minestrone (Mixed Vegetable Soup)

Metric/Imperial
1 onion, peeled and sliced
1 garlic clove, peeled and crushed (optional)
1 carrot, peeled and diced
1 turnip, peeled and diced
1 leek, trimmed and sliced
1 celery stick, sliced
225 g / 8 oz tomatoes, skinned and roughly chopped
50 g / 2 oz broken pasta or long-grain rice
1.2 litres / 2 pints stock
salt
freshly ground black pepper
¼ small cabbage, shredded
100 g / 4 oz runner beans, sliced
grated Parmesan cheese to serve

American
1 onion, peeled and sliced
1 garlic clove, peeled and crushed (optional)
1 carrot, peeled and diced
1 turnip, peeled and diced
1 leek, trimmed and sliced
1 celery stalk, sliced
1 cup skinned and chopped tomatoes
½ cup broken pasta or long-grain rice
5 cups stock
salt
freshly ground black pepper
¼ small cabbage, shredded
½ cup sliced string beans
grated Parmesan cheese to serve

Beetroot (beet) and orange soup; Minestrone (Mixed vegetable soup); Chilled pea soup

Put the onion, garlic, carrot, turnip, leek, celery, tomatoes and pasta or rice in a large pan. Stir in the stock and add salt and pepper to taste.

Bring to the boil, then lower the heat, cover and simmer for 30 minutes until the vegetables are tender.

Add the cabbage and beans and cook for a further 5 to 10 minutes until tender. Taste and adjust seasoning, then serve hot with Parmesan cheese handed separately.

Serves 6

Chilled Pea Soup

Metric/Imperial	American
350 g / 12 oz shelled peas (about 750 g / 1½ lb fresh peas in the pod)	2¼ cups shelled peas (about 1½ lb fresh peas in the shell)
1 onion, peeled and chopped	1 onion, peeled and chopped
1 large mint sprig	1 large mint sprig
finely grated rind and juice of ½ lemon	finely grated rind and juice of ½ lemon
900 ml / 1½ pints stock	3¾ cups stock
salt	salt
freshly ground black pepper	freshly ground black pepper
150 ml / ¼ pint natural yogurt or milk	⅔ cup unflavored yogurt or milk
1 tablespoon chopped mint to garnish	1 tablespoon chopped mint to garnish

Put the peas in a pan with the onion, mint, lemon rind and juice, stock and salt and pepper to taste.

Bring to the boil, then lower the heat, cover and simmer for 30 minutes until the peas are soft. Work the soup to a purée through a sieve (strainer) or in an electric blender. Leave to cool.

Stir in the yogurt or milk, taste and adjust seasoning, then chill in the refrigerator.

Sprinkle with chopped mint and serve chilled.

Serves 4 to 6

Jerusalem Cocottes

Eggs are baked in a nest of creamed artichokes for this delicious starter.

Metric/Imperial	American
450 g / 1 lb Jerusalem artichokes, scrubbed	1 lb Jerusalem artichokes, scrubbed
salt	salt
150 ml / ¼ pint natural yogurt	²/₃ cup unflavored yogurt
freshly ground white pepper	freshly ground white pepper
4 eggs	4 eggs
chopped parsley to garnish	chopped parsley to garnish

Cook the artichokes in boiling salted water for about 20 minutes until tender. Peel off the skins and mash the artichokes well. Stir in the yogurt with salt and pepper to taste. Alternatively, work the ingredients to a smooth purée in an electric blender.

Spread the mixture in 4 individual ovenproof dishes or in one large baking dish. Make 4 hollows for the eggs and crack 1 egg into each hollow.

Bake in a preheated moderate oven (180°C / 350°F, Gas Mark 4) for 10 to 15 minutes until the eggs are just set. Garnish with parsley and serve hot.

Serves 4

Guacamole

This Mexican avocado pâté makes an interesting starter or a party dip. In Mexico they serve it very hot and fiery and usually add chilli peppers. If the guacamole is not to be used immediately, reserve the avocado stones (seeds), bury them in the mixture and cover the dish – this helps to prevent the avocados from browning.

Metric/Imperial	American
2 large very ripe avocado pears	2 large very ripe avocado pears
juice of 1 lemon	juice of 1 lemon
4 tomatoes, skinned, seeded and chopped	4 tomatoes, skinned, seeded and chopped
1 small onion, peeled and grated	1 small onion, peeled and grated
1 garlic clove, peeled and crushed	1 garlic clove, peeled and crushed
¼ teaspoon Tabasco sauce	¼ teaspoon Tabasco sauce
salt	salt
freshly ground black pepper	freshly ground black pepper
1 small lettuce to serve (optional)	1 small head of lettuce to serve (optional)

Cut the avocados in half and remove the stones (seeds). Scoop out the pulp into a bowl and immediately pour over the lemon juice to prevent browning.

Mash the avocados well, then add the remaining ingredients, except the lettuce, and beat well until smooth. Alternatively, put all the ingredients in an electric blender and work to a smooth purée.

Transfer to a serving bowl, or serve on individual plates, lined with lettuce leaves. Serve immediately with toasted wholewheat bread.

Serves 4 to 6

Tomato Tart

Metric/Imperial	American
wholewheat pastry made with 175 g / 6 oz flour (see page 145)	wholewheat dough made with 1½ cups flour (see page 145)
750 g / 1½ lb tomatoes	1½ lb tomatoes
1 onion, peeled and chopped	1 onion, peeled and chopped
1 garlic clove, peeled and chopped (optional)	1 garlic clove, peeled and chopped (optional)
4 thyme sprigs	4 thyme sprigs
salt	salt
freshly ground black pepper	freshly ground black pepper

Roll out the pastry dough on a lightly floured surface and use to line a 20 cm / 8 inch flan dish or flan ring placed on a baking sheet. Prick the base lightly with a fork, cover with foil, then weigh down with baking beans or rice.

Bake in a preheated moderately hot oven (200°C / 400°F, Gas Mark 6) for 15 minutes. Remove the beans or rice and the foil, return the flan case to the oven and bake for a further 5 minutes.

Meanwhile, make the filling: skin 450 g / 1 lb of the tomatoes, then chop them roughly. Put the tomatoes in a pan with the onion, garlic if using, thyme and salt and pepper to taste. Cover and simmer gently until the tomatoes are reduced to a pulp. Discard the thyme sprigs.

Spread the tomato mixture in the flan case. Slice the remaining tomatoes and arrange overlapping around the edge of the tart.

Return to the oven and bake for a further 15 minutes. Serve hot or cold.

Serves 4 to 6

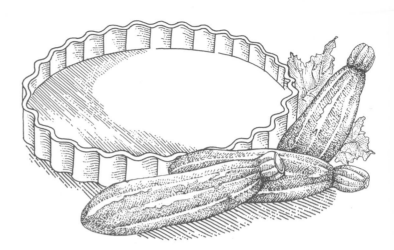

Mushrooms à la Grècque

Metric/Imperial	American
2 tablespoons oil	2 tablespoons oil
1 large onion, peeled and sliced	1 large onion, peeled and sliced
1 large carrot, peeled and sliced	1 large carrot, peeled and sliced
1 celery stick, sliced	1 celery stalk, sliced
1 large garlic clove, peeled and crushed	1 large garlic clove, peeled and crushed
150 ml / ¼ pint dry white wine	⅔ cup dry white wine
3 tomatoes, skinned, quartered and seeded	3 tomatoes, skinned, quartered and seeded
3 tablespoons chopped parsley	3 tablespoons chopped parsley
1 tablespoon thyme leaves	1 tablespoon thyme leaves
1 bay leaf	1 bay leaf
salt	salt
freshly ground black pepper	freshly ground black pepper
450 g / 1 lb button mushrooms	4 cups button mushrooms

Heat the oil in a large pan. Add the onion, carrot and celery and fry gently for 3 minutes, stirring occasionally. Add the garlic and fry for a further 1 minute.

Stir in the wine, tomatoes, 1 tablespoon parsley, thyme, bay leaf and salt and pepper to taste. Bring to the boil, then lower the heat and add the mushrooms. Simmer gently for 10 minutes.

Leave to cool, then pour into a serving dish and chill in the refrigerator. Sprinkle with the remaining parsley and serve chilled.

Serves 4

Courgette (Zucchini) Quiche

Metric/Imperial	American
wholewheat pastry made with 175 g / 6 oz flour (see page 145)	wholewheat dough made with 1½ cups flour (see page 145)
2 tablespoons oil	2 tablespoons oil
2 onions, peeled and sliced	2 onions, peeled and sliced
450 g / 1 lb courgettes, sliced	1 lb zucchini, sliced
salt	salt
freshly ground black pepper	freshly ground black pepper
2 eggs, beaten with 150 ml / ¼ pint milk	2 eggs, beaten with ⅔ cup milk
2 tablespoons grated Parmesan cheese	2 tablespoons grated Parmesan cheese

Roll out the pastry dough on a lightly floured surface and use to line a 20 cm / 8 inch flan dish or flan ring, placed on a baking sheet. Prick the base lightly with a fork, cover with foil, then weigh down with baking beans or rice.

Bake in a preheated moderately hot oven (200°C / 400°F, Gas Mark 6) for 15 minutes. Remove the beans or rice and the foil, return the flan case to the oven and bake for a further 5 minutes.

Meanwhile, make the filling: heat the oil in a frying pan (skillet). Add the onions and courgettes (zucchini) and fry gently for about 10 minutes until lightly browned, stirring occasionally.

Remove the onions and courgettes (zucchini) from the pan with a slotted spoon, then place in the flan case. Add salt and pepper to taste to the egg and milk mixture, then pour into the flan case. Sprinkle with the Parmesan cheese.

Bake in a preheated moderately hot oven (190°C / 375°F, Gas Mark 5) for 25 to 30 minutes until the filling is set and lightly browned on top. Serve hot or cold.

Serves 4 to 6

Italian Bean Soup

Metric/Imperial

225 g / 8 oz dried white
   beans (haricot, butter
   beans, etc)
600 ml / 1 pint water
1 large onion, peeled and
   chopped
1 garlic clove, peeled and
   crushed (optional)
1 celery stick, sliced
1 large carrot, peeled and
   sliced
4 tomatoes, skinned and
   chopped
finely grated rind and juice
   of ½ lemon
1 bay leaf
salt
freshly ground black pepper
2 tablespoons chopped
   parsley (optional)

American

1 cup dried white beans
   (navy, lima, etc)
2½ cups water
1 large onion, peeled and
   chopped
1 garlic clove, peeled and
   crushed (optional)
1 celery stalk, sliced
1 large carrot, peeled and
   sliced
4 tomatoes, skinned and
   chopped
finely grated rind and juice
   of ½ lemon
1 bay leaf
salt
freshly ground black pepper
2 tablespoons chopped
   parsley (optional)

Put the beans in a large bowl, cover with the water, then leave to soak overnight. Alternatively, pour over boiling water and soak for several hours. Drain the beans, reserving the water. Make up to 1.2 litres / 2 pints / 5 cups with stock or more water.

Place the beans and liquid in a large pan, then add all the remaining ingredients, except the parsley. Bring to the boil, then lower the heat, cover and simmer for 1 to 1½ hours until the beans are tender, adding more water if necessary. Discard the bay leaf.

Transfer about half the beans and some of the liquid into an electric blender. Work to a smooth purée.

Return the purée to the soup and bring to the boil, stirring constantly. Taste and adjust the seasoning, and add more liquid if the soup is too thick. Sprinkle with parsley if liked, and serve hot.

Serves 4 to 6

ABOVE: Mediterranean lentil stew; Italian bean soup
RIGHT: Black eye fish hors d'oeuvre

Black Eye Fish Hors D'Oeuvre

Metric/Imperial

100 g / 4 oz black eye peas
600 ml / 1 pint water
225 g / 8 oz white fish fillets
(cod, haddock, etc),
cooked, skinned and
flaked
1 × 100 g / 4 oz can tuna
fish, drained and flaked
100 g / 4 oz peeled prawns
1 small onion, peeled and
grated
150 ml / ¼ pint vinaigrette
dressing (see page 80)
finely grated rind and juice
of ½ lemon
dash of Tabasco sauce
2 teaspoons tomato purée
2 tablespoons chopped
parsley
salt
freshly ground black pepper
TO GARNISH:
few unshelled prawns
parsley sprigs

American

½ cup black eye peas
2½ cups water
½ lb white fish fillets (cod,
haddock, etc), cooked,
skinned and flaked
1 × 4 oz can tuna fish,
drained and flaked
½ cup shelled shrimp
1 small onion, peeled and
grated
⅔ cup French dressing (see
page 80)
finely grated rind and juice
of ½ lemon
dash of Tabasco sauce
2 teaspoons tomato paste
2 tablespoons chopped
parsley
salt
freshly ground black pepper
TO GARNISH:
few unshelled shrimp
parsley sprigs

Put the peas in a large bowl, cover with the water, then leave to soak overnight. Alternatively, pour over boiling water and soak for several hours.

Transfer the peas and water to a pan and bring to the boil. Lower the heat, cover and simmer for 1 to 1½ hours until the beans are tender, adding more water if necessary.

Drain the peas and place in a bowl. Add the flaked fish and prawns (shrimp) and fold lightly to mix.

Mix together the remaining ingredients, then fold in the salad. Leave to marinate for at least 1 hour.

Turn into a serving dish, garnish with the prawns (shrimp) and parsley, and serve cold.

Serves 6 as a starter, 4 as a main course

Mediterranean Lentil Stew

Lentils do not need soaking before cooking, and mixed with vegetables they make a delicious stew in which most of the liquid has been absorbed to give a moist sauce.

Metric/Imperial

2 tablespoons oil
2 onions, peeled and
chopped
1 garlic clove, peeled and
crushed
2 celery sticks, sliced
4 small courgettes, sliced
4 tomatoes, skinned and
quartered
900 ml / 1½ pints water or
stock
¼ teaspoon ground
coriander
salt
freshly ground black pepper
225 g / 8 oz brown lentils
2 tablespoons chopped
parsley (optional)

American

2 tablespoons oil
2 onions, peeled and
chopped
1 garlic clove, peeled and
crushed
2 celery stalks, sliced
4 small zucchini, sliced
4 tomatoes, skinned and
quartered
3¾ cups water or stock
¼ teaspoon ground
coriander
salt
freshly ground black pepper
1 cup brown lentils
2 tablespoons chopped
parsley (optional)

Heat the oil in a large pan. Add the onions, garlic, celery and courgettes (zucchini) and fry gently for 10 minutes until lightly browned, stirring frequently.

Add the tomatoes, water or stock, coriander and salt and pepper to taste. Bring to the boil. Add the lentils, then cover and simmer for 1 to 1½ hours until the lentils are tender.

Alternatively, transfer the ingredients to a casserole, cover and bake in a preheated moderate oven (180°C / 350°F, Gas Mark 4) for 1½ hours to 2 hours.

Sprinkle with the chopped parsley, if liked, and serve hot.

Serves 4

Haricot (Navy) Bean Paprika

Metric/Imperial	American
350 g / 12 oz haricot beans, soaked overnight	1½ cups navy beans, soaked overnight
salt	salt
2 tablespoons oil	2 tablespoons oil
1 large onion, peeled and sliced	1 large onion, peeled and sliced
1 clove garlic, peeled and crushed	1 clove garlic, peeled and crushed
1 tablespoon paprika	1 tablespoon paprika
2 tablespoons tomato purée	2 tablespoons tomato paste
50 g / 2 oz canned pimento, sliced	½ cup sliced canned pimento
1 × 500 g / 1 lb can tomatoes	1 lb can tomatoes
150 ml / ¼ pint water	⅔ cup water
4 tablespoons soured cream	4 tablespoons sour cream

Drain the haricot (navy) beans, and cook in boiling salted water for 45 minutes or until almost tender; drain.

Meanwhile, heat the oil in a large pan and sauté the onion and garlic until soft. Stir in the paprika and cook, stirring, for 2 to 3 minutes.

Add the beans, tomato purée (paste), pimento, tomatoes and water. Bring to the boil, cover and simmer gently for about 10 minutes.

Stir in the soured cream just before serving.

Serves 4

Southern Baked Beans

Metric/Imperial	American
225 g / 8 oz haricot beans	1 cup navy beans
600 ml / 1 pint water	2½ cups water
1 large onion, peeled and chopped	1 large onion, peeled and chopped
2 celery sticks, sliced	2 celery stalks, sliced
1 red pepper, cored, seeded and sliced	1 red pepper, cored, seeded and sliced
4 tomatoes, skinned and chopped	4 tomatoes, skinned and chopped
1 tablespoon molasses or honey	1 tablespoon molasses or honey
1 tablespoon tomato purée	1 tablespoon tomato paste
2 tablespoons vinegar	2 tablespoons vinegar
2 teaspoons Worcestershire sauce	2 teaspoons Worcestershire sauce
2 teaspoons mustard powder	2 teaspoons mustard powder
salt	salt
freshly ground black pepper	freshly ground black pepper
100 g / 4 oz salami, thickly sliced and skinned	¼ lb salami, thickly sliced and skinned

Put the beans in a large bowl, cover with the water, then leave to soak overnight. Alternatively, pour over boiling water and soak for several hours.

Drain the beans, reserving the water. Make up to 600 ml / 1 pint / 2½ cups with more water.

Place the beans and liquid in a large pan, then bring to the boil. Lower the heat, cover and simmer for 1 to 1½ hours until the beans are tender, adding more water if necessary. Drain and reserve 300 ml / ½ pint / 1¼ cups cooking liquid.

Put the beans in layers in a casserole dish with the onion, celery, red pepper and tomatoes.

Mix the reserved cooking liquid with the remaining ingredients, except the salami. Pour over the beans.

Cover and bake in a preheated moderate oven (180°C / 350°F, Gas Mark 4) for 1 hour. Arrange the salami on top and bake for a further 30 minutes until the beans are tender and well-flavoured with the salami. Serve hot.

Serves 4 to 6

Lentil Patties

Metric/Imperial	American
2 tablespoons oil	2 tablespoons oil
1 clove garlic, peeled and crushed	1 clove garlic, peeled and crushed
1 onion, peeled and finely chopped	1 onion, peeled and finely chopped
1 celery stick, chopped	1 celery stalk, chopped
1 carrot, peeled and chopped	1 carrot, peeled and chopped
225 g / 8 oz brown lentils	1 cup brown lentils
450 ml / ¾ pint water	2 cups water
salt	salt
freshly ground black pepper	freshly ground black pepper
4 tablespoons wholemeal flour	4 tablespoons wholewheat flour
½ teaspoon ground ginger	½ teaspoon ground ginger
½ teaspoon ground cumin	½ teaspoon ground cumin
1 teaspoon curry powder	1 teaspoon curry powder
1 tablespoon mango chutney, chopped	1 tablespoon mango chutney, chopped
oil for shallow frying	oil for shallow frying
DRESSING:	DRESSING:
150 ml / ¼ pint natural yogurt	⅔ cup unflavored yogurt
1 clove garlic, peeled and crushed	1 clove garlic, peeled and crushed
1 tablespoon chopped parsley	1 tablespoon chopped parsley

Heat the oil in a large pan. Add the garlic, onion, celery and carrot and sauté until the vegetables begin to soften.

Add the lentils, water, salt and pepper. Bring to the boil, then lower the heat, cover and simmer for about 1 hour until the lentils are soft and all the liquid is absorbed.

Add 2 tablespoons flour, the spices and chutney to the pan and mix well. Continue to cook gently for 2 to 3 minutes, stirring constantly. Adjust the seasoning, if necessary. Turn the mixture onto a plate and leave until cool enough to handle.

Divide the mixture into 18 equal pieces and form each one into a patty, about 1 cm / ½ inch thick. Coat with the remaining flour. Heat a little oil in a frying pan (skillet) and fry the lentil patties, a few at a time, until crisp and golden brown, turning once.

Mix together the yogurt, garlic and parsley for the dressing. Serve the patties on a bed of rice, topped with the yogurt dressing.

Serves 6

Butter (Lima) Bean, Herb and Tomato Soufflé

The puréed butter (lima) beans form the sauce for this simple soufflé.

Metric/Imperial	American
100 g / 4 oz butter beans	½ cup lima beans
600 ml / 1 pint water	2½ cups water
150 ml / ¼ pint milk	⅔ cup milk
1 large onion, peeled and grated	1 large onion, peeled and grated
4 tomatoes, skinned and chopped	4 tomatoes, skinned and chopped
1 tablespoon chopped parsley	1 tablespoon chopped parsley
1 tablespoon chopped thyme	1 tablespoon chopped thyme
1 teaspoon chopped sage	1 teaspoon chopped sage
salt	salt
freshly ground white pepper	freshly ground white pepper
4 eggs, separated	4 eggs, separated

Put the beans in a large bowl, cover with the water, then leave to soak overnight. Alternatively, pour over boiling water and soak for several hours.

Transfer the beans and water to a pan, then bring to the boil. Lower the heat, cover and simmer for about 1½ hours until the beans are soft, adding more water if necessary.

Drain the beans, return to the rinsed-out pan and mash well. Add the milk and onion and bring to the boil, stirring constantly. Simmer for 1 minute.

Remove the pan from the heat, then stir in the tomatoes, herbs and salt and pepper to taste. Stir in the egg yolks and leave to cool slightly.

Beat the egg whites until just stiff, then fold into the bean sauce. Pour the mixture into a 1.5 litre / 2½ pint / 6¼ cup soufflé dish. Bake in a preheated moderate oven (180°C / 350°F, Gas Mark 4) for 1 hour until the soufflé has risen and is lightly browned on top. Serve immediately.

Serves 4 to 6

Chick Pea (Garbanzos) Salad

This Middle Eastern dish makes an unusual start to a meal. Serve with pitta bread.

Metric/Imperial	American
175 g / 6 oz chick peas	1 cup garbanzos
600 ml / 1 pint water	2½ cups water
1 large garlic clove, peeled and crushed	1 large garlic clove, peeled and crushed
juice of 1 lemon	juice of 1 lemon
4 tablespoons tahini (sesame seed paste), or sesame seeds	¼ cup tahini (sesame seed paste), or sesame seeds
150 ml / ¼ pint natural yogurt	⅔ cup unflavored yogurt
salt	salt
freshly ground white pepper	freshly ground white pepper
TO GARNISH:	TO GARNISH:
1 small lettuce	1 small head of lettuce
2 tomatoes, sliced	2 tomatoes, sliced
12 black olives	12 ripe olives
2 tablespoons chopped parsley	2 tablespoons chopped parsley

Put the chick peas (garbanzos) in a large bowl, cover with the water, then leave to soak overnight. Alternatively, pour over boiling water and soak for several hours.

Transfer the chick peas (garbanzos) and water to a pan and bring to the boil. Lower the heat, cover and simmer for about 1 hour until they are soft, adding more water if necessary.

Drain the chick peas (garbanzos), then mash them to a purée. Stir in the garlic, lemon juice, tahini or sesame seeds, yogurt and salt and pepper to taste.

Beat to a smooth, creamy paste, adding a little water if too thick. Alternatively, work all the ingredients to a smooth purée in an electric blender, adding more water as necessary to blend.

To serve: arrange the lettuce leaves on individual serving plates, then divide the purée equally between them, piling it up in the centre. Garnish with tomato slices, olives and parsley and serve cold.

Serves 6 as a starter, 4 as a main course

Soya Bean Moussaka

This Greek dish is traditionally made with minced (ground) lamb or beef, but soya beans are substituted in this recipe to make a cheap and tasty dish. Omit the bacon for a vegetarian dish.

Metric/Imperial	American
225 g / 8 oz soya beans	1 cup soy beans
600 ml / 1 pint water	2½ cups water
4 tablespoons oil	¼ cup oil
50 g / 2 oz streaky bacon, derinded and chopped	3 fatty bacon slices, derinded and chopped
2 onions, peeled and chopped	2 onions, peeled and chopped
2 celery sticks, sliced	2 celery stalks, sliced
1 large carrot, peeled and sliced	1 large carrot, peeled and sliced
100 g / 4 oz mushrooms, sliced	1 cup sliced mushrooms
4 tomatoes, skinned and chopped	4 tomatoes, skinned and chopped
1 tablespoon tomato purée	1 tablespoon tomato paste
1 teaspoon dried marjoram	1 teaspoon dried marjoram
salt	salt
freshly ground black pepper	freshly ground black pepper
1 bay leaf	1 bay leaf
675 g / 1½ lb aubergines, stalks removed and thinly sliced	1½ lb eggplants, stalks removed and thinly sliced
CHEESE SAUCE:	CHEESE SAUCE:
25 g / 1 oz vegetable margarine	2 tablespoons vegetable margarine
25 g / 1 oz flour	¼ cup flour
300 ml / ½ pint milk	1¼ cups milk
100 g / 4 oz Cheddar cheese, grated	1 cup grated Cheddar cheese
1 egg, beaten	1 egg, beaten
½ teaspoon prepared mustard	½ teaspoon prepared mustard

Put the soya beans in a large bowl, cover with the water, then leave to soak overnight. Alternatively, pour over boiling water and soak for several hours.

Drain the beans, reserving the water. Make up to 1.2 litres / 2 pints / 5 cups with more water.

Place the beans and liquid in a large pan, then bring to the boil. Skim then lower the heat, cover and simmer for about 2 hours until the beans are just tender. Drain and reserve 300 ml / ½ pint / 1¼ cups cooking liquid.

Heat 1 tablespoon oil in a large pan. Add the bacon, onions, celery and carrot and fry gently for 5 minutes. Add the mushrooms and fry for a further 2 minutes. Stir in the reserved cooking liquid together with the tomatoes, tomato purée (paste), marjoram and salt and pepper to taste.

Bring to the boil, stirring constantly. Add the beans and bay leaf, cover and simmer for 1 hour until the beans are tender and most of the liquid has been absorbed to give a moist mixture. Discard the bay leaf.

Meanwhile, put the aubergine (eggplant) slices in a colander, sprinkling the layers with salt. Leave for about 1 hour to allow the water to drain off and remove the bitterness. Rinse under cold running water to remove the salt, then pat dry.

Place the aubergine (eggplant) slices in a single layer on a grill (broiler) pan. Brush lightly with oil and grill (broil) for about 5 minutes until lightly browned, turning once. Repeat with the remaining aubergine (eggplant) slices.

Place one third of the aubergines (eggplants) in the bottom of a 1.75 litre / 3 pint / 7½ cup casserole dish. Cover with half the bean mixture, then another third of the aubergines (eggplants). Spread the remaining bean mixture on top, then finish with a neat layer of aubergines (eggplants).

To make the sauce: melt the margarine in a pan, add the flour and cook for 1 to 2 minutes, stirring constantly. Remove from the heat and stir in the milk gradually, beating vigorously after each addition. Return to the heat and bring to the boil, stirring constantly. Simmer for 2 minutes until thick, then stir in half the cheese and the beaten egg. Add the mustard and salt and pepper to taste.

Pour the cheese sauce over the top of the moussaka, then sprinkle with the remaining cheese. Bake in a preheated moderate oven (180°C / 350°F, Gas Mark 4) for 30 minutes until the topping is browned. Garnish with parsley and serve hot.

Serves 6

Chick pea (garbanzos) salad; Soya bean moussaka; Southern baked beans (page 92)

Leeks à la Grècque

Metric/Imperial	American
300 ml / ½ pint water (or 150 ml / ¼ pint dry white wine and 150 ml / ¼ pint water)	1¼ cups water (or ⅔ cup dry white wine and ⅔ cup water)
finely grated rind and juice of 1 lemon	finely grated rind and juice of 1 lemon
2 shallots, peeled and thinly sliced	2 shallots, peeled and thinly sliced
4 parsley sprigs	4 parsley sprigs
1 small celery stick, with leaves	1 small celery stalk, with leaves
1 fennel sprig or few fennel seeds	1 fennel sprig or few fennel seeds
1 thyme sprig	1 thyme sprig
6 peppercorns	6 peppercorns
3 coriander seeds	3 coriander seeds
salt	salt
450 g / 1 lb leeks, trimmed and cleaned	1 lb leeks, trimmed and cleaned

Put all the ingredients in a large pan, except the leeks. Bring to the boil, then lower the heat, cover and simmer for 10 minutes.

Add the leeks to the pan, cover and simmer gently for 10 to 15 minutes until tender but not broken up.

Transfer the leeks to a serving dish. Boil the cooking liquid until reduced by half. Strain if preferred, then pour over the leeks and leave to cool. Serve cold.

Serves 4

Courgettes (Zucchini) Provençal

Metric/Imperial	American
450 g / 1 lb courgettes, sliced	1 lb zucchini, sliced
4 tomatoes, sliced	4 tomatoes, sliced
1 small onion, peeled and grated	1 small onion, peeled and grated
2 tablespoons chopped parsley	2 tablespoons chopped parsley
1 tablespoon thyme leaves	1 tablespoon thyme leaves
salt	salt
freshly ground black pepper	freshly ground black pepper
5 tablespoons stock	⅓ cup stock

Arrange the courgettes (zucchini) and tomatoes in layers in a baking dish or casserole, sprinkling each layer with the onion, half of the parsley, the thyme and salt and pepper to taste. Pour in the stock.

Cover and bake in a preheated moderate oven (180°C / 350°F, Gas Mark 4) for 30 to 40 minutes until the courgettes (zucchini) are tender but not soft.

Alternatively, put all the ingredients, except half the parsley, in a large saucepan. Cover and cook gently for 10 minutes until just tender, stirring occasionally.

Taste and adjust the seasoning. Sprinkle with the remaining parsley and serve hot or cold.

Serves 4

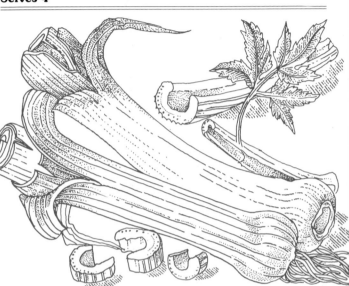

Celery with Orange and Nuts

Metric/Imperial	American
1 celery head, trimmed and cut into 5 cm / 2 inch lengths, leaves reserved	1 celery head, trimmed and cut into 2 inch lengths, leaves reserved
finely grated rind of ½ orange	finely grated rind of ½ orange
juice of 1 orange	juice of 1 orange
1 orange, peel and pith removed and divided into segments	1 orange, peel and pith removed and divided into segments
25 g / 1 oz sultanas	3 tablespoons seedless white raisins
25 g / 1 oz walnuts	¼ cup walnuts
salt	salt
freshly ground black pepper	freshly ground black pepper

Put the celery and leaves in a baking dish. Add the orange rind, juice and segments, then sprinkle with the sultanas (seedless white raisins), nuts and salt and pepper to taste.

Cover and bake in a preheated moderate oven (180°C / 350°F, Gas Mark 4) for 30 to 40 minutes until the celery is just tender.

Alternatively, put all the ingredients in a large saucepan. Cover and cook gently for 15 to 20 minutes until just tender, stirring occasionally. If necessary, add a little water towards the end of cooking.

Taste and adjust the seasoning. Serve hot.

Serves 4

Spinach Fried with Garlic

This is a very quick and nutritious way to cook spinach – it is fried quickly with onions and garlic until just tender. To make a quick lunch or supper dish, add 100 g / 4 oz / ½ cup chopped bacon with the onion.
The spinach stalks may be cooked separately and served like asparagus spears. Alternatively, they may be chopped and added with the leaves, but they will take a little longer to cook than the leaves.

Metric/Imperial	American
2 tablespoons oil	2 tablespoons oil
1 large onion, peeled and chopped	1 large onion, peeled and chopped
1 large garlic clove, peeled and crushed	1 large garlic clove, peeled and crushed
450 g / 1 lb spinach leaves	1 lb spinach leaves
1 tablespoon lemon juice	1 tablespoon lemon juice
salt	salt
freshly ground black pepper	freshly ground black pepper

Heat the oil in a large pan. Add the onion and garlic and fry gently for 5 minutes, stirring frequently.

Wash the spinach thoroughly, then add to the pan with only the water clinging to the leaves. Add the lemon juice and salt and pepper to taste. Fry gently for 3 to 5 minutes until the spinach is just tender but still bright green, stirring constantly. Taste and adjust the seasoning, then serve immediately.
Serves 4

Cabbage Braised with Apple and Yogurt

Metric/Imperial	American
450 g / 1 lb cabbage, shredded	6 cups shredded cabbage
1 onion, peeled and grated	1 onion, peeled and grated
1 cooking apple, peeled, cored and grated	1 baking apple, peeled, cored and grated
salt	salt
freshly ground white pepper	freshly ground white pepper
150 ml / ¼ pint natural yogurt	⅔ cup unflavored yogurt
pinch of grated nutmeg	pinch of grated nutmeg

Put half the cabbage in a baking dish. Sprinkle with half the onion and apple and salt and pepper to taste. Spoon over half the yogurt.

Add the remaining cabbage, then top with the remaining apple and onion and sprinkle with salt and pepper to taste. Spoon over the remaining yogurt and sprinkle with the nutmeg.

Bake in a preheated moderately hot oven (190°C / 375°F, Gas Mark 5) for about 20 minutes or until the cabbage is just tender. Serve hot.
Serves 4

Vegetable Strudel

Metric/Imperial	American
2 tablespoons oil	2 tablespoons oil
1 small onion, peeled and chopped	1 small onion, peeled and chopped
1 clove garlic, peeled and crushed	1 clove garlic, peeled and crushed
1 celery stick, sliced	1 celery stalk, sliced
100 g / 4 oz button mushrooms, sliced	1 cup sliced button mushrooms
2 tablespoons flour	2 tablespoons flour
150 ml / ¼ pint light stock	⅔ cup light stock
1 tablespoon tomato purée	1 tablespoon tomato paste
225 g / 8 oz tomatoes, skinned and chopped	2 cups chopped tomatoes
1 small cauliflower, cooked and roughly chopped	1 small cauliflower, cooked and roughly chopped
1 tablespoon chopped parsley	1 tablespoon chopped parsley
¼ teaspoon dried basil	¼ teaspoon dried basil
salt	salt
freshly ground black pepper	freshly ground black pepper
1 × 375 g / 13 oz packet frozen puff pastry, thawed	1 × 13 oz package frozen puff paste, thawed
1 egg, beaten	1 egg, beaten

Heat the oil in a frying pan (skillet) and sauté the onion, garlic and celery until soft. Add the mushrooms and cook for 1 minute. Add the flour, then gradually stir in the stock and tomato purée (paste). Bring to the boil, stirring.

Remove from the heat, and add the tomatoes, cauliflower and herbs. Season with salt and pepper to taste, then leave to cool.

Roll out the pastry to a 36 cm / 14 inch square. Spread the cooked vegetable filling over the pastry, leaving a 2.5 cm / 1 inch border around the edge. Brush this border with beaten egg. Fold the pastry in half and press the edges together to seal. Brush the pastry with beaten egg and roll up like a Swiss (jelly) roll.

Carefully place on a baking tray. Brush with beaten egg to glaze and make several slits along the top of the strudel. Bake in a moderately hot oven (200°C / 400°F, Gas Mark 6) for 30 minutes. Cut into slices and serve with a crisp green salad.
Serves 4

Leek Pie

The bacon may be omitted for a vegetarian dish.

Metric/Imperial

PASTRY:
175 g / 6 oz wholemeal flour
pinch each of salt and pepper
75 g / 3 oz vegetable margarine
75 g / 3 oz mature Cheddar cheese, finely grated
2 tablespoons cold water
beaten egg or milk to glaze
FILLING:
1 tablespoon vegetable margarine
100 g / 4 oz streaky bacon, rinds removed and chopped
750 g / 1 ½ lb leeks, trimmed and sliced into 1 cm / ½ inch rounds
25 g / 1 oz flour
300 ml / ½ pint stock (or milk and water mixed)
finely grated rind and juice of ½ lemon
¼ teaspoon grated nutmeg
50 g / 2 oz shelled hazelnuts
50 g / 2 oz seedless raisins
salt
freshly ground black pepper

American

DOUGH:
1 ½ cups wholewheat flour
pinch each of salt and pepper
⅓ cup vegetable margarine
¾ cup finely grated mature Cheddar cheese
2 tablespoons cold water
beaten egg or milk to glaze
FILLING:
1 tablespoon vegetable margarine
½ cup chopped fatty bacon
1 ½ lb leeks, trimmed and sliced into ½ inch rounds
¼ cup flour
1 ¼ cups stock (or milk and water mixed)
finely grated rind and juice of ½ lemon
¼ teaspoon grated nutmeg
⅜ cup shelled filberts
⅓ cup seedless raisins
salt
freshly ground black pepper

To make the pastry dough: put the flour and salt and pepper in a bowl, then add the margarine in pieces. Rub into the flour until the mixture resembles breadcrumbs, then stir in the cheese. Add the water and mix to a firm dough. Chill in the refrigerator until required.

To make the filling: melt the margarine in a pan. Add the bacon and fry gently for 3 minutes, stirring occasionally. Add the leeks and fry gently for a further 5 minutes, stirring constantly until soft but not brown.

Stir in the flour and cook for 1 to 2 minutes, then gradually stir in the stock or milk and water. Bring to the boil, then lower the heat and simmer until the sauce is thick and smooth, stirring constantly. Add the remaining filling ingredients, simmer for 2 minutes, then transfer to a 1 litre / 1 ¾ pint / 4 ¼ cup pie dish. Leave to cool.

Meanwhile, roll out the pastry dough on a lightly floured surface until 2.5 cm / 1 inch larger than the circumference of the pie dish. Cut a 1 cm / ½ inch strip from the edge, then press it onto the moistened rim of the dish. Moisten the strip, then cover the dish with the remaining pastry dough, pressing the edges firmly to seal. Trim and flute the edge and decorate the top of the pie with the trimmings.

Brush with beaten egg or milk. Bake in a preheated moderately hot oven (200°C / 400°F, Gas Mark 6) for 30 minutes until the pastry is crisp and golden brown. Serve hot or cold.

Serves 4

Mixed Vegetable Curry

If you do not have all the individual spices for this curry, substitute 1-2 tablespoons curry powder.

Metric/Imperial
2 tablespoons oil
225 g / 8 oz onions, peeled and sliced
1 garlic clove, peeled and crushed
1 cooking apple, peeled, cored and chopped
2.5 cm / 1 inch piece fresh root ginger, peeled and grated
1 tablespoon mustard seeds
1 teaspoon ground turmeric
1 teaspoon ground coriander
1 teaspoon ground cumin
1/2 teaspoon ground fenugreek
1/4 teaspoon chilli powder
450 ml / 3/4 pint stock
finely grated rind and juice of 1/2 lemon
salt
freshly ground black pepper
225 g / 8 oz potatoes, peeled and diced
225 g / 8 oz carrots, peeled and sliced
225 g / 8 oz tomatoes, skinned and roughly chopped
225 g / 8 oz cauliflower florets
225 g / 8 oz runner beans, sliced
50 g / 2 oz sultanas
50 g / 2 oz shelled Brazil nuts
1 tablespoon grated fresh coconut

American
2 tablespoons oil
2 onions, peeled and sliced
1 garlic clove, peeled and crushed
1 baking apple, peeled, cored and chopped
1 inch piece fresh ginger root, peeled and grated
1 tablespoon mustard seeds
1 teaspoon ground turmeric
1 teaspoon ground coriander
1 teaspoon ground cumin
1/2 teaspoon ground fenugreek
1/4 teaspoon chili powder
2 cups stock
finely grated rind and juice of 1/2 lemon
salt
freshly ground black pepper
1 1/3 cups peeled and diced raw potato
1 1/2 cups peeled and sliced carrots
1 cup skinned and roughly chopped tomatoes
2 cups cauliflower florets
1 cup sliced green beans
1/3 cup seedless white raisins
1/2 cup shelled Brazil nuts
1 tablespoon grated fresh coconut

Heat the oil in a large pan. Add the onions, garlic, apple and ginger and fry gently for 5 minutes, stirring occasionally. Stir in the spices and fry gently for a further 3 minutes, stirring constantly.

Add the stock and bring to the boil, stirring constantly, until the sauce thickens slightly. Add the lemon rind and juice and salt and pepper to taste, then lower the heat and simmer for 2 minutes.

Add the potatoes, carrots and tomatoes. Cover the pan and simmer for 10 minutes.

Add the cauliflower, beans, sultanas (seedless white raisins) and nuts. Cover and simmer for a further 10 minutes or until the vegetables are just tender but still crisp and not broken up.

Taste and adjust the seasoning. Sprinkle with the coconut and serve hot. Alternatively, serve cold as a salad.

Serves 4

Underground Hotpot

Other root vegetables such as turnips, swedes (rutabaga) or celeriac may be substituted. Whole peanuts are usually obtainable but if not, substitute salted peanuts and decrease the quantity of salt in the recipe.

Metric/Imperial	American
450 g / 1 lb potatoes, peeled and thinly sliced	4 medium potatoes, peeled and thinly sliced
225 g / 8 oz onions, peeled and sliced	2 onions, peeled and sliced
225 g / 8 oz carrots, peeled and sliced	1½ cups peeled and sliced carrots
225 g / 8 oz parsnips, peeled and sliced	1½ cups peeled and sliced parsnips
225 g / 8 oz Jerusalem artichokes, peeled and sliced	1½ cups peeled and sliced Jerusalem artichokes
2 celery sticks, sliced	2 celery stalks, sliced
100 g / 4 oz whole peanuts, shelled	½ cup whole shelled peanuts
100 g / 4 oz mature Cheddar cheese, grated	1 cup grated mature Cheddar cheese
2 tablespoons rosemary leaves	2 tablespoons rosemary leaves
salt	salt
freshly ground black pepper	freshly ground black pepper
300 ml / ½ pint stock	1¼ cups stock

Put half the potato slices in the bottom of a 1.75 litre / 3 pint / 7½ cup casserole dish.

Arrange the remaining vegetables in the dish in layers, sprinkling each layer with the nuts, cheese, rosemary and salt and pepper to taste. Reserve a little cheese for the topping.

Finish with a layer of potatoes arranged neatly in circles on top, then pour on the stock and sprinkle with the reserved cheese.

Bake in a preheated moderately hot oven (190°C / 375°F, Gas Mark 5) for 1½ hours until the top is browned and the vegetables are tender when pierced with a skewer. Serve hot.

Serves 4 to 6

Brazil Mushroom Casserole

Metric/Imperial	American
450 g / 1 lb button mushrooms	4 cups button mushrooms
4 tomatoes, sliced	4 tomatoes, sliced
4 spring onions, trimmed and chopped	4 scallions, trimmed and chopped
1 tablespoon chopped oregano or marjoram	1 tablespoon chopped oregano or marjoram
1 tablespoon chopped basil	1 tablespoon chopped basil
1 teaspoon rosemary leaves	1 teaspoon rosemary leaves
salt	salt
freshly ground black pepper	freshly ground black pepper
4 tablespoons dry white wine or stock	¼ cup dry white wine or stock
100 g / 4 oz Brazil nuts, coarsely ground	1 cup coarsely ground Brazil nuts
50 g / 2 oz fresh wholemeal breadcrumbs	1 cup fresh wholewheat breadcrumbs

Wipe the mushrooms and cut the larger ones into halves or quarters, leaving the small ones whole. Arrange the mushrooms, tomatoes and spring onions (scallions) in layers in a casserole dish, sprinkling each layer with the herbs and salt and pepper to taste. Pour on the wine or stock.

Mix the nuts and breadcrumbs together and sprinkle over the top of the casserole. Bake in a preheated moderately hot oven (190°C / 375°F, Gas Mark 5) for 20 to 30 minutes until the mushrooms are tender and the topping is browned. Serve hot.

Serves 4

Stuffed Peppers

Metric/Imperial	American
175 g / 6 oz brown rice	1 cup brown rice
300 ml / ½ pint water	1¼ cups water
salt	salt
4 tomatoes, skinned and chopped	4 tomatoes, skinned and chopped
1 onion, peeled and grated	1 onion, peeled and grated
50 g / 2 oz pine nuts	½ cup pine nuts
25 g / 1 oz seedless raisins	3 tablespoons seedless raisins
100 g / 4 oz Cheddar cheese, grated	1 cup grated Cheddar cheese
2 tablespoons chopped parsley	2 tablespoons chopped parsley
pinch of ground cinnamon	pinch of ground cinnamon
freshly ground black pepper	freshly ground black pepper
4 green peppers, cored and seeded, tops reserved	4 green peppers, cored and seeded, tops reserved
5 tablespoons stock or water	⅓ cup stock or water

Cook the rice in the boiling salted water for 30 minutes or until the rice is tender and all the water has been absorbed. Remove from the heat and gently fold in the tomatoes, onion, pine nuts and raisins.

Fold in most of the cheese, reserving a little for the topping, then fold in the parsley, cinnamon and salt and pepper to taste.

Stand the peppers upright in a baking dish, cutting a small slice off the bottoms if necessary. Divide the filling equally between the peppers, sprinkle with the reserved cheese and replace the lids.

Pour the stock or water into the dish and cover with foil. Bake in a preheated moderately hot oven (190°C / 375°F, Gas Mark 5) for 30 to 40 minutes until the peppers are tender. Serve hot or cold.

Serves 4

Stuffed Marrow (Squash) Rings

This recipe may also be used to stuff courgettes (zucchini). Cut a wedge from the top of each courgette (zucchini) to make a boat shape for the stuffing, or if they are small scoop out the inside with an apple corer and fill the central hole with stuffing.

Metric/Imperial	American
1 × 1 kg / 2 lb marrow, cut crosswise into 5 cm / 2 inch thick rings, seeds removed	1 × 2 lb squash, cut crosswise into 2 inch thick rings, seeds removed
1 tablespoon oil	1 tablespoon oil
1 onion, peeled and chopped	1 onion, peeled and chopped
100 g / 4 oz mushrooms, chopped	1 cup chopped mushrooms
100 g / 4 oz cooked ham, diced	½ cup diced cooked ham
25 g / 1 oz fresh wholemeal breadcrumbs	½ cup fresh wholewheat breadcrumbs
1 tablespoon chopped parsley	1 tablespoon chopped parsley
1 tablespoon chopped marjoram or oregano	1 tablespoon chopped marjoram or oregano
salt	salt
freshly ground black pepper	freshly ground black pepper

Put the marrow (squash) in a lightly greased baking dish. Set aside.

Heat the oil in a pan. Add the onion and fry gently for 3 minutes, stirring occasionally. Add the mushrooms and fry for a further 3 minutes. Remove from the heat, add the remaining ingredients and mix well.

Spoon the stuffing mixture into the centre of the marrow (squash) rings, then cover the dish with foil. Bake in a preheated moderate oven (180°C / 350°F, Gas Mark 4) for 20 to 30 minutes until the marrow (squash) is just tender. Serve hot.

Serves 4

Wholewheat Pizza

To save time, substitute 225 g / 8 oz / ½ lb wholemeal scone dough (wholewheat biscuit dough) for the yeast dough specified in this recipe.

Metric/Imperial
DOUGH:
225 g / 8 oz strong
  wholemeal flour
1 teaspoon salt
7 g / ¼ oz fresh yeast, or 1
  teaspoon dried yeast and
  ¼ teaspoon caster sugar
150 ml / ¼ pint lukewarm
  water
TOPPING:
1 tablespoon oil
1 large onion, peeled and
  chopped
1 garlic clove, peeled and
  crushed (optional)
4 tomatoes, skinned and
  roughly chopped
1 tablespoon chopped
  oregano or marjoram
salt
freshly ground black pepper
1 tomto, sliced
100 g / 4 oz Mozzarella or
  Bel Paese cheese, thinly
  sliced
1 × 50 g / 2 oz can
  anchovy fillets, drained
few black olives

American
DOUGH:
2 cups wholewheat flour
1 teaspoon salt
¼ cake compressed yeast,
  or 1 teaspoon active dry
  yeast and ¼ teaspoon
  sugar
⅔ cup lukewarm water
TOPPING:
1 tablespoon oil
1 large onion, peeled and
  chopped
1 garlic clove, peeled and
  crushed (optional)
4 tomatoes, skinned and
  roughly chopped
1 tablespoon chopped
  oregano or marjoram
salt
freshly ground black pepper
1 tomato, sliced
¼ lb Mozzarella or Bel
  Paese cheese, thinly
  sliced
1 × 2 oz can anchovy
  fillets, drained
few ripe olives

To make the dough: put the flour and salt in a bowl. Blend the fresh yeast with the water until dissolved. (For dried yeast, dissolve the sugar in the water, add the yeast, then leave in a warm place for about 15 minutes until frothy.) Pour the yeast liquid into the flour and mix to a firm dough.

Turn the dough out onto a lightly floured surface and knead well for about 10 minutes until no longer sticky. Put the dough in a warm, greased bowl, cover with greased polythene (plastic) and leave to rise in a warm place for about 1 hour or until doubled in size.

Meanwhile, make the topping: heat the oil in a pan. Add the onion and garlic and fry gently for 5 minutes until soft, stirring occasionally. Add the tomatoes and herbs and cook gently for about 10 minutes until reduced to a pulp. Add salt and pepper to taste.

When the dough has risen, turn out onto the floured surface again and knead for 2 minutes. Roll out to a 23 cm / 9 inch circle and place on a lightly greased baking sheet.

Spread the tomato mixture over the dough, then arrange the tomato slices around the edge, and the cheese slices overlapping in the centre. Arrange the anchovies and olives on top. Leave the pizza to rise in a warm place for 15 minutes until puffy.

Bake in a preheated hot oven (220°C / 425°F, Gas Mark 7) for 20 to 25 minutes until risen and light brown around the edge. Serve hot or cold.
Serves 4

Wholewheat pizza; Pasta with ratatouille sauce (page 104); Broccoli pancakes (crêpes)

Broccoli Pancakes (Crêpes)

Metric/Imperial

PANCAKE BATTER:
100 g / 4 oz wholemeal
   flour
pinch of salt
1 egg, beaten
150 ml / ¼ pint milk
150 ml / ¼ pint water
oil for frying
FILLING:
450 g / 1 lb broccoli spears
salt
25 g / 1 oz vegetable
   margarine
25 g / 1 oz flour
300 ml / ½ pint milk
100 g / 4 oz Gruyère or
   Cheddar cheese, grated
freshly ground black pepper
1 × 50 g / 2 oz can
   anchovy fillets, drained

American

CRÊPE BATTER:
1 cup wholewheat flour
pinch of salt
1 egg, beaten
⅔ cup milk
⅔ cup water
oil for frying
FILLING:
1 lb broccoli spears
salt
2 tablespoons vegetable
   margarine
¼ cup flour
1¼ cups milk
1 cup grated Gruyère or
   Cheddar cheese
freshly ground black pepper
1 × 2 oz can anchovy
   fillets, drained

To make the pancakes (crêpes): put the flour and salt in a bowl and make a well in the centre. Add the egg and milk and stir well to give a smooth batter, then beat in the water to give a pouring consistency.

Heat a little oil in a 20 cm / 8 inch frying pan (skillet). When the oil is hot, quickly pour in enough batter to thinly coat the bottom of the pan, tilting the pan to spread the batter evenly. Cook until the top of the batter is set and the underside is golden brown. Turn or toss the pancake (crêpe) over and cook the other side.

Slide onto a warm plate, cover and keep warm by standing the plate over a pan of hot water. Continue making the pancakes (crêpes) in this way until all the batter is used up, making 8 pancakes (crêpes) in all.

To make the filling: cook the broccoli in boiling salted water for 5 to 10 minutes until just tender, then drain thoroughly and keep warm.

Meanwhile, melt the margarine in a pan. Add the flour and cook for 1 to 2 minutes, stirring constantly. Remove from the heat and gradually stir in the milk, beating well after each addition. Return to the heat and simmer until the sauce is thick and smooth, stirring constantly. Stir in the cheese, reserving a little for the topping, then add pepper to taste.

Divide the broccoli and anchovies equally between the pancakes (crêpes), then roll up and place in a baking dish. Pour over the sauce and sprinkle with the reserved cheese.

Bake in a preheated moderately hot oven (200°C / 400°F, Gas Mark 6) for 10 to 15 minutes until heated through. Serve hot.

Alternatively, leave the pancakes (crêpes) until cold before filling, then cover and bake in a preheated moderately hot oven for 15 minutes. Remove the lid and bake for a further 10 to 15 minutes until hot and bubbling. Serve hot.
Serves 4

Stuffed Cabbage Leaves

Metric/Imperial	American
8 large cabbage leaves	8 large cabbage leaves
salt	salt
1 tablespoon oil	1 tablespoon oil
1 onion, peeled and chopped	1 onion, peeled and chopped
1 cooking apple, peeled, cored and chopped	1 baking apple, peeled, cored and chopped
1 garlic clove, peeled and crushed	1 garlic clove, peeled and crushed
225 g / 8 oz minced pork or veal	1 cup ground pork or veal
50 g / 2 oz fresh wholemeal breadcrumbs	1 cup fresh wholewheat breadcrumbs
finely grated rind and juice of ½ lemon	finely grated rind and juice of ½ lemon
1 tablespoon chopped sage	1 tablespoon chopped sage
1 tablespoon chopped parsley	1 tablespoon chopped parsley
freshly ground black pepper	freshly ground black pepper
4 tomatoes, cut into wedges	4 tomatoes, cut into wedges

Blanch the cabbage leaves in boiling salted water for 2 minutes or until soft enough to roll up. Drain thoroughly and set aside.

Heat the oil in a pan. Add the onion, apple and garlic and fry gently for 5 minutes, stirring occasionally. Add the pork or veal and fry for a further 5 minutes, stirring constantly to break up the meat. Remove from the heat and stir in the breadcrumbs, lemon rind and juice, herbs and salt and pepper to taste.

Divide the stuffing mixture equally between the cabbage leaves, then roll up, from the stalk end, folding in the edges to enclose the stuffing completely.

Put the stuffed cabbage in a shallow baking dish and surround with the tomato wedges.

Cover and bake in a preheated moderate oven (180°C / 350°F, Gas Mark 4) for 20 to 30 minutes until the cabbage is tender. Serve hot.

Serves 4

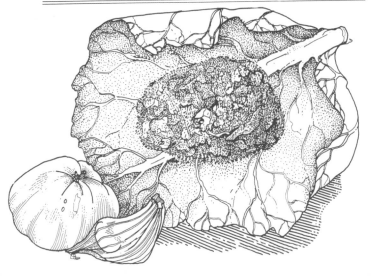

Pasta with Ratatouille Sauce

This Mediterranean vegetable stew is traditionally cooked in oil and served as an accompaniment to meat. In this recipe the vegetables are cooked in their own juices for a healthier, more concentrated flavour. Served with pasta, ratatouille makes a meal in itself. It is also good served cold as a starter, without pasta.

Metric/Imperial	American
1 large onion, peeled and chopped	1 large onion, peeled and chopped
1 garlic clove, peeled and crushed	1 garlic clove, peeled and crushed
450 g / 1 lb courgettes, sliced	3 cups sliced zucchini
1 large aubergine, diced	1 large eggplant, diced
1 green pepper, cored, seeded and diced	1 green pepper, cored, seeded and diced
450 g / 1 lb tomatoes, skinned and chopped	2 cups skinned and chopped tomatoes
1 tablespoon chopped oregano or basil	1 tablespoon chopped oregano or basil
salt	salt
freshly ground black pepper	freshly ground black pepper
450 g / 1 lb pasta (spaghetti, noodles, etc)	1 lb pasta (spaghetti, noodles, etc)
1 tablespoon chopped parsley	1 tablespon chopped parsley
grated Parmesan cheese to serve	grated Parmesan cheese to serve

Put all the ingredients in a large pan, except the pasta and cheese. Cover and cook gently for 30 minutes until the vegetables are tender and the juices have thickened slightly, stirring occasionally.

Meanwhile, cook the pasta in a large pan containing plenty of boiling salted water until just tender (about 5 minutes for freshly made pasta and 15 minutes for dried). Drain and pile into a warmed serving dish.

Taste and adjust the seasoning of the sauce, then pour over the pasta. Sprinkle with the parsley and grated Parmesan cheese. Serve hot.

Serves 4 to 6

Cauliflower Cheese Timbale

In this recipe, cauliflower is cooked in a savoury egg custard, similar to a baked soufflé but much easier to control. It is a very useful way of turning leftover cooked vegetables into a tasty substantial dish.

Metric/Imperial	American
450 g / 1 lb cauliflower, chopped, with leaves and stalks finely chopped	1 lb cauliflower, chopped, with leaves and stalks finely chopped

1 large onion, peeled and
  chopped
300 ml / ½ pint water
salt
4 eggs, lightly beaten
50 g / 2 oz fresh wholemeal
  breadcrumbs
100 g / 4 oz Cheddar
  cheese, grated
pinch of grated nutmeg
freshly ground white pepper
300 ml / ½ pint milk

1 large onion, peeled and
  chopped
1¼ cups water
salt
4 eggs, lightly beaten
1 cup fresh wholewheat
  breadcrumbs
1 cup grated Cheddar
  cheese
pinch of grated nutmeg
freshly ground white pepper
1¼ cups milk

Put the cauliflower and onion in a large pan with the water and salt. Bring to the boil, then lower the heat, cover and simmer for about 10 minutes until the cauliflower is just tender. Drain thoroughly.

Put the eggs in a bowl with the breadcrumbs, cheese, nutmeg and salt and pepper to taste. Mix well. Heat the milk, but do not allow to boil, then stir into the egg mixture.

Put the cauliflower in a 1.5 litre / 2½ pint / 6¼ cup baking dish or greased ring mould. Pour over the egg custard to cover the cauliflower.

Stand the dish or mould in a roasting pan, half-filled with hot water. Bake in a preheated moderate oven (180°C / 350°F, Gas Mark 4) for 45 minutes or until the custard is set and a skewer comes out clean when inserted in the centre.

Alternatively, cover the dish or mould and steam over boiling water for about 1 hour until set.

Serve straight from the dish, or leave to stand for a few minutes, then turn out of the mould onto a warmed serving platter. Serve hot with a mushroom or tomato sauce.

The timbale can also be served cold, in which case it should be left to cool in the mould before turning out onto a serving platter.

Serves 4

Spinach Roulade

A simple spinach soufflé mixture is first baked flat, then filled with an onion and mushroom sauce and rolled up like a Swiss (jelly) roll. It makes a delicious light main course.

Metric/Imperial	American
ROULADE:	ROULADE:
450 g / 1 lb spinach leaves	1 lb spinach leaves
4 eggs, separated	4 eggs, separated
pinch of grated nutmeg	pinch of grated nutmeg
salt	salt
freshly ground black pepper	freshly ground black pepper
FILLING:	FILLING:
25 g / 1 oz vegetable margarine	2 tablespoons vegetable margarine
100 g / 4 oz streaky bacon, derinded and chopped	½ cup chopped fatty bacon
2 onions, peeled and sliced	2 onions, peeled and sliced

2 onions, peeled and sliced
100 g / 4 oz button
  mushrooms, sliced
25 g / 1 oz flour
300 ml / ½ pint milk
1 teaspoon lemon juice
1 tablespoon grated
  Parmesan cheese

1 cup sliced button
  mushrooms
¼ cup flour
1¼ cups milk
1 teaspoon lemon juice
1 tablespoon grated
  Parmesan cheese

To make the roulade: wash the spinach thoroughly, then put in a large pan with only the water clinging to the leaves. Cook gently for about 5 minutes until tender, then drain thoroughly.

Chop the spinach finely, then put in a bowl with the egg yolks, nutmeg and salt and pepper to taste. Beat well. Whisk the egg whites until stiff, then fold into the spinach mixture.

Line a 32 × 23 cm / 13 × 9 inch roasting pan with oiled greaseproof paper or non-stick parchment so that it comes above the sides of the pan. Spoon in the spinach and smooth the surface.

Bake in a preheated moderately hot oven (200°C / 400°F, Gas Mark 6) for 10 to 15 minutes until the roulade is well risen, firm and just beginning to brown.

Meanwhile, make the filling: melt the margarine in a pan. Add the bacon and onions and fry gently for 5 minutes, stirring occasionally. Add the mushrooms and fry gently for a further 2 minutes.

Add the flour and cook for 1 to 2 minutes, stirring constantly. Remove from the heat and gradually stir in the milk, beating well after each addition. Return to the heat and simmer until the sauce is thick and smooth, stirring constantly. Add the lemon juice and salt and pepper to taste.

Sprinkle the Parmesan cheese over a large sheet of greaseproof (wax) paper. Turn the roulade out onto the paper, then carefully peel off the lining paper on top of the roulade.

Spread the sauce over the roulade, leaving a 2.5 cm / 1 inch margin all round. Roll up the roulade like a Swiss (jelly) roll, gently lifting the paper so that the roulade falls over the filling. Lift carefully onto a warmed serving dish and serve immediately.

Serves 4

Heat the oil in a wok or large frying pan (skillet). Add the bacon, onion, garlic, ginger and mushrooms and fry briskly for 3 minutes, stirring constantly.

Add the peas and cabbage and fry for a further 2 minutes, stirring constantly.

Add the remaining ingredients and stir-fry over moderate heat for about 5 minutes until the vegetables are tender but still crisp, and most of the liquid has evaporated. Taste and adjust the seasoning and serve immediately.

Serves 4

Chinese Stir-Fried Vegetables

Traditionally cooked in a Chinese wok, the vegetables are cooked very quickly to retain their natural flavour and crispness.
Whole peanuts are usually obtainable but if not, substitute salted peanuts and decrease the quantity of salt in the recipe.

Metric/Imperial	American
1 tablespoon oil	1 tablespoon oil
50 g / 2 oz streaky bacon, derinded and chopped	¼ cup chopped fatty bacon
1 large onion, peeled and chopped	1 large onion, peeled and chopped
1 garlic clove, peeled and crushed	1 garlic clove, peeled and crushed
1 tablespoon peeled and grated fresh root ginger	1 tablespoon peeled and grated fresh ginger root
50 g / 2 oz mushrooms, sliced	½ cup sliced mushrooms
450 g / 1 lb mange-tout peas, topped and tailed	1 lb snow peas, topped and tailed
450 g / 1 lb Chinese or other cabbage, shredded	6 cups shredded Chinese or other cabbage
100 g / 4 oz bean sprouts	2 cups bean sprouts
50 g / 2 oz whole peanuts, shelled	¼ cup whole shelled peanuts
1 tablespoon soy sauce	1 tablespoon soy sauce
5 tablespoons stock or water	⅓ cup stock or water
salt	salt
freshly ground black pepper	freshly ground black pepper

Vegetable Kebabs with Pilaf

Bacon rolls, pieces of chicken breast, cubes of lamb, pork or steak may be substituted for some of the vegetables on the skewers.

Metric/Imperial	American
PILAF:	PILAF:
2 tablespoons oil	2 tablespoons oil
1 large onion, peeled and chopped	1 large onion, peeled and chopped
2 celery sticks, sliced	2 celery stalks, sliced
225 g / 8 oz brown rice	1¼ cups brown rice
600 ml / 1 pint stock	2½ cups stock
50 g / 2 oz seedless raisins	⅓ cup seedless raisins
50 g / 2 oz dried apricots, roughly chopped	⅓ cup roughly chopped dried apricots
50 g / 2 oz walnuts, roughly chopped	½ cup roughly chopped walnuts
1 cinnamon stick	1 cinnamon stick
1 bay leaf	1 bay leaf
salt	salt
freshly ground black pepper	freshly ground black pepper
KEBABS:	KEBABS:
225 g / 8 oz courgettes, sliced	1½ cups sliced zucchini
8 small tomatoes	8 small tomatoes
1 large onion, cut into wedges with skin	1 large onion, cut into wedges with skin
8 button mushrooms	8 button mushrooms
1 green pepper, cored, seeded and cut into 8 pieces	1 green pepper, cored, seeded and cut into 8 pieces
1 tablespoon oil	1 tablespoon oil
1 tablespoon lemon juice	1 tablespoon lemon juice
1 tablespoon thyme leaves	1 tablespoon thyme leaves

To make the pilaf: heat the oil in a pan. Add the onion and celery and fry gently for 5 minutes until golden brown. Add the rice and cook for 1 minute, stirring constantly. Pour on the stock, then add the raisins, apricots and walnuts.

Bring to the boil, stirring occasionally, then add the cinnamon, bay leaf and salt and pepper to taste. Lower the heat, cover the pan and simmer for 30 minutes or until the rice is tender and all the stock has been absorbed.

To make the kebabs: blanch the courgettes (zucchini) in boiling water for 1 minute, then drain. Thread the vegetables onto 4 large kebab skewers, alternating the different ingredients.

Mix together the oil, lemon juice, thyme and salt and pepper to taste, then brush over the vegetables. Cook on a barbecue or under the grill (broiler) for 5 to 10 minutes until cooked through, turning and basting from time to time.

Spoon the pilaf into a warmed shallow serving dish and arrange the kebabs on top. Serve immediately.

Serves 4

Carrot Soufflé

Metric/Imperial	American
450 g / 1 lb carrots, peeled and chopped	3 cups peeled and chopped carrots
1 onion, peeled and chopped	1 onion, peeled and chopped
450 ml / ³/₄ pint water	2 cups water
salt	salt
freshly ground white pepper	freshly ground white pepper
25 g / 1 oz vegetable margarine	2 tablespoons vegetable margarine
1 tablespoon flour	1 tablespoon flour
150 ml / ¹/₄ pint milk	²/₃ cup milk
100 g / 4 oz cooked ham, diced	¹/₂ cup diced cooked ham
4 eggs, separated	4 eggs, separated

Put the carrots in a pan with the onion, water and salt. Bring to the boil, then lower the heat, cover and simmer for about 20 minutes or until the carrots are soft. Drain, then mash or work to a purée in an electric blender. Add salt and pepper to taste.

Melt the margarine in a pan. Add the flour and cook for 1 to 2 minutes, stirring constantly. Remove from the heat, and gradually stir in the milk, beating well after each addition. Return to the heat and simmer until the sauce is thick and smooth, stirring constantly.

Stir the sauce into the carrot purée with the ham. Beat in the egg yolks.

Beat the egg whites until stiff, then fold gently into the carrot mixture. Pour into a greased 1.5 litre / 2¹/₂ pint / 6¹/₄ cup soufflé dish.

Bake in a preheated moderate oven (180°C / 350°F, Gas Mark 4) for 45 minutes until well risen and set. Serve immediately.

Serves 4

TOP LEFT: Chinese stir-fried vegetables
LEFT: Vegetable kebabs with pilaf
ABOVE: Carrot soufflé

FRUIT & NUTS

Like vegetables, the main contribution that fruits give to the diet are vitamins (especially vitamin C), minerals and fibre. They also provide a wide variety of colour, texture and flavour and a refreshing juiciness. This juiciness is due to the high water content – up to 95 per cent depending on the type of fruit.

Fruits especially high in vitamin C are black and red currants, strawberries, citrus fruits, gooseberries, raspberries and blackberries. Those high in vitamin A are apricots, peaches, blackcurrants, oranges and bananas. As vitamin C is easily destroyed by heat, it is best to eat fruit raw, although obviously some fruits like gooseberries, rhubarb and cooking apples, are inedible raw and therefore must be cooked. As far as possible avoid peeling fruit – especially apples, pears, plums, peaches and grapes – as their skins provide fibre and look attractive.

Served as a dessert, fruit is all too frequently combined with generous amounts of sugar and rich foods, such as butter and cream, which dilute the flavour of the fruit and render the dish less satisfactory from a health point of view. Fruit desserts can be delicious without being sweet or rich. For example, a lemon mousse has a more refreshing flavour when the cream is eliminated; all that is required is lemons, eggs, a little sugar and gelatine. In many recipes, cream can be replaced by yogurt and, or, whisked egg whites which give added volume and texture without the richness. Instead of using whipped cream for decoration, try draining natural (unflavored) yogurt through a sieve lined with muslin (cheesecloth) until it is the consistency of whipped cream and can be piped. The yogurt gives a refreshing flavour which goes well with many fruits.

A little sugar has to be added to many fruits to make them appetizing; if possible use unrefined sugars or honey, which impart a better flavour.

Dried fruit

Fruit is primarily dried as a means of preservation. In the drying process, nutritional content, flavour, texture and colour are changed, giving us an even wider variety of fruits to include in our diet. Most common of the dried fruits are grapes in the form of raisins, sultanas (white raisins) and currants, but dried peaches, figs, dates, plums, pears, apples and bananas are also available.

They can all be eaten or added to dishes in their dried form, but if reconstituted and cooked with water they are extremely useful in sauces, mousses and soufflés, as they cook to a thick purée which needs no extra thickening and only a little sugar. The nutrients are of course more diluted then, but if you cook the fruit in its soaking water you will retain much of their goodness.

Dried fruit can easily be prepared at home, which is particularly useful if you have an abundance of apples or pears in the garden during autumn. To prepare dried apples: peel, core and slice into rings, about 5 mm/¼ inch thick, and immediately immerse in a salt solution (1 tablespoon salt to 1.2 litres/2 pints/5 cups) water. Leave for 1 minute, then drain and dry thoroughly. Spread the apple rings on a slatted drying tray and leave in a warm place for several hours until they are soft and springy to touch. Cool, then pack in polythene (plastic) bags.

Dried fruits are normally used in sweet dishes, but they can also be added to savoury foods to give extra flavour, colour and texture.

Nuts

Nuts are increasingly being recognized as a valuable food, lending themselves to both sweet and savoury dishes. Almonds, walnuts, hazelnuts and similar filberts, brazils, chestnuts, pistachios, cashews, peanuts and coconut are the most popular varieties. Pecans, pine kernels, sesame and sunflower seeds can also be included in the diet.

The different varieties vary in their nutritional content but, in general, nuts are a rich source of nutrients. They are widely used by vegetarians to make savoury dishes because of their high protein content.

Mixed with breadcrumbs and flavourings, nuts make substantial dishes; they can also be added to meat dishes, soups or stuffings. Ground or chopped, they make a good base for mousses, soufflés, flans or cakes; very finely ground nuts can replace flour completely in a whisked sponge cake. Used simply on their own, they make attractive and nutritious decorations for sweet dishes.

Walnut and Cheese Burgers

Metric/Imperial	American
175 g / 6 oz shelled walnuts	1½ cups shelled walnuts
50 g / 2 oz wholemeal bread, cubed	2 large slices wholewheat bread, cubed
100 g / 4 oz Cheddar cheese, grated	1 cup grated Cheddar cheese
1 onion, peeled and grated	1 onion, peeled and grated
salt	salt
freshly ground black pepper	freshly ground black pepper
1 egg	1 egg
1 tablespoon tomato purée	1 tablespoon tomato paste
oil for shallow frying	oil for shallow frying
TO GARNISH:	TO GARNISH:
tomatoes	tomatoes
watercress	watercress

Put the nuts in an electric blender, reserving 50 g / 2 oz / ½ cup for the coating. Add the bread and grind coarsely. Transfer to a bowl, add the cheese, onion and salt and pepper to taste and stir well. Beat the egg with the tomato purée (paste). Add to the nut mixture and stir until well combined.

Divide the mixture into 4 on a lightly floured surface. Shape into burgers, about 8 cm / 3½ inches in diameter and 1 cm / ½ inch thick. Chop the reserved walnuts and press into both sides of the burgers.

Heat a little oil in a frying pan (skillet), add the burgers and fry for about 5 minutes until browned on both sides, turning once. Alternatively, place the burgers on a lightly greased baking sheet and bake in a preheated moderately hot oven (200°C / 400°F, Gas Mark 6) for 20 minutes until browned.

Serve hot or cold, garnished with tomatoes and watercress.

Serves 4

RIGHT: Preparing Walnut and cheese burgers
ABOVE RIGHT: Preparing Herb and nut roast; Brazil nut loaf

Herb and Nut Roast

Metric/Imperial	American
100 g / 4 oz hazelnuts	¾ cup filberts
100 g / 4 oz wholemeal bread, cubed	2 large slices wholewheat bread, cubed
100 g / 4 oz vegetable margarine	½ cup vegetable margarine
450 g / 1 lb onions, peeled and chopped	1 lb onions, peeled and chopped
1 tablespoon yeast extract	1 tablespoon yeast extract
100 g / 4 oz unsalted cashews or peanuts	1 cup unsalted cashews or peanuts
2 tablespoons chopped parsley	2 tablespoons chopped parsley
2 tablespoons chopped mixed herbs	2 tablespoons chopped mixed herbs
salt	salt
freshly ground black pepper	freshly ground black pepper

Put the hazelnuts (filberts) in an electric blender, reserving about 12 whole ones. Add the bread and grind coarsely.

Melt the margarine in a large pan, add the onions and fry gently for 10 minutes until soft. Stir in the yeast extract.

Remove from the heat, then stir in the ground nuts and bread, cashews or peanuts, herbs, salt and pepper to taste.

Press the mixture into a 900 ml / 1½ pint / 3¾ cup pie dish or casserole. Press the reserved nuts into the top. Bake in a preheated moderate oven (180°C / 350°F, Gas Mark 4) for 40 minutes until lightly browned on top. Serve hot.

Serves 4 to 6

Brazil Nut Loaf

Metric/Imperial

225 g / 8 oz shelled Brazil nuts
100 g / 4 oz wholemeal bread, cubed with crusts
1 tablespoon oil
100 g / 4 oz bacon, derinded and chopped
2 onions, peeled and chopped
1 garlic clove, peeled and crushed
1 tablespoon chopped parsley
1 tablespoon chopped thyme
salt
freshly ground black pepper
1 egg
1 teaspoon Worcestershire sauce

American

½ lb shelled Brazil nuts
2 large slices wholewheat bread, cubed with crusts
1 tablespoon oil
4 bacon slices, derinded and chopped
2 onions, peeled and chopped
1 garlic clove, peeled and crushed
1 tablespoon chopped parsley
1 tablespoon chopped thyme
salt
freshly ground black pepper
1 egg
1 teaspoon Worcestershire sauce

Put the nuts and bread in an electric blender and grind coarsely.

Heat the oil in a pan, add the bacon, onions and garlic and fry gently for 4 to 5 minutes until soft. Remove the pan from the heat, then add the ground nuts and bread, herbs and salt and pepper to taste. Mix well. Beat the egg with the Worcestershire sauce, add to the nut mixture and bind thoroughly.

Press the mixture into a lightly greased 450 g / 1 lb / 4½ × 2½ × 1½ inch loaf tin and level the surface. Bake in a preheated moderately hot oven (190°C / 375°F, Gas Mark 5) for 40 minutes until the top is crisp and lightly browned.

Turn the loaf out onto a serving dish and serve hot. Alternatively leave to cool in the tin, then turn out and serve cold with sliced tomatoes.

Serves 4 to 6

Chestnut Soup

This soup will have a better flavour if the chestnuts are first roasted to remove their skins, rather than boiled.

Metric/Imperial	American
450 g / 1 lb chestnuts	1 lb chestnuts
1 large onion, peeled and chopped	1 large onion, peeled and chopped
2 celery sticks, chopped	2 celery stalks, chopped
1.2 litres / 2 pints turkey or chicken stock	5 cups turkey or chicken stock
1 bay leaf	1 bay leaf
salt	salt
freshly ground black pepper	freshly ground black pepper

Make a small cut through the skins of the chestnuts, then place on a baking sheet and bake on the top shelf of a hot oven (200°C / 400°F, Gas Mark 6) until the skins crack. Alternatively, put the chestnuts in a pan, cover with water and bring to the boil. Peel off both layers of skin while the chestnuts are still hot.

Put the peeled chestnuts in a pan, add the remaining ingredients and bring to the boil. Lower the heat, cover and simmer for 45 minutes until the chestnuts and celery are tender. Discard the bay leaf.

Transfer the soup to an electric blender, reserving a few whole chestnuts for the garnish. Blend to a smooth purée, then return to the rinsed-out pan. Reheat gently, then taste and adjust the seasoning. Stir in a little milk if the soup is too thick.

Serve hot, garnished with the reserved chestnuts.

Serves 6

Spinach and Peanut Galette

Metric/Imperial	American
PANCAKES:	PANCAKES:
100 g / 4 oz wholemeal flour	1 cup wholewheat flour
1 egg, beaten	1 egg, beaten
300 ml / ½ pint milk	1¼ cups milk
oil for shallow frying	oil for shallow frying
FILLING:	FILLING:
1 tablespoon oil	1 tablespoon oil
1 small onion, peeled and sliced	1 small onion, peeled and sliced
225 g / 8 oz button mushrooms, sliced	1 cup sliced button mushrooms
450 g / 1 lb frozen spinach, cooked and drained	1 lb frozen spinach, cooked and drained
salt	salt
freshly ground black pepper	freshly ground black pepper
SAUCE:	SAUCE:
25 g / 1 oz butter	2 tablespoons butter
50 g / 2 oz shelled peanuts	½ cup shelled peanuts
2 tablespoons flour	2 tablespoons flour
300 ml / ½ pint chicken stock	1¼ cups chicken stock

To make the pancakes: put the flour in a bowl and make a well in the centre. Pour in the egg and milk and beat well to give a smooth batter.

Heat a little oil in a 20 cm / 8 inch frying pan (skillet). Pour in enough batter to coat the bottom of the pan thinly. Cook until set and golden brown underneath, then turn the pancake and cook the other side. Repeat with the remaining batter to make 8 pancakes.

To prepare the filling: heat the oil in a pan and sauté the onion and mushrooms until soft. Stir in the spinach and season with salt and pepper to taste.

Spread each pancake with a little of the spinach filling and pile the pancakes on top of one another in a straight-sided ovenproof serving dish.

To make the sauce: heat the butter in a pan and fry the peanuts until golden brown. Stir in the flour and cook for 1 minute. Add the stock gradually, stirring constantly. Cook, stirring, until thickened.

Pour the sauce over the galette and cook in a preheated moderately hot oven (200°C / 400°F, Gas Mark 6) for 30 minutes. Serve hot.

Serves 4 to 6

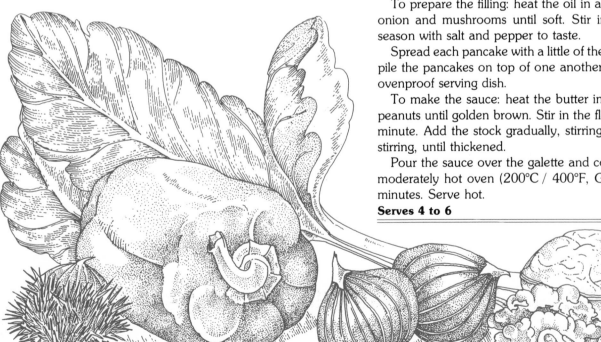

Greek Rice Ring

Metric/Imperial	American
3 tablespoons oil	3 tablespoons oil
1 onion, peeled and sliced	1 onion, peeled and sliced
1 clove garlic, peeled and crushed	1 clove garlic, peeled and crushed
225 g / 8 oz brown rice	1 1/3 cups brown rice
750 ml / 1 1/4 pints water	3 cups water
salt	salt
1 green pepper, cored, seeded and chopped	1 green pepper, cored, seeded and chopped
50 g / 2 oz dried apricots, soaked and sliced	1/3 cup dried apricots, soaked and sliced
50 g / 2 oz dried prunes, soaked, stoned and sliced	1/3 cup dried prunes, soaked pitted and sliced
75 g / 3 oz walnuts, roughly chopped	3/4 cup roughly chopped walnuts
50 g / 2 oz black olives, halved and stoned	1/3 cup ripe olives, halved and pitted
freshly ground black pepper	freshly ground black pepper

Heat the oil in a large pan and sauté the onion and garlic until soft. Stir in the rice and cook, stirring, for 1 minute. Add the water and salt. Bring to the boil, cover and simmer for 20 minutes.

Stir in the green pepper, apricots and prunes. Continue to simmer, covered, for about 20 minutes or until the rice is cooked and the liquid absorbed. Stir in the walnuts, olives and salt and pepper to taste.

Turn the mixture into a greased 900 ml / 1 1/2 pint / 3 3/4 cup ring mould and cook in a preheated moderate oven (180°C / 350°F, Gas Mark 4) for 30 minutes. Turn out and serve hot or cold. Fill the centre with courgettes (zucchini) provençal (page 96), or a crisp green salad if preferred.
Serves 4

Broccoli and Almonds

Metric/Imperial	American
500 g / 1 lb broccoli spears	4 cups broccoli spears
salt	salt
2 tablespoons olive oil	2 tablespoons olive oil
1 onion, peeled and sliced	1 onion, peeled and sliced
1 clove garlic, peeled and crushed	1 clove garlic, peeled and crushed
50 g / 2 oz blanched almonds	1/2 cup blanched almonds
5 tomatoes, skinned and chopped	5 tomatoes, skinned and chopped
freshly ground black pepper	freshly ground black pepper
1 tablespoon chopped parsley	1 tablespoon chopped parsley

Cook the broccoli spears in boiling salted water for about 15 minutes until just tender.

Heat the oil in a pan and sauté the onion, garlic and almonds until the onion is soft and the almonds are beginning to brown. Stir in the tomatoes and heat through. Season with salt and pepper to taste.

Drain the broccoli and place in a heated serving dish. Spoon the sauce over the broccoli and sprinkle with chopped parsley. Serve hot.
Serves 4

Apricot Tart

Metric/Imperial	American
PASTRY:	DOUGH:
100 g / 4 oz wholemeal flour	1 cup wholewheat flour
75 g / 3 oz vegetable margarine	1/3 cup vegetable margarine
75 g / 3 oz ground almonds	3/4 cup ground almonds
50 g / 2 oz sugar	1/4 cup sugar
1 egg yolk, mixed with 2 teaspoons cold water	1 egg yolk, mixed with 2 teaspoons cold water
4 drops almond essence	4 drops almond extract
FILLING:	FILLING:
300 ml / 1/2 pint milk	1 1/4 cups milk
2 eggs	2 eggs
2 tablespoons cornflour	2 tablespoons cornstarch
2 tablespoons caster sugar	2 tablespoons sugar
150 ml / 1/4 pint natural yogurt	2/3 cup unflavored yogurt
1 tablespoon sherry	1 tablespoon sherry
450 g / 1 lb apricots	1 lb apricots
4 tablespoons apricot jam	1/4 cup apricot jam
2 tablespoons orange juice	2 tablespoons orange juice
25 g / 1 oz shelled almonds	1/4 cup shelled almonds

To make the pastry dough: put the flour in a bowl. Add the margarine and rub into the flour until the mixture resembles breadcrumbs. Stir in the almonds and sugar, then the egg yolk mixture and almond essence (extract). Mix to a firm dough.

Turn onto a lightly floured surface, roll out and use to line a 20 cm / 8 inch flan dish or flan ring placed on a baking sheet. Line the dough with foil, then fill with baking beans or rice.

Bake in a preheated moderately hot oven (200°C / 400°F, Gas Mark 6) for 15 minutes, then remove the beans or rice and foil and bake for a further 5 to 10 minutes until the bottom of the pastry is crisp. Remove from the oven and leave to cool.

To make the filling: heat the milk to just below boiling point. Put the eggs in a bowl with the cornflour (cornstarch) and sugar. Beat lightly, then gradually stir in the hot milk. Return to the pan and bring to the boil, stirring constantly. Simmer for 2 minutes until the custard is thick and smooth.

Leave to cool, stirring occasionally to prevent a skin forming. Whisk in the yogurt and sherry, then spoon the custard into the flan case and level the surface.

Cut the apricots in half and remove the stones (seeds). Put the jam and orange juice in a pan and heat gently until the jam has melted. Add the apricots to the pan, cut side down, and simmer for 5 to 10 minutes until tender. Arrange the apricots and almonds on top. Pour over the syrup from the pan, then leave to cool and set. Serve cold.

Serves 4 to 6

Hazelnut (Filbert) and Raspberry Torte

Use hazelnuts (filberts) with their skins on to give colour and flavour to this torte. Ground hazelnuts (filberts) are used instead of flour for the cake mixture, and the filling is a purée of apples and raspberries.

Metric/Imperial	American
TORTE:	TORTE:
4 eggs, separated	4 eggs, separated
100 g / 4 oz soft brown sugar	2/3 cup brown sugar
100 g / 4 oz shelled hazelnuts, coarsely ground	3/4 cup shelled filberts, coarsely ground
FILLING:	FILLING:
450 g / 1 lb cooking apples, peeled, cored and sliced	1 lb baking apples, peeled, cored and sliced
finely grated rind and juice of 1/2 lemon	finely grated rind and juice of 1/2 lemon
225 g / 8 oz raspberries	1 3/4 cups raspberries
50 g / 2 oz light soft brown sugar	1/3 cup light brown sugar
TO DECORATE:	TO DECORATE:
150 ml / 1/4 pint natural yogurt	2/3 cup unflavored yogurt
few whole hazelnuts	few whole filberts

To make the torte: beat the egg yolks and sugar together until thick and creamy. Beat the egg whites until just stiff. Fold the ground hazelnuts (filberts) and egg whites carefully into the creamed mixture.

Apricot tart; Spiced fruit compote; Hazelnut (filbert) and raspberry torte

Line the bottoms of two greased 23 cm / 9 inch sandwich tins (layer cake pans) with greased greaseproof paper or non-stick parchment. Divide the mixture equally between the tins and level the surface.

Bake in a preheated moderate oven (180°C / 350°F, Gas Mark 4) for 30 minutes until risen and firm to touch. Leave in the tins until cold; do not turn out onto a wire rack or the cakes will stick.

To make the filling: put the apples in a pan with the lemon rind and juice, raspberries and sugar. Cook for 10 to 15 minutes until pulpy, stirring occasionally. Remove from the heat and beat until smooth, or rub through a sieve (strainer) for a smoother texture. Leave to cool.

Meanwhile, place a sieve (strainer) over a bowl and line with a piece of muslin (cheesecloth). Pour in the yogurt and leave to drain for about 3 hours until most of the liquid has drained through, leaving the yogurt with a smooth, creamy consistency in the sieve (strainer).

To assemble the torte: lift the cakes carefully out of the tins and peel off the paper. Place one cake on a serving plate and spread with the filling mixture. Cover with the other cake, then pipe the creamy yogurt in rosettes on the top. Decorate with whole hazelnuts (filberts).

Serves 6 to 8

Spiced Fruit Compote

Metric/Imperial	American
450 g / 1 lb mixed dried fruit (apples, apricots, figs, peaches, pears, prunes, sultanas, etc)	3 cups mixed dried fruit (apples, apricots, figs, peaches, pears, prunes, seedless white raisins, etc)
300 ml / ½ pint orange juice	1¼ cups orange juice
300 ml / ½ pint water	1¼ cups water
1 cinnamon stick	1 cinnamon stick
2 cloves	2 cloves
50 g / 2 oz blanched slivered almonds	½ cup blanched slivered almonds

Put the dried fruit in a bowl and pour over the orange juice and water. Add the spices and leave to soak overnight. Alternatively, pour over boiling juice and water and soak for a few hours.

Transfer to a pan and bring to the boil. Lower the heat, cover and simmer for about 20 minutes or until the fruit is tender, adding more water if the syrup becomes absorbed.

Sprinkle with the almonds and serve warm or cold.

Serves 4 to 6

Pears in Cassis

Pears cooked in white wine and blackcurrants turn a beautiful rich crimson colour – perfect for a dinner party as they can be cooked in advance.

Metric/Imperial
300 ml / ½ pint medium or sweet white wine
100 g / 4 oz blackcurrants, stalks removed
4 tablespoons honey
1 cinnamon stick
2 strips lemon rind
4-6 pears
1 teaspoon arrowroot

American
1¼ cups medium or sweet white wine
1 cup blackcurrants, stalks removed
¼ cup honey
1 cinnamon stick
2 strips lemon rind
4-6 pears
1 teaspoon arrowroot

Pour the wine into a pan, then add the blackcurrants, honey, cinnamon and lemon rind. Heat gently until the honey has dissolved, then bring to the boil. Boil for 1 minute.

Peel the pears, leaving the stalks attached. Put the pears in the pan, submerging them as much as possible in the wine mixture. Cover and cook gently for about 20 minutes until the pears are tender, turning occasionally.

Lift the pears carefully out of the pan and transfer to a serving bowl. Discard the cinnamon stick and lemon rind.

Blend the arrowroot with a little cold water, then pour into the wine mixture. Bring to the boil, then lower the heat and simmer for 1 minute until the sauce thickens, stirring constantly. Pour over the pears. Serve hot or cold.

Serves 4 to 6

Almond and Strawberry Malakoff

Metric/Imperial
18 sponge fingers
finely grated rind and juice of 2 oranges
2 tablespoons sherry
FILLING:
100 g / 4 oz vegetable margarine
100 g / 4 oz light soft brown sugar
225 g / 8 oz curd cheese
175 g / 6 oz ground almonds
350 g / 12 oz strawberries

American
18 ladyfingers
finely grated rind and juice of 2 oranges
2 tablespoons sherry
FILLING:
½ cup vegetable margarine
⅔ cup light brown sugar
1 cup cottage cheese
1½ cups ground almonds
¾ lb strawberries

Line the bottom of a 15 × 7 cm / 6 × 3 inch round cake tin with greased greaseproof paper or non-stick parchment. Trim one end off the sponge fingers (ladyfingers) so that they fit the depth of the tin; reserve the trimmings.

Mix the orange juice with the sherry. Dip in the sponge fingers (ladyfingers), one at a time, for a few seconds to soften slightly, then arrange them, rounded end down, around the edge of the tin. Reserve any remaining juice for the filling.

To make the filling: beat together the margarine and sugar until light and creamy. Add the cheese, ground almonds, orange rind and reserved juice and beat well. Set aside about one third of the strawberries; slice the remainder.

Spread one third of the almond mixture in the bottom of the tin. Cover with half the sliced strawberries and sponge trimmings. Spread another third of the almond mixture on top, then the remaining sliced strawberries and sponge trimmings. Finish with the remaining almond mixture and level the surface.

Cover with a small plate or saucer, place a weight on top, then chill in the refrigerator for at least 4 hours until firm.

To serve: invert the malakoff onto a serving plate and decorate the top with the reserved strawberries.

Serves 6

Peach and Raspberry Cheesecake

If you do not have a loose-bottomed cake tin, make this cheesecake in an ordinary cake tin and turn it out onto a serving plate so that the crust is on top rather than underneath.

Metric/Imperial	American
BISCUIT CRUST:	CRACKER CRUST:
75 g / 3 oz vegetable margarine	1/3 cup vegetable margarine
175 g / 6 oz digestive biscuits, crushed	1 1/2 cups Graham crackers, crushed
1 tablespoon demerara sugar	1 tablespoon raw sugar
FILLING:	FILLING:
350 g / 12 oz cottage cheese, sieved	1 1/2 cups cottage cheese, sieved
150 ml / 1/4 pint natural yogurt	2/3 cup unflavored yogurt
50 g / 2 oz caster sugar	1/4 cup sugar
finely grated rind and juice of 1 lemon	finely grated rind and juice of 1 lemon
15 g / 1/2 oz gelatine	1 envelope unflavored gelatin
2 tablespoons water	2 tablespoons water
2 egg whites	2 egg whites
TOPPING:	TOPPING:
2 large peaches	2 large peaches
225 g / 8 oz raspberries	2 cups raspberries

To make the crust: melt the margarine in a pan, then stir in the biscuits (crackers) and sugar. Spoon the mixture into a lightly greased 18-20 cm / 7-8 inch loose-bottomed cake tin, spread evenly and press down with the back of a spoon. Chill in the refrigerator.

Meanwhile, make the filling: put the cottage cheese in a bowl with the yogurt, sugar, lemon rind and juice, reserving 1 tablespoon of lemon juice for the topping. Beat well.

Sprinkle the gelatine over the water in a small cup. Stand the cup in a pan of hot water and stir until the gelatine has dissolved. Fold into the cheese mixture.

Beat the egg whites until stiff, then fold into the cheese mixture. Pour on top of the crust in the tin and level the surface. Chill in the refrigerator until set.

To serve: run a knife around the edge of the cheesecake, then remove from the tin. Cut the peaches in half, remove the stones (seeds), then slice the flesh. Brush the cut surfaces with the reserved lemon juice. Arrange the peach slices on top of the cheesecake with the raspberries. Serve chilled.

Serves 6 to 8

Apricot Syllabub

Metric/Imperial	American
225 g / 8 oz dried apricots	1 1/2 cups dried apricots
600 ml / 1 pint water	2 1/2 cups water
finely grated rind and juice of 1 lemon	finely grated rind and juice of 1 lemon
150 ml / 1/4 pint natural yogurt	1 1/4 cups unflavored yogurt
2 tablespoons Grand Marnier or other liqueur	2 tablespoons Grand Marnier or other liqueur
50 g / 2 oz soft brown sugar	1/3 cup brown sugar
2 egg whites	2 egg whites
lemon twists or chopped nuts, to decorate	lemon twists or chopped nuts, to decorate

Put the apricots in a bowl, pour over the water, then add the lemon rind and juice. Leave to soak overnight. Alternatively, pour over boiling water and soak for a few hours.

Transfer to a pan and bring to the boil. Lower the heat, cover and simmer for 20 to 30 minutes until the apricots are soft, adding more water if necessary.

Work the mixture to a smooth purée in an electric blender, then transfer to a bowl and leave to cool.

Stir the yogurt, liqueur and sugar into the purée until well blended. Beat the egg whites until just stiff, then fold into the mixture.

Spoon into a serving bowl or 6 individual dishes or glasses, then chill in the refrigerator for at least 1 hour before serving. Decorate with lemon twists or nuts.

Serves 6

ABOVE: Raspberry chantilly; Strawberry and orange soufflé; Peach and raspberry cheesecake (page 117)
BELOW LEFT: Apricot syllabub

Raspberry Chantilly

Metric/Imperial	American
450 g / 1 lb raspberries	3 cups raspberries
2 tablespoons Grand Marnier or other liqueur	2 tablespoons Grand Marnier or other liqueur
2 egg whites	2 egg whites
grated rind of 1/2 lemon	grated rind of 1/2 lemon
1 tablespoon caster sugar	1 tablespoon sugar
25 g / 1 oz flaked almonds, toasted	1/4 cup toasted sliced almonds

Put the raspberries in 4 glasses and spoon over the liqueur.

Just before serving, beat the egg whites until stiff. Fold in the yogurt carefully with the lemon rind and sugar. Spoon over the raspberries and sprinkle with the almonds.

Serves 4

Strawberry and Orange Soufflé

The flavour of orange combines well with strawberries. This soufflé has a strong natural flavour as no cream is used to mask the flavour of the fruit and the yogurt gives it a tangy, refreshing taste.

Metric/Imperial	American
450 g / 1 lb strawberries, hulled	3 cups hulled strawberries
4 eggs, separated	4 eggs, separated
100 g / 4 oz caster sugar	1/2 cup sugar
finely grated rind and juice of 1 large orange	finely grated rind and juice of 1 large orange
15 g / 1/2 oz gelatine	1 envelope gelatin
150 ml / 1/4 pint natural yogurt	2/3 cup unflavored yogurt
25 g / 1 oz flaked almonds, toasted and chopped	1/4 cup toasted sliced almonds, chopped
1 orange, peeled and segmented, to decorate	1 orange, peeled and segmented, to decorate

Mash the strawberries or work to a purée in an electric blender, reserving a few whole ones for decoration.

Put the egg yolks in a bowl with the sugar, orange rind and half the juice. Stand the bowl over a pan of gently simmering water and whisk until the mixture is thick and pale. Remove from the heat and continue whisking until cool.

Pour the remaining orange juice into a small cup and sprinkle the gelatine on top. Stand the cup in a pan of hot water and stir until the gelatine has dissolved.

Stir the strawberry purée into the egg mixture with the yogurt and mix well. Stir in the dissolved gelatine. Leave in a cool place until thick and just beginning to set. Beat the egg whites until just stiff and fold into the mixture.

Tie a collar of greaseproof (wax) paper around a 900 ml / 1 1/2 pint / 3 3/4 cup soufflé dish so that it stands 5 cm / 2 inches above the rim of the dish. Pour in the soufflé mixture. Chill in the refrigerator for at least 2 hours before serving.

Remove the collar carefully before serving. Press the chopped nuts around the side. Decorate the top with the reserved strawberries and the orange segments.

Serves 4 to 6

Rhubarb, Orange and Ginger Fool

Metric/Imperial	American
450 g / 1 lb rhubarb, trimmed and chopped	1 lb rhubarb trimmed and chopped
finely grated rind and juice of 1 orange	finely grated rind and juice of 1 orange
4 tablespoons light soft brown sugar	1/4 cup light brown sugar
150 ml / 1/4 pint milk	2/3 cup milk
1 egg, lightly beaten	1 egg, lightly beaten
1 tablespoon cornflour	1 tablespoon cornstarch
1 tablespoon sugar	1 tablespoon sugar
1/4 teaspoon vanilla essence	1/4 teaspoon vanilla extract
150 ml / 1/4 pint natural yogurt	2/3 cup unflavored yogurt
1 tablespoon finely chopped preserved ginger	1 tablespoon finely chopped preserved ginger
few orange slices to decorate	few orange slices to decorate

Put the rhubarb in a pan with the orange rind and juice and the brown sugar. Cover and simmer gently for 10 to 15 minutes until tender. Mash the rhubarb to a pulp by beating vigorously with a wooden spoon, or work to a purée in an electric blender. Leave to cool.

Heat the milk to just below boiling point. Put the egg in a bowl with the cornflour (cornstarch)), sugar and vanilla essence (extract). Beat lightly, then gradually stir in the hot milk. Pour the mixture back into the pan and bring to the boil slowly, stirring constantly. Cook, stirring, until the custard thickens.

Leave to cool, stirring occasionally to prevent a skin from forming, then whisk in the yogurt. Stir the custard into the rhubarb purée with the ginger.

Spoon into a large serving bowl or individual dishes or glasses. Chill in the refrigerator, then decorate with orange slices before serving. Serve chilled.

Serves 4

Bramble Mousse

Metric/Imperial	American
450 g / 1 lb blackberries	4 cups blackberries
225 g / 8 oz cooking apples, peeled, cored and sliced	1 1/2 cups peeled, cored and sliced baking apples
finely grated rind and juice of 1 orange or lemon	finely grated rind and juice of 1 orange or lemon
4 tablespoons soft brown sugar	1/4 cup brown sugar
15 g / 1/2 oz gelatine	1 envelope gelatin
2 tablespoons water	2 tablespoons water
150 ml / 1/4 pint natural yogurt	2/3 cup unflavored yogurt
2 egg whites	2 egg whites

Put the blackberries in a pan, reserving a few for decoration. Add the apples, orange or lemon rind and juice and the sugar. Cover and heat gently for 10 to 15 minutes until the fruit is soft, stirring occasionally. Rub through a sieve (strainer) into a bowl.

Sprinkle the gelatine over the water in a small cup. Stand the cup in a pan of hot water and stir until the gelatine has dissolved.

Stir the gelatine into the fruit purée with the yogurt and mix well. Leave in a cool place until thick and just beginning to set.

Beat the egg whites until just stiff, then fold into the mousse. Transfer to a large serving bowl or individual dishes or glasses. Chill in the refrigerator until set, then decorate with the reserved blackberries. Serve chilled.

Serves 4 to 6

Gingered Pear and Yogurt Mousse

Metric/Imperial

1 kg / 2 lb pears, peeled,
   cored and chopped
finely grated rind and juice
   of 1 lemon
1/4 teaspoon ground ginger
3-4 pieces preserved ginger
   in syrup
2 eggs, separated
300 ml / 1/2 pint natural
   yogurt
15 g / 1/2 oz gelatine
2 tablespoons water

American

2 lb pears, peeled, cored
   and chopped
finely grated rind and juice
   of 1 lemon
1/4 teaspoon ground ginger
3-4 pieces preserved ginger
   in syrup
2 eggs, separated
1 1/4 cups unflavored yogurt
2 envelopes gelatin
2 tablespoons water

Put the pears in a pan with the lemon rind and juice, ginger and 2 tablespoons syrup from the preserved ginger. Cover and cook gently for 10 to 15 minutes until the pears are tender, stirring occasionally. Take out the preserved ginger; chop one of the pieces, slice the remainder and set aside.

Put the pears and juice, egg yolks and yogurt in an electric blender and blend to a smooth purée. Alternatively, rub the pears and juice through a sieve (strainer), then beat in the egg yolks and yogurt.

Sprinkle the gelatine over the water in a small cup. Stand the cup in a pan of hot water and stir until the gelatine has dissolved. Stir into the pear purée, with the chopped ginger. Leave in a cool place until thick and just beginning to set.

Beat the egg whites until stiff, then fold into the mixture. Spoon into 6 individual glasses or dishes and chill in the refrigerator until set. Decorate with slices of preserved ginger. Serve chilled.

Serves 6

Prune and Orange Ring

Metric/Imperial

225 g / 8 oz prunes
finely grated rind of 1
   orange
juice of 2 large oranges
15 g / 1/2 oz gelatine
juice of 1 lemon
2 egg whites
2 oranges, peel and pith
   removed and sliced, to
   serve

American

1 1/3 cups prunes
finely grated rind of 1
   orange
juice of 2 large oranges
1 envelope gelatin
juice of 1 lemon
2 egg whites
2 oranges, peel and pith
   removed and sliced, to
   serve

Put the prunes and orange rind in a bowl. Make the orange juice up to 300 ml / 1/2 pint / 1 1/4 cups with water, then pour over the prunes. Leave to soak overnight. Alternatively, pour over boiling juice and water and soak for a few hours.

Transfer to a pan and bring to the boil. Lower the heat, cover and simmer for 20 minutes until the prunes are tender, then drain, reserving the juice.

Measure the juice and make up to 300 ml / 1/2 pint / 1 1/4 cups with water. Remove the stones (seeds) from the prunes. Put the prune flesh and juice in an electric blender and work to a smooth purée.

Sprinkle the gelatine over the lemon juice in a small cup. Stand the cup in a pan of hot water and stir until the gelatine has dissolved. Stir into the prune purée.

Beat the egg whites until just stiff, then fold into the mixture. Pour into a 900 ml / 1 1/2 pint / 3 3/4 cup ring mould or serving bowl and chill in the refrigerator until set.

To serve: dip the mould in hot water for a few seconds, then invert onto a serving plate. Fill the centre of the ring with the orange slices.

Serves 4 to 6

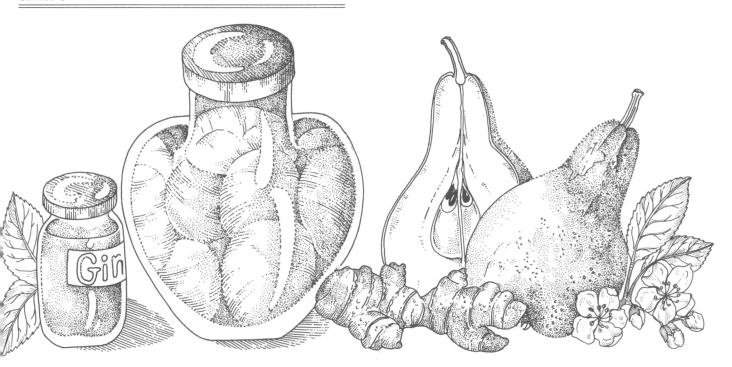

Chestnut Whip

If fresh chestnuts are unobtainable, use one 450 g / 1 lb can unsweetened chestnut purée instead of making your own.

Metric/Imperial	American
450 g / 1 lb chestnuts	1 lb chestnuts
600 ml / 1 pint water	2½ cups water
200 ml / ⅓ pint milk	1 cup milk
¼ teaspoon vanilla essence	¼ teaspoon vanilla extract
finely grated rind and juice of 1 small orange	finely grated rind and juice of 1 small orange
2 tablespoons rum	2 tablespoons rum
100 g / 4 oz soft brown sugar	⅔ cup brown sugar
2 egg whites	2 egg whites
orange twists, to decorate	orange twists, to decorate

Chestnut whip

Put the chestnuts in a pan and cover with the water. Bring to the boil, then lower the heat and simmer for 10 minutes. Drain and leave until cool enough to handle.

Peel off the skins with a sharp knife, then return the chestnuts to the pan and add the milk and vanilla essence (extract). Cover and cook gently for about 15 minutes until the chestnuts are soft and have absorbed the milk, stirring occasionally.

Rub through a sieve (strainer) to give a thick, dry purée, then stir in the orange rind and juice, rum and sugar. Beat the egg whites until just stiff, then fold into the chestnut mixture.

Spoon into a serving bowl or 6 individual dishes or glasses. Chill in the refrigerator for at least 1 hour before serving, then decorate with orange twists.

Serves 6

Orange and Lemon Mousse

Metric/Imperial	American
4 large eggs, separated	4 large eggs, separated
100 g / 4 oz light soft brown sugar	⅔ cup light brown sugar
finely grated rind and juice of 2 lemons	finely grated rind and juice of 2 lemons
finely grated rind and juice of 2 oranges	finely grated rind and juice of 2 oranges
15 g / ½ oz gelatine	1 envelope gelatin
150 ml / ¼ pint natural yogurt	⅔ cup unflavored yogurt

Put the egg yolks and sugar in a bowl. Add the lemon rind and juice, orange rind and half of the orange juice.

Pour the remaining orange juice into a small cup and sprinkle on the gelatine. Stand the cup in a pan of hot water and stir until the gelatine has dissolved.

Stand the bowl with the egg yolk mixture over a pan of gently simmering water and whisk until the mixture is thick and pale. Remove from the heat and continue whisking until cool.

Stir the yogurt into the mixture with the dissolved gelatine. Leave in a cool place until thick and just beginning to set.

Beat the egg whites until just stiff, then fold into the mousse. Pour into a serving bowl and chill in the refrigerator for at least 2 hours before serving. Serve chilled.

Alternatively, pour into a 900 ml / 1½ pint / 3¾ cup soufflé dish tied with a collar of greaseproof (wax) paper so that the mousse will set above the rim of the dish. Remove the collar carefully before serving.

Serves 4 to 6

LEFT: Orange and lemon mousse

ABOVE: Minted apple snow

Minted Apple Snow

Metric/Imperial	**American**
1 kg / 2 lb cooking apples, peeled, cored and sliced	6 cups peeled, cored and sliced baking apples
finely grated rind and juice of 1 orange	finely grated rind and juice of 1 orange
3 tablespoons honey	3 tablespoons honey
4 large mint sprigs	4 large mint sprigs
2 large egg whites	2 large egg whites

Put the apples in a pan, then add the orange rind and juice and the honey. Add the mint, reserving the top leaves for decoration. Cover and cook gently for about 15 minutes until the apples are cooked to a pulp, stirring occasionally.

Discard the mint, then beat the pulp vigorously with a wooden spoon until smooth. Alternatively, rub through a sieve (strainer) or work to a purée in an electric blender. Leave to cool.

Beat the egg whites until stiff, then fold into the apple purée. Spoon into a serving bowl or individual dishes or glasses. Decorate with the reserved mint leaves. Serve chilled.

Serves 4

Sunshine Fruit Salad

Metric/Imperial	American
juice of 2 large oranges	juice of 2 large oranges
juice of 1 lemon	juice of 1 lemon
2 tablespoons Cointreau, Grand Marnier or other liqueur (optional)	2 tablespoons Cointreau, Grand Marnier or other liqueur (optional)
225 g / 8 oz strawberries, hulled and halved	2 cups strawberries, hulled and halved
2 large peaches	2 large peaches
2 large bananas	2 large bananas
2 passion fruit or pomegranates	2 passion fruit or pomegranates

Put the orange and lemon juices in a serving bowl, then stir in the liqueur, if using. Add the strawberries.

Cut the peaches in half, remove the stones (seeds), then slice the flesh. Peel and slice the bananas. Cut the passion fruit or pomegranates in half, then scoop out the flesh with the seeds. Add the prepared fruit to the strawberries and fold gently to coat with the juice. Serve chilled.

Serves 4

Frosted Almond Creams

Metric/Imperial	American
2 eggs, separated	2 eggs, separated
50 g / 2 oz soft brown sugar	1/3 cup brown sugar
50 g / 2 oz chopped almonds, toasted	1/2 cup toasted chopped almonds
300 ml / 1/2 pint natural yogurt	1 1/4 cups unflavored yogurt
2 tablespoons Grand Marnier or other liqueur	2 tablespoons Grand Marnier or other liqueur
25 g / 1 oz toasted slivered almonds, to decorate	1/4 cup toasted slivered almonds, to decorate

Beat the egg yolks and sugar together until thick and creamy. Stir in the chopped almonds, yogurt and liqueur. Beat the egg whites until just stiff, then fold into the almond mixture. Pour into 6 individual ramekin dishes and freeze until firm.

To serve: remove from the freezer and leave to soften slightly at room temperature for 15 minutes, or in the refrigerator for 30 minutes. Sprinkle with slivered almonds before serving.

Serves 6

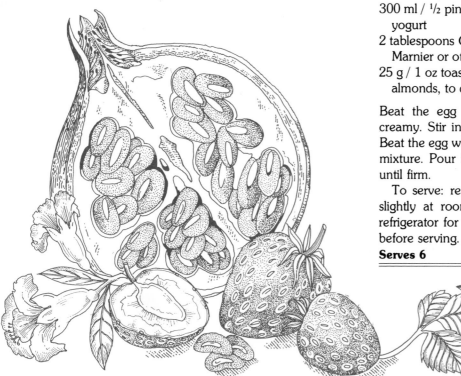

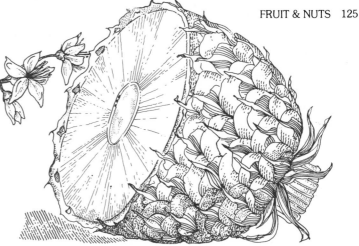

Blackcurrant and Orange Ice Cream

Something between an ice cream and a sorbet (sherbet), this rich-flavoured dessert uses yogurt and egg yolks as well as the usual egg whites.

Metric/Imperial	American
225 g / 8 oz blackcurrants, stalks removed	2 cups blackcurrants, stalks removed
finely grated rind and juice of 1 orange	finely grated rind and juice of 1 orange
6-8 mint leaves	6-8 mint leaves
4 tablespoons soft brown sugar	1/4 cup brown sugar
300 ml / 1/2 pint natural yogurt	1 1/4 cups unflavored yogurt
2 eggs, separated	2 eggs, separated
4-6 small mint sprigs to decorate	4-6 small mint sprigs to decorate

Put the blackcurrants in an electric blender, reserving a few for decoration. Add the orange rind and juice, the mint leaves, sugar, yogurt and egg yolks. Blend until smooth.

Transfer the purée to a bowl, then place in the freezer, or freezing compartment of the refrigerator; freeze until half frozen and beginning to thicken.

Beat the egg whites until stiff, then fold into the ice cream. Freeze until half frozen, then beat again to prevent large ice crystals forming, then freeze until firm.

To serve: allow the ice cream to soften slightly at room temperature for about 10 minutes, or in the refrigerator for 20 minutes. Spoon into individual dishes or glasses, then decorate with the reserved blackcurrants and the mint sprigs.

Serves 4 to 6

Pineapple Sorbet (Sherbet)

Traditionally, sorbets (sherbets) are made with a sweet sugar syrup, but this recipe simply uses puréed pineapple flavoured with orange and folded in with the beaten egg whites.

Metric/Imperial	American
1 × 1.5 kg / 3 lb pineapple	1 × 3 lb pineapple
finely grated rind and juice of 1 large orange	finely grated rind and juice of 1 large orange
sugar to taste	sugar to taste
2 egg whites	2 egg whites

Cut the pineapple in half lengthwise, leaving the green leaves attached. Scoop out the pineapple flesh and discard the central core. Reserve the pineapple shells for serving. Alternatively, slice the top off the pineapple and scoop out the flesh.

Work the pineapple flesh to a purée with the orange rind and juice in an electric blender. Add sugar to taste. Transfer the purée to a bowl, then place in the freezer, or freezing compartment of the refrigerator; freeze until half frozen and beginning to thicken.

Beat the egg whites until stiff. Beat the sorbet (sherbet) well to break down the ice crystals, then fold in the beaten egg whites. Spoon the mixture into the pineapple shells and return to the freezer or freezing compartment. If there is too much sorbet (sherbet) to fill the shells, freeze in a separate container.

To serve: allow the sorbet (sherbet) to soften slightly at room temperature for 10 to 15 minutes, or in the refrigerator for 20 minutes.

Serves 6 to 8

Walnut Pie

Metric/Imperial

PASTRY:

175 g / 6 oz wholemeal
    flour
100 g / 4 oz vegetable
    margarine
50 g / 2 oz soft brown sugar
1 tablespoon ground mixed
    spice
2 tablespoons beaten egg

FILLING:

2 eggs, separated
100 g / 4 oz soft brown
    sugar
100 g / 4 oz walnut halves,
    chopped
finely grated rind and juice
    of 1 lemon
few walnut halves, to
    decorate

American

DOUGH:

1½ cups wholewheat flour
½ cup vegetable margarine
⅓ cup brown sugar
2 teaspoons ground allspice
1 teaspoon ground
    cinnamon
2 tablespoons beaten egg

FILLING:

2 eggs, separated
⅔ cup brown sugar
1 cup chopped walnuts
finely grated rind and juice
    of 1 lemon
few walnut halves, to
    decorate

To make the pastry dough: put the flour in a bowl, then rub in the margarine until the mixture resembles breadcrumbs. Stir in the sugar and spice, then the egg. Mix to a firm dough.

Turn the dough out onto a lightly floured surface, then roll out and use to line a 20 cm / 8 inch flan dish or flan ring placed on a baking sheet. Line the dough with foil, then fill with baking beans or rice. Bake in a preheated moderately hot oven (200°C / 400°F, Gas Mark 6) for 15 minutes, then remove the foil and beans or rice.

Meanwhile, make the filling: beat the egg yolks and sugar together until light and creamy. Stir in the walnuts and lemon rind and juice. Beat the egg whites until just stiff, then fold into the walnut mixture.

Pour the filling into the flan case. Bake in a preheated moderate oven (180°C / 350°F, Gas Mark 4) for 30 minutes until lightly browned and risen. Decorate with walnut halves and serve hot or cold.

Serves 6

Spiced Cranberry and Apple Pie

Metric/Imperial

PASTRY:

175 g / 6 oz wholemeal
    flour
50 g / 2 oz soft brown sugar
1 tablespoon ground mixed
    spice
100 g / 4 oz vegetable
    margarine
50 g / 2 oz chopped nuts
1 egg, beaten

FILLING:

450 g / 1 lb cooking apples,
    peeled, cored and sliced
finely grated rind and juice
    of 1 orange
225 g / 8 oz cranberries
75 g / 3 oz sugar

American

DOUGH:

1½ cups wholewheat flour
⅓ cup brown sugar
2 teaspoons ground allspice
1 teaspoon ground
    cinnamon
½ cup vegetable margarine
½ cup chopped nuts
1 egg, beaten

FILLING:

4 cups peeled, cored and
    sliced baking apples
finely grated rind and juice
    of 1 orange
2 cups cranberries
⅓ cup sugar

To make the pastry dough: put the flour, sugar and spice in a bowl and mix well. Add the margarine in pieces and rub into the flour until the mixture resembles breadcrumbs.

Stir in the nuts, then 2 tablespoons of beaten egg and mix to a firm dough. Turn out onto a lightly floured surface and knead lightly, then cover and chill until required.

To make the filling: put all the ingredients in a bowl and mix well. Spoon into a 900 ml / 1½ pint / 3¾ cup pie dish.

Roll out the dough on the lightly floured surface to a shape 2.5 cm / 1 inch larger than the circumference of the pie dish. Cut a 1 cm / ½ inch strip of dough from around the edge and press it onto the moistened rim of the pie dish. Moisten the strip, then place the large piece of dough on top. Press firmly to seal, then trim and flute the edge.

Decorate the top of the pie with the trimmings and make a slit in the centre. Brush with the remaining beaten egg.

Bake in a preheated moderately hot oven (200°C / 400°F, Gas Mark 6) for 30 to 40 minutes until the pastry is crisp and brown. Serve hot.

Serves 4 to 6

Spiced cranberry and apple pie; Walnut pie; French orange flans (page 128)

Plum and Orange Cobbler

Metric/Imperial	American
FILLING:	FILLING:
450 g / 1 lb Victoria plums	1 lb purple plums
juice of 2 oranges	juice of 2 oranges
1 orange, peel and pith removed and divided into segments	1 orange, peel and pith removed and divided into segments
3 tablespoons honey	3 tablespoons honey
SCONES:	BISCUITS:
225 g / 8 oz wholemeal flour	2 cups wholewheat flour
1 teaspoon ground mixed spice	½ teaspoon ground allspice
2 teaspoons baking powder	½ teaspoon ground cinnamon
½ teaspoon salt	2 teaspoons baking powder
25 g / 1 oz vegetable margarine	½ teaspoon salt
25 g / 1 oz soft brown sugar	2 tablespoons vegetable margarine
finely grated rind of 1 orange	3 tablespoons brown sugar
150 ml / ¼ pint natural yogurt or milk	finely grated rind of 1 orange
milk or beaten egg to glaze	⅔ cup unflavored yogurt
	milk or beaten egg to glaze

To make the filling: place the plums in a baking dish. Add the orange juice and segments and spoon over the honey.

To make the scones (biscuits): put the flour, spice, baking powder and salt in a bowl and stir well. Rub in the margarine, then stir in the sugar and orange rind. Add the yogurt and mix to a soft dough.

Turn the dough out onto a lightly floured surface and roll out to about 1 cm / ½ inch thickness. Cut out 8 to 10 rounds with a 4 cm / 1½ inch biscuit cutter, then arrange overlapping around the edge of the dish. Brush with a little milk or beaten egg.

Bake in a preheated hot oven (220°C / 425°F, Gas Mark 7) for about 15 minutes until the scones (biscuits) are risen and brown and the plums are just tender when pierced with a skewer. Serve hot.

Serves 4

French Orange Flans

Metric/Imperial	American
PASTRY:	DOUGH:
175 g / 6 oz wholemeal flour	1½ cups wholewheat flour
50 g / 2 oz soft brown sugar	⅓ cup brown sugar
1 tablespoon ground mixed spice	2 teaspoons ground allspice
100 g / 4 oz vegetable margarine	1 teaspoon ground cinnamon
2 tablespoons beaten egg	½ cup vegetable margarine
TOPPING:	2 tablespoons beaten egg
2 small thin-skinned oranges, thinly sliced	TOPPING:
2 tablespoons clear honey	2 small thin-skinned oranges, thinly sliced
FILLING:	2 tablespoons clear honey
1 egg, beaten	FILLING:
50 g / 2 oz ground almonds	1 egg, beaten
1 tablespoon sugar	½ cup ground almonds
	1 tablespoon sugar

To make the pastry dough: put the flour, sugar and spice in a bowl and mix well. Add the margarine in pieces and rub into the flour until the mixture resembles breadcrumbs.

Add the beaten egg and mix to a firm dough. Turn out onto a lightly floured surface and knead lightly. Cover and chill in the refrigerator until required.

To make the topping: put the orange slices in a pan and simmer for about 30 minutes until the peel is tender. Drain.

Divide the dough into 4 pieces. Roll out on a lightly floured surface and use to line individual flan rings, about 10 cm / 4 inches in diameter. Alternatively, roll out four 10 cm / 4 inch circles and place on a baking sheet.

Line the dough with foil, then fill with baking beans or rice. Bake in a preheated moderately hot oven (200°C / 400°F, Gas Mark 6) for 15 minutes, then remove the beans or rice and foil.

To make the filling: put the egg, almonds and sugar in a bowl and beat well to mix. Spread in the bottom of the flan cases then arrange the orange slices on top, overlapping each other. Spoon over the honey.

Bake in a moderate oven (180°C / 350°F, Gas Mark 4) for 20 minutes. Serve hot or cold.

Serves 4

Black Pear Pudding

Metric/Imperial	American
4 pears, peeled, cored and sliced	4 pears, peeled, cored and sliced
100 g / 4 oz blackberries	1 cup blackberries
finely grated rind and juice of 1 lemon	finely grated rind and juice of 1 lemon
75 g / 3 oz soft brown sugar	½ cup brown sugar
50 g / 2 oz vegetable margarine	¼ cup vegetable margarine
1 large egg, beaten	1 large egg, beaten
100 g / 4 oz wholemeal flour	1 cup wholewheat flour
1 teaspoon ground cinnamon	1 teaspoon ground cinnamon
2 teaspoons baking powder	2 teaspoons baking powder
1 tablespoon milk	1 tablespoon milk

Put the pears and blackberries in a 900 ml / 1½ pint / 3¾ cup pie dish. Sprinkle over the lemon rind and juice and 2 tablespoons sugar.

Cream the margarine and remaining sugar together until pale and fluffy. Beat in the egg with a little of the flour and the cinnamon.

Fold in the remaining flour and baking powder to give a soft dropping consistency, then spread the mixture over the fruit and level the surface.

Bake in a preheated moderate oven (180°C / 350°F, Gas Mark 4) for 45 minutes until the topping is risen and brown. Serve hot.

Serves 4

Cherry Custard Pudding

This pudding separates out on cooking to give a layer of custard and cherries with a light sponge topping.

Metric/Imperial	American
350 g / 12 oz cherries, stoned	3 cups pitted cherries
50 g / 2 oz vegetable margarine	¼ cup vegetable margarine
50 g / 2 oz caster sugar	¼ cup sugar
finely grated rind and juice of 1 large lemon	finely grated rind and juice of 1 large lemon
2 eggs, separated	2 eggs, separated
300 ml / ½ pint milk	1¼ cups milk
50 g / 2 oz self-raising flour	½ cup self-rising flour
½ teaspoon ground cinnamon	½ teaspoon ground cinnamon

Put the cherries in a baking dish.

Cream together the margarine, sugar and lemon rind until pale and fluffy. Beat in the egg yolks a little at a time, then stir in the milk, lemon juice, flour and cinnamon to give a loose, curd-like mixture.

Beat the egg whites until just stiff, then fold into the mixture and spoon on top of the cherries.

Place the dish in a roasting pan, then pour in enough hot water to come half way up the sides of the pan. Bake in a preheated moderate oven (180°C / 350°F, Gas Mark 4) for 40 to 45 minutes until the top is set, firm and golden. Serve hot.

Serves 4

Gooseberry and Almond Crumble

Metric/Imperial	American
450 g / 1 lb gooseberries, topped and tailed	2¾ cups gooseberries, topped and tailed
2 tablespoons sugar	2 tablespoons sugar
finely grated rind and juice of 1 orange	finely grated rind and juice of 1 orange
CRUMBLE:	CRUMBLE:
100 g / 4 oz wholemeal flour or rolled oats	1 cup wholewheat flour or rolled oats
50 g / 2 oz vegetable margarine	¼ cup vegetable margarine
50 g / 2 oz soft brown sugar	⅓ cup brown sugar
50 g / 2 oz blanched almonds, flaked or chopped	½ cup flaked or chopped blanched almonds

Put the gooseberries in a 900 ml / 1½ pint / 3¾ cup pie dish. Sprinkle over the sugar, then pour over the orange juice, reserving the rind for the crumble.

To make the crumble: put the flour in a bowl, then rub in the margarine. Stir in the brown sugar, almonds and reserved orange rind, then spoon on top of the gooseberries to cover them completely.

Bake in a preheated moderately hot oven (200°C / 400°F, Gas Mark 6) for 30 minutes until the crumble is crisp and brown. Serve hot.

Serves 4

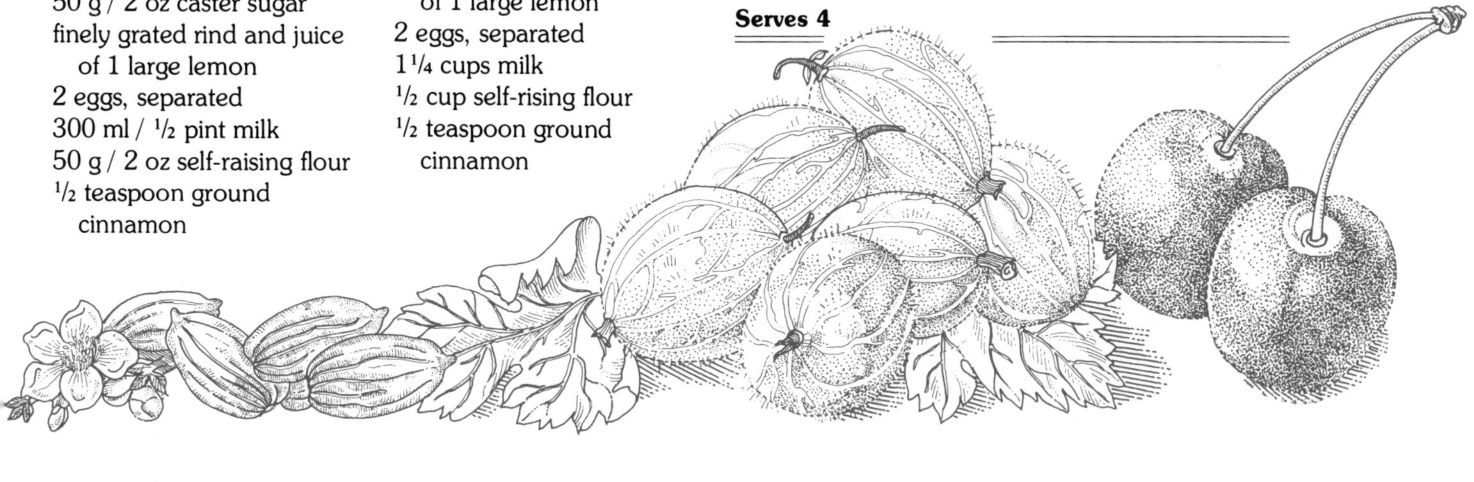

Blackberry and Orange Stuffed Apples

Metric/Imperial
4 large cooking apples
225 g / 8 oz blackberries
finely grated rind and juice
  of 1 large orange
4 tablespoons soft brown
  sugar
1 tablespoon chopped mint

American
4 large baking apples
2 cups blackberries
finely grated rind and juice
  of 1 large orange
¼ cup brown sugar
1 tablespoon chopped mint

Remove the cores from the apples, making a large hole for the stuffing. Make a shallow cut through the skin around the centre of each apple to prevent the skins bursting.

To make the stuffing: mix the blackberries with the orange rind, sugar and mint. Place the apples in a baking dish and divide the stuffing equally between the apples, pressing it well down into the centres. Spoon any remaining stuffing around the apples, then spoon over the orange juice.

Bake in a preheated moderate oven (180°C / 350°F, Gas Mark 4) for 45 minutes or until the apples are tender. Serve hot.

Serves 4

Baked Grapefruit Soufflé

Metric/Imperial	American
finely grated rind of 2 large grapefruit	finely grated rind of 2 large grapefruit
25 g / 1 oz vegetable margarine	2 tablespoons vegetable margarine
25 g / 1 oz flour	¼ cup flour
juice of 1 large grapefruit	juice of 1 large grapefruit
1 grapefruit, peel and pith removed and divided into segments	1 grapefruit, peel and pith removed and divided into segments
50 g / 2 oz sugar	¼ cup sugar
4 egg yolks	4 egg yolks
5 egg whites	5 egg whites

Put the grapefruit rind and margarine in a pan and heat gently until the margarine has melted. Stir in the flour, then the grapefruit juice. Bring to the boil, stirring constantly to give a thick smooth sauce.

Add the grapefruit segments and simmer for 1 minute. Stir in the sugar, then remove from the heat and leave to cool slightly.

Beat the egg yolks into the grapefruit sauce. Beat the egg whites until stiff, then fold gently into the grapefruit mixture.

Pour into a 1.5 litre / 2½ pint / 6¼ cup soufflé dish. Bake in a preheated moderate oven (180°C / 350°F, Gas Mark 4) for 45 minutes until the soufflé is well risen, set and golden brown on top. Serve immediately.

Serves 4

LEFT: Blackberry and orange stuffed apples; Spiced stuffed peaches
BELOW: Grapefruit soufflé

Spiced Stuffed Peaches

Metric/Imperial	American
4 large peaches	4 large peaches
juice of 2 oranges	juice of 2 oranges
2 tablespoons redcurrant jelly	2 tablespoons redcurrant jelly
1 cinnamon stick	1 cinnamon stick
2 cloves	2 cloves
½ teaspoon whole allspice	½ teaspoon whole allspice
2-3 tablespoons brandy (optional)	2-3 tablespoons brandy (optional)
FILLING:	FILLING:
1 egg, lightly beaten	1 egg, lightly beaten
50 g / 2 oz ground almonds	½ cup ground almonds
1 tablespoon finely chopped preserved ginger	1 tablespoon finely chopped preserved ginger
1 tablespoon soft brown sugar	1 tablespoon brown sugar

Cut the peaches in half. Remove the stones (seeds). Scoop out and reserve some of the flesh from the centre of each peach half to allow room for the filling.

To make the filling: put the egg in a bowl with the almonds, ginger, sugar and reserved peach flesh. Mix well, then spoon into the peach halves. Place the peaches in a baking dish.

Put the orange juice, redcurrant jelly and spices in a small pan. Heat gently until the jelly has dissolved, then bring to the boil. Pour over the peaches.

Bake in a preheated moderate oven (180°C / 350°F, Gas Mark 4) for about 20 minutes until the peaches are tender when pierced with a skewer. If liked, warm the brandy, pour over the peaches and set alight. Serve hot or cold.

Serves 4

Hot Berry Snow

Metric/Imperial	American
450 g / 1 lb mixed red berries (strawberries, raspberries, redcurrants), hulled and stalks removed	3-4 cups mixed red berries (strawberries, raspberries, redcurrants), hulled and stalks removed
1 tablespoon honey	1 tablespoon honey
150 ml / ¼ pint natural yogurt	⅔ cup unflavored yogurt
2 eggs, separated	2 eggs, separated
1 tablespoon flour	1 tablespoon flour
25 g / 1 oz ground almonds	¼ cup ground almonds
2 tablespoons soft brown sugar	2 tablespoons brown sugar

Wash the fruit and place in a baking dish. Spoon over the honey.

Put the yogurt in a bowl, then beat in the egg yolks, flour and almonds.

Beat the egg whites until stiff, then fold into the yogurt mixture. Spoon over the fruit and sprinkle with the sugar.

Bake in a preheated moderately hot oven (200°C / 400°F, Gas Mark 6) for 15 to 20 minutes until the topping is risen and golden brown. Serve immediately.

Serves 4

Hot Harlequin Soufflé

Metric/Imperial	American
175 g / 6 oz mixed dried fruit	1 cup mixed dried fruit
450 ml / ¾ pint water	2 cups water
finely grated rind and juice of 1 lemon	finely grated rind and juice of 1 lemon
25 g / 1 oz soft brown sugar	3 tablespoons brown sugar
4 egg whites	4 egg whites

Put the dried fruit in a bowl, pour over the water and lemon rind and juice and leave to soak overnight. Alternatively, pour over boiling water and soak for a few hours.

Transfer to a pan and bring to the boil. Lower the heat, cover and simmer for 30 minutes or until the fruit is tender. Drain and reserve the liquid.

Remove any stones (seeds) from the fruit. Make up the liquid to 150 ml / ¼ pint / ⅔ cup with water if necessary, then work the fruit and liquid to a smooth purée in an electric blender. Transfer to a large bowl, stir in the sugar and leave to cool.

Beat the egg whites until just stiff, then fold into the purée. Pour into a 1.5 litre / 2½ pint / 6¼ cup soufflé dish.

Bake in a preheated moderately hot oven (200°C / 400°F, Gas Mark 6) for 20 minutes until the soufflé has risen and the top is lightly browned. Serve immediately.

Serves 4

Hot Fruit Compote

Metric/Imperial
175 g / 6 oz dried apricots
450 ml / ³⁄₄ pint dry cider
3 tablespoons clear honey
150 ml / ¹⁄₄ pint water
1 cinnamon stick
2 cloves
50 g / 2 oz seedless raisins
1 large grapefruit, peel and
   pith removed and divided
   into segments
2 bananas, peeled and cut
   into chunks

American
1 cup dried apricots
2 cups hard cider
3 tablespoons clear honey
²⁄₃ cup water
1 cinnamon stick
2 cloves
¹⁄₃ cup seedless raisins
1 large grapefruit, peel and
   pith removed and divided
   into segments
2 bananas, peeled and cut
   into chunks

Soak the apricots in the cider for 2 to 3 hours.

Place the apricots, cider, honey, water, cinnamon and cloves in a large pan. Bring to the boil, then lower the heat, cover and simmer gently for 15 to 25 minutes, until the apricots are just soft. Add the raisins and simmer for 5 minutes.

Discard the cinnamon stick and cloves. Add the grapefruit segments and banana chunks to the pan and heat through gently. Serve warm, with yogurt if liked.

Serves 4

WHOLEGRAIN BAKING

Home-baked cakes, scones and biscuits (cookies) might seem inevitably to contain too many 'unhealthy ingredients' and too many calories to have any place in a healthy diet, but this need not follow, if ingredients are chosen carefully. The recipes in this chapter are based upon wholewheat flour and natural sugars rather than the refined ingredients normally used for baking.

A wheat grain has three components: the starchy inner endosperm, the outer bran, and the wheatgerm. The refining of flour removes the bran and the wheatgerm, leaving only the starchy endosperm. The extraction rate describes the percentage of the original grain that remains in the flour.

Wholewheat (or wholemeal) flour has a 100 per cent extraction rate because it contains all the original grain and it has a coarse texture. Wheatmeal or brown flour, with an 80 or 90 per cent extraction rate, contains a proportion of bran and germ and the texture is finer than that of wholewheat flour. Wheaten flour is brown flour with extra pieces of whole grain added. Granary flour has malted wheat and rye grains added to a brown flour base.

Although the vitamin and mineral contents are lowered as the extraction rate drops, millers are required by law to restore them to that of an 80 or 90 per cent extraction rate. White flour should therefore be as nutritious as brown flour, but all the fibre supplied by the bran is lost.

Most people prefer white bread, yet wholewheat bread is certainly better for us because of the higher proportion of roughage it provides and it is delicious – especially when home-made. A number of other cereals can be used in baking. Oatmeal and muesli make good and nourishing cakes and biscuits (cookies) with a distinctive 'nutty' flavour.

Fats are required for most cakes and biscuits (cookies). To moderate the intake of animal fats use vegetable margarine rather than butter; it gives an excellently light texture to cakes and is easier to blend.

Sweetening is essential in cake-baking, but refined sugars can easily be avoided. Natural brown sugars, to which nothing is added or taken away, impart excellent flavour and colour to cakes and biscuits (cookies). Demerara (raw) sugar has a crunchy texture and is good for biscuits (cookies) and cake toppings. Unrefined Muscovado or Barbados sugar is soft and sticky, finely grained, and comes in dark and light varieties so that it can be used in all types of cakes. Molasses or Black Barbados sugar is very dark and strongly flavoured – perfect for gingerbread and fruit cakes.

Honey is a natural sweetener which has traces of minerals and vitamins. The simple sugars contained in honey – glucose and fructose – are quickly absorbed by the body and utilized for energy. A little honey added to bread dough, cakes and biscuits (cookies) will greatly improve the flavour. In cake recipes, a proportion of one-quarter honey to three-quarters sugar will give an excellent flavour and the cake will keep longer. Honey whipped into a little cream or vegetable margarine makes a good filling for cakes or a topping for wholewheat biscuits (cookies).

There is no special trick in wholewheat baking, except to remember that flours have different absorption rates. Liquid should be added gradually and mixed in carefully until completely absorbed. If wholewheat flour is substituted for white flour in a recipe, it may be necessary to add a little more liquid to get a satisfactory consistency.

Wholewheat recipes are generally a little more 'chewy' and flavoursome than those made with white flour, and are delicious served at any time of the day.

Farmhouse bread (page 136); Fruit malt loaf (page 137); Bran bread (page 136); Wholewheat baps (page 136)

Farmhouse Bread

Metric/Imperial	American
1.5 kg / 3 lb wholemeal bread flour	12 cups wholewheat flour
25 g / 1 oz sea salt	1 tablespoon coarse salt
25 g / 1 oz Muscovado sugar	1½ tablespoons Barbados sugar
25 g / 1 oz fresh yeast	1 cake compressed yeast
900 ml / 1½ pints lukewarm water	3¾ cups lukewarm water
1 tablespoon vegetable oil	1 tablespoon vegetable oil
beaten egg to glaze	beaten egg to glaze

Put the flour, salt and sugar in a warm bowl and mix well. Blend the yeast with a little of the water, then stir into the remaining water and add to the dry ingredients with the oil. Mix to a soft dough.

Turn out onto a lightly floured surface and knead for 5 minutes until smooth. Place the dough in a warm, greased bowl. Cover with a damp cloth and leave in a warm place for about 1 hour until doubled in size.

Turn out onto the floured surface and knead again for 5 minutes, then divide the dough into 4 pieces. Fold each piece into 3, then place in greased, warmed 450 g / 1 lb / 8 × 4½ × 2½ inch loaf tins. Cover with a damp cloth and leave in a warm place for about 30 minutes until the dough rises to the tops of the tins.

Brush the dough with beaten egg, then bake in a preheated hot oven (230°C / 450°F, Gas Mark 8) for 40 minutes. Turn out onto a wire rack and leave to cool.

Makes four 450 g / 1 lb loaves

Bran Bread

Metric/Imperial	American
550 g / 1¼ lb wholemeal bread flour	5 cups wholewheat flour
100 g / 4 oz bran	2 cups bran
15 g / ½ oz sea salt	1½ teaspoons coarse salt
25 g / 1 oz Muscovado sugar	1½ tablespoons Barbados sugar
25 g / 1 oz fresh yeast	1 cake compressed yeast
450 ml / ¾ pint lukewarm water	2 cups lukewarm water
1 tablespoon corn oil	1 tablespoon corn oil
TO FINISH:	TO FINISH:
2 tablespoons cold water	2 tablespoons cold water
pinch of salt	pinch of salt
2 tablespoons rolled oats	2 tablespoons rolled oats

Put the flour, bran, salt and sugar in a warm bowl and mix well. Blend the yeast with a little of the water, then stir into the remaining water and add to the dry ingredients with the oil. Mix to a firm dough.

Turn out onto a lightly floured surface and knead for 5 minutes until smooth. Shape the dough into a ball and place in a greased polythene (plastic) bag. Tie loosely and leave in a warm place for about 1 hour until doubled in size.

Remove the dough and knead again on the floured surface for 5 minutes, then divide in half. Shape each piece of dough and place in greased, warmed 450 g / 1 lb / 8 × 4½ × 2½ inch loaf tins, tucking in the corners lightly but firmly. Cover with greased polythene (plastic) and leave in a warm place for about 30 minutes until the dough rises to the tops of the tins.

Mix the cold water and salt together, then brush over the tops of the loaves and sprinkle with the oats. Bake in a preheated hot oven (230°C / 450°F, Gas Mark 8) for 35 minutes until well-risen and crisp. Turn out onto a wire rack and leave to cool.

Makes two 450 g / 1 lb loaves

Wholewheat Baps (Buns)

Metric/Imperial	American
675 g / 1½ lb wholemeal bread flour	6 cups wholewheat flour
1 teaspoon sea salt	1 teaspoon coarse salt
25 g / 1 oz Muscovado sugar	1½ tablespoons Barbados sugar
25 g / 1 oz fresh yeast	1 cake compressed yeast
450 ml / ¾ pint lukewarm water	2 cups lukewarm water
1 tablespoon oil	1 tablespoon oil

Put the flour, salt and sugar in a warm bowl and mix well. Blend the yeast with a little of the water, then stir into the remaining water and add to the dry ingredients with the oil. Mix to a soft dough.

Turn out onto a lightly floured surface and knead for 5 minutes until smooth. Place the dough in a warm, greased bowl. Cover and leave in a warm place for about 15 minutes until doubled in size.

Turn out onto the floured surface and knead again for 2 minutes, then divide the dough into 12 pieces and shape into round flat baps (buns). Place the baps (buns) on greased, warmed baking sheets and sprinkle with a little wholemeal (wholewheat) flour. Cover with a piece of oiled polythene (plastic) and leave to rise in a warm place until doubled in size.

Bake in a preheated hot oven (220°C / 425°F, Gas Mark 7) for 15 minutes. Remove the baps (buns) from the baking sheets, then wrap them in a clean cloth; this will keep them soft by trapping the steam as they cool.

Makes 12 baps (buns)

Cheese Loaf

Metric/Imperial	American
225 g / 8 oz wholemeal bread flour	2 cups wholewheat flour
1 teaspoon sea salt	1 teaspoon coarse salt
1 teaspoon mustard powder	1 teaspoon mustard powder
100 g / 4 oz Cheddar cheese, grated	1 cup grated Cheddar cheese
15 g / ½ oz fresh yeast	½ cake compressed yeast
150 ml / ¼ pint lukewarm water	⅔ cup lukewarm water

Put the flour, salt, mustard and cheese in a warm bowl and mix well. Blend the yeast with a little of the water, then stir into the remaining water and add to the dry ingredients. Mix to a soft dough.

Turn out onto a lightly floured surface and knead for 5 minutes until smooth. Place the dough in a warm, greased bowl. Cover and leave in a warm place for about 1 hour until doubled in size.

Turn out onto the floured surface and knead again for 2 minutes, then fold into 3 and place in a greased, warmed 450 g / 1 lb / 8 × 4½ × 2½ inch loaf tin. Cover with a clean cloth and leave in a warm place for about 20 minutes until the dough rises to the top of the tin.

Bake in a preheated hot oven (220°C / 425°F, Gas Mark 7) for 10 minutes, then reduce the heat to moderately hot (190°C / 375°F, Gas Mark 5) and bake for a further 35 minutes. Turn out onto a wire rack and leave to cool.

Makes one 450 g / 1 lb loaf

Fruit Malt Loaf

Metric/Imperial	American
225 g / 8 oz wholemeal flour	2 cups wholewheat flour
¼ teaspoon sea salt	¼ teaspoon coarse salt
100 g / 4 oz sultanas	¾ cup seedless white raisins
25 g / 1 oz vegetable margarine	2 tablespoons vegetable margarine
50 g / 2 oz malt extract	3 tablespoons malt extract
25 g / 1 oz black treacle	1½ tablespoons molasses
25 g / 1 oz fresh yeast	1 cake compressed yeast
75 ml / 2½ fl oz lukewarm water	⅓ cup lukewarm water
1 tablespoon clear honey to glaze	1 tablespoon clear honey to glaze

Put the flour, salt and sultanas (seedless white raisins) in a warm bowl and mix well. Put the margarine, malt extract and black treacle (molasses) in a pan and heat gently until the margarine has melted. Leave to cool for 5 minutes.

Blend the yeast with the water, then add to the dry ingredients with the melted mixture. Mix to a soft dough.

Turn out onto a lightly floured surface and knead for 5 minutes until smooth. Place the dough in a warmed, greased bowl. Cover and leave in a warm place for about 1 hour until doubled in size.

Turn out onto the floured surface and knead again for 5 minutes. Fold the dough into 3, then place in a greased, warmed 450 g / 1 lb / 8 × 4½ × 2½ inch loaf tin. Cover with a clean damp cloth and leave in a warm place for about 20 minutes until the dough rises to the top of the tin.

Bake in a preheated moderately hot oven (200°C / 400°F, Gas Mark 6) for 45 minutes. Turn out onto a wire rack, brush with honey, then leave to cool.

Makes one 450 g / 1 lb loaf

Farmhouse Scones

Metric/Imperial	American
225 g / 8 oz wholemeal flour	2 cups wholewheat flour
pinch of sea salt	pinch of coarse salt
1 teaspoon baking powder	1 teaspoon baking powder
50 g / 2 oz vegetable margarine	1/4 cup vegetable margarine
25 g / 1 oz Muscovado sugar	1 1/2 tablespoons Barbados sugar
25 g / 1 oz sultanas	3 tablespoons seedless white raisins
1 egg	1 egg
5 tablespoons milk	1/3 cup milk
milk to glaze	milk to glaze

Put the flour, salt and baking powder in a bowl and mix well. Rub in the margarine until the mixture resembles coarse breadcrumbs, then stir in the sugar and sultanas (seedless white raisins). Beat the egg with the milk, then gradually add to the dry mixture and mix to a soft dough.

Cottage Cheese Griddlecakes

Metric/Imperial	American
25 g / 1 oz vegetable margarine, melted	2 tablespoons vegetable margarine, melted
100 g / 4 oz cottage cheese	1/2 cup cottage cheese
2 eggs, beaten	2 eggs, beaten
50 g / 2 oz wholemeal self-raising flour	1/2 cup wholewheat self-rising flour
1 tablespoon milk	1 tablespoon milk

Put the margarine and cottage cheese in a bowl and mix well. Beat in the eggs, then stir in the flour and milk and beat to a smooth thick batter.

Grease a griddle or heavy-based frying pan (skillet) very lightly with fat, then heat until very hot.

Drop tablespoonfuls of the batter onto the hot surface. Cook for 1 minute until just set, then turn over and cook for a further 1 minute. Turn over again and continue cooking until the griddlecakes are set and golden in colour.

Transfer to a wire rack and cover with a clean cloth to keep hot while cooking the remaining batter. Serve hot with honey or a savoury spread.

Makes 10 to 12 griddlecakes

ABOVE: Cottage cheese griddlecakes
RIGHT: Yogurt wholewheat scones; Farmhouse scones

Turn out onto a lightly floured surface and roll out to 1 cm / ¹/₂ inch thickness. Cut out 12 rounds with a 5 cm / 2 inch biscuit cutter and place on a greased baking sheet.

Brush the tops with a little milk to glaze, then bake in a preheated moderately hot oven (200°C / 400°F, Gas Mark 6) for 15 minutes. Transfer to a wire rack and leave to cool.

Makes 12 scones

Yogurt Wholewheat Scones

Metric/Imperial
225 g / 8 oz wholemeal
 flour
¹/₂ teaspoon salt
1¹/₂ teaspoons baking
 powder
25 g / 1 oz vegetable
 margarine
150 ml / ¹/₄ pint natural
 yogurt

American
2 cups wholewheat flour
¹/₂ teaspoon salt
1¹/₂ teaspoons baking
 powder
2 tablespoons vegetable
 margarine
²/₃ cup unflavored yogurt

Put the flour, salt and baking powder in a bowl and stir well to mix. Rub in the margarine, then stir in the yogurt and mix to a soft dough.

Turn out onto a lightly floured surface and knead lightly for 30 seconds. Roll out to 2 cm / ³/₄ inch thickness, cut out 10 rounds with a 5 cm / 2 inch biscuit cutter and place on a greased baking sheet.

Bake in a preheated moderately hot oven (200°C / 400°F, Gas Mark 6) for 12 minutes. Transfer to a wire rack and leave to cool. Serve with honey or a cheese spread.

Makes 10 scones

Honey Fruit Loaf

Metric/Imperial	American
75 g / 3 oz vegetable margarine	1/3 cup vegetable margarine
75 g / 3 oz Muscovado sugar	1/2 cup Barbados sugar
1 egg. beaten	1 egg, beaten
2 tablespoons honey	2 tablespoons honey
225 g / 8 oz wholemeal self-raising flour	2 cups wholewheat self-rising flour
1/4 teaspoon salt	1/4 teaspoon salt
1 teaspoon ground mixed spice	1/2 teaspoon ground allspice
175 g / 6 oz mixed dried fruit	1/2 teaspoon ground cinnamon
4 tablespoons milk	1 cup mixed dried fruit
	1/4 cup milk

Cream the margarine and sugar until light and fluffy, then beat in the egg and honey. Stir in the flour, salt and spice, then beat in the fruit and milk until thoroughly mixed.

Spoon the mixture into a greased 750 g / 1½ lb / 10 × 4 × 4 inch loaf pan, then bake in a preheated moderately hot oven (190°C / 375°F, Gas Mark 5) for 45 minutes. Turn out onto a wire rack and leave to cool.

Makes one 750 g / 1½ lb fruit loaf

Walnut Squares

Metric/Imperial	American
1 egg, beaten	1 egg, beaten
225 g / 8 oz Muscovado sugar	1 1/3 cups Barbados sugar
75 g / 3 oz wholemeal flour	3/4 cup wholewheat flour
1 teaspoon bicarbonate of soda	1 teaspoon baking soda
1/4 teaspoon salt	1/4 teaspoon salt
100 g / 4 oz walnuts, finely chopped	1 cup finely chopped walnuts

Put the egg and sugar in a bowl and mix well. Mix the flour, soda and salt together, then stir into the egg mixture. Stir in the nuts.

Spread the mixture in a greased 20 cm / 8 inch square tin (pan). Bake in a preheated moderate oven (180°C / 350°F, Gas Mark 4) for 20 minutes. Leave to cool in the tin, then cut into squares before serving.

Makes 16 squares

Honey Cake

Metric/Imperial	American
100 g / 4 oz vegetable margarine	1/2 cup vegetable margarine
50 g / 2 oz Muscovado sugar	1/3 cup Barbados sugar
3 tablespoons honey	3 tablespoons honey
2 eggs, lightly beaten	2 eggs, lightly beaten
225 g / 8 oz wholemeal flour	2 cups wholewheat flour
1 tablespoon baking powder	1 tablespoon baking powder
1 teaspoon ground cinnamon	1 teaspoon ground cinnamon
120 ml / 4 fl oz milk (approximately)	1/2 cup milk (approximately)
25 g / 1 oz flaked almonds	1/4 cup sliced almonds

Cream the margarine and sugar until light and fluffy, then beat in the honey. Add the eggs a little at a time, adding a little of the flour after each addition.

Mix the remaining flour with the baking powder and cinnamon, then beat into the creamed mixture with enough milk to make a soft dropping consistency.

Sprinkle the almonds over the base of a greased 18 cm / 7 inch square cake tin. Spoon in the mixture.

Bake in a preheated moderate oven (180°C / 350°F, Gas Mark 4) for 1 hour. Turn out onto a wire rack and leave to cool.

Makes one 18 cm / 7 inch square cake

Parkin

Metric/Imperial
100 g / 4 oz wholemeal
  flour
350 g / 12 oz medium
  oatmeal
1 teaspoon ground ginger
100 g / 4 oz vegetable
  margarine
100 g / 4 oz honey
100 g / 4 oz black treacle
4 tablespoons milk
½ teaspoon bicarbonate of
  soda

American
1 cup wholewheat flour
2 cups medium oatmeal
1 teaspoon ground ginger
½ cup vegetable margarine
⅓ cup honey
⅓ cup molasses
¼ cup milk
½ teaspoon baking soda

Put the flour, oatmeal and ginger in a bowl and mix well. Put the margarine, honey and black treacle (molasses) in a pan and heat gently until the margarine has melted. Add to the dry ingredients and mix well.

Heat the milk until lukewarm, stir in the soda, then add to the flour mixture and beat well. Pour the mixture into a greased 28 × 18 cm / 11 × 7 inch cake tin.

Bake in a preheated moderate oven (160°C / 325°F, Gas Mark 3) for 1½ hours. Leave to cool in the tin for 10 minutes, then turn out onto a wire rack and leave to cool completely.

Store in an airtight tin for 3 to 4 days before cutting.
Makes one 28 × 18 cm / 11 × 7 inch cake

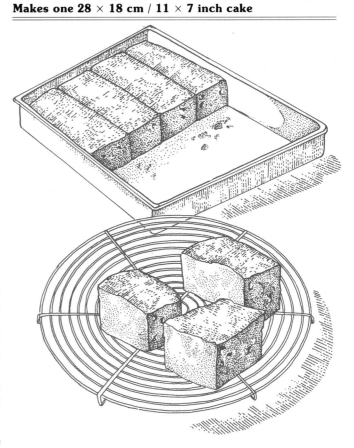

Ginger Honey Cake

Metric/Imperial
75 g / 3 oz vegetable
  margarine
50 g / 2 oz Muscovado
  sugar
2 tablespoons honey
1 egg, beaten with 1 egg
  yolk
175 g / 6 oz wholemeal
  self-raising flour
pinch of salt
1 teaspoon ground ginger
1 teaspoon ground
  cinnamon
6 tablespoons milk
  (approximately)

American
⅓ cup vegetable margarine
⅓ cup Barbados sugar
2 tablespoons honey
1 egg, beaten with 1 egg
  yolk
1½ cups wholewheat
  self-rising flour
pinch of salt
1 teaspoon ground ginger
1 teaspoon ground
  cinnamon
6 tablespoons milk
  (approximately)

Cream the margarine and sugar until light and fluffy, then beat in the honey. Add the egg mixture a little at a time, adding a little of the flour after each addition.

Mix the remaining flour with the salt, ginger and cinnamon, then beat into the creamed mixture with enough milk to make a soft dropping consistency.

Spoon the mixture into a greased 18 cm / 7 inch round cake tin lined with greased greaseproof paper or non-stick parchment.

Bake in a preheated moderate oven (180°C / 350°F, Gas Mark 4) for 50 minutes. Turn out onto a wire rack, carefully remove the paper and leave to cool.
Makes one 18 cm / 7 inch round cake

Oatmeal crunchies (page 144); Wholewheat cheese biscuits (crackers); Digestive biscuits (Graham crackers); Fruit slices; Nutty fruit chews

Nutty Fruit Chews

For these, use a mixture of raisins, sultanas (seedless white raisins), figs, dates, prunes and apricots.

Metric/Imperial	American
450 g / 1 lb mixed dried fruit	3 cups mixed dried fruit
100 g / 4 oz chopped mixed nuts	1 cup chopped mixed nuts
100 g / 4 oz clear honey	1/3 cup clear honey

Put the large fruit in a bowl and pour on enough boiling water to cover. Leave to stand for 5 minutes, then drain off the water. Put all the fruit through the fine blade of a mincer (grinder), then stir in the nuts and honey until well mixed.

Spread the mixture in a 20 cm / 8 inch square tin lined with foil. Cover with more foil, then place weights on top so that the surface is evenly pressed down. Leave in a cool place for 12 hours. Cut into squares before serving.

Makes 16 squares

Fruit Slices

Metric/Imperial	American
wholewheat pastry made with 225 g / 8 oz flour (see page 145)	wholewheat dough made with 2 cups flour (see page 145)
100 g / 4 oz currants	²/₃ cup currants
100 g / 4 oz sultanas	²/₃ cup seedless white raisins
1 large cooking apple, peeled, cored and grated	1 large baking apple, peeled, cored and grated
finely grated rind of 1 orange	finely grated rind of 1 orange
juice of ¹/₂ lemon	juice of ¹/₂ lemon
50 g / 2 oz demerara sugar	¹/₃ cup raw sugar
TOPPING:	TOPPING:
1 egg white, lightly beaten	1 egg white, lightly beaten
little demerara sugar	little raw sugar

Divide the pastry dough in half. Roll out one piece and use to line the base of a shallow 28 × 20 cm / 11 × 8 inch tin.

Mix the fruit, orange rind, lemon juice and sugar together, then spread this mixture over the dough. Roll out the remaining dough and use to cover the fruit mixture.

Brush with egg white and sprinkle with sugar. Bake in a preheated hot oven (220°C / 425°F, Gas Mark 7) for 25 minutes. Leave to cool in the tin. Cut into slices before serving.

Makes 16 slices

Digestive Biscuits (Graham Crackers)

Metric/Imperial	American
350 g / 12 oz wholemeal flour	3 cups wholewheat flour
2 teaspoons sea salt	2 teaspoons coarse salt
150 g / 5 oz vegetable margarine	⁵/₈ cup vegetable margarine
50 g / 2 oz Muscovado sugar	¹/₃ cup Barbados sugar
1 egg, beaten with 4 tablespoons cold water	1 egg, beaten with ¹/₄ cup cold water

Put the flour and salt in a bowl, then rub in the margarine until the mixture resembles fine breadcrumbs. Stir in the sugar, then add the egg and water mixture and mix to a soft dough.

Turn out onto a lightly floured surface and knead lightly. Roll out to 5 mm / ¹/₄ inch thickness, then cut out 40 rounds with a 6 cm / 2¹/₂ inch biscuit cutter.

Place the rounds on greased baking sheets and prick each one 4 times with a fork. Bake in a preheated moderate oven (180°C / 350°F, Gas Mark 4) for 25 minutes. Transfer to a wire rack and leave to cool.

Makes 40 biscuits (crackers)

Wholewheat Cheese Biscuits (Crackers)

Metric/Imperial	American
100 g / 4 oz wholemeal flour	1 cup wholewheat flour
¹/₂ teaspoon sea salt	¹/₂ teaspoon coarse salt
1 teaspoon mustard powder	1 teaspoon mustard powder
25 g / 1 oz vegetable margarine	2 tablespoons vegetable margarine
225 g / 8 oz Cheddar cheese, finely grated	2 cups finely grated Cheddar cheese
2 tablespoons cold water	2 tablespoons cold water

Put the flour, salt and mustard in a bowl and mix well. Rub in the margarine, then stir in the cheese. Add the water and mix to a firm dough.

Turn out onto a lightly floured surface and knead lightly. Roll out to 5 mm / ¹/₄ inch thickness, then cut out 30 rounds with a 5 cm / 2 inch biscuit cutter.

Place the rounds on greased baking sheets and prick each one 3 times with a fork. Bake in a preheated hot oven (230°C / 450°F, Gas Mark 8) for 6 minutes. Transfer to a wire rack and leave to cool.

Makes 30 biscuits (crackers)

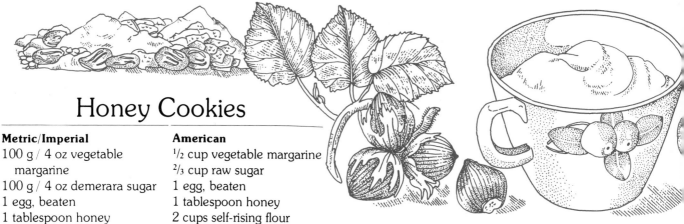

Honey Cookies

Metric/Imperial	American
100 g / 4 oz vegetable margarine	½ cup vegetable margarine
100 g / 4 oz demerara sugar	⅔ cup raw sugar
1 egg, beaten	1 egg, beaten
1 tablespoon honey	1 tablespoon honey
225 g / 8 oz self-raising flour	2 cups self-rising flour
pinch of salt	pinch of salt
50 g / 2 oz chopped mixed nuts	½ cup chopped mixed nuts

Cream the margarine and sugar until light and fluffy, then beat in the egg and honey. Sift the flour and salt together, then beat gradually into the creamed mixture. Add the nuts and mix well.

Divide the dough into 36 pieces, about the size of walnuts, and roll each one into a ball. Place on greased baking sheets, flattening each ball with a fork dipped in cold water. Bake in a preheated moderate oven (180°C / 350°F, Gas Mark 4) for 12 minutes. Transfer carefully to a wire rack and leave to cool.

Makes 36 cookies

Oatmeal Crunchies

Metric/Imperial	American
225 g / 8 oz wholemeal flour	2 cups wholewheat flour
75 g / 3 oz medium oatmeal	½ cup oatmeal
75 g / 3 oz bran	1½ cups bran
150 g / 5 oz Muscovado sugar	¾ cup Barbados sugar
½ teaspoon ground ginger	½ teaspoon ground ginger
½ teaspoon ground mixed spice	¼ teaspoon ground allspice
100 g / 4 oz vegetable margarine	¼ teaspoon ground cinnamon
150 ml / ¼ pint cold water (approximately)	½ cup vegetable margarine
	⅔ cup cold water (approximately)

Put the dry ingredients in a bowl and mix well. Rub in the margarine until the mixture resembles coarse breadcrumbs, then add enough water to make a stiff dough.

Turn out onto a lightly floured surface, then roll out to 1 cm / ½ inch thickness. Cut out 48 rounds with a 6 cm / 2½ inch biscuit cutter.

Place on greased baking sheets, then bake in a preheated moderate oven (180°C / 350°F, Gas Mark 4) for 25 minutes. Transfer to a wire rack and leave to cool.

Makes 48 crunchies

Muesli Flapjacks

Metric/Imperial	American
150 g / 5 oz vegetable margarine	2/3 cup vegetable margarine
75 g / 3 oz Muscovado sugar	1/2 cup Barbados sugar
1 tablespoon honey	1 tablespoon honey
225 g / 8 oz muesli	1 1/2 cups muesli
50 g / 2 oz hazelnuts, chopped	1/2 cup chopped filberts

Heat the margarine gently in a pan until melted. Remove from the heat and stir in the sugar and honey. Add the muesli and nuts and mix thoroughly.

Press the mixture firmly into a greased 18 cm / 7 inch square cake tin. Bake in a preheated moderately hot oven (190°C / 375°F, Gas Mark 5) for 25 minutes. Mark into 9 squares while still hot, then leave in the tin until almost cold. Transfer carefully to a wire rack and leave to cool completely.

Makes 9 flapjacks

Wholewheat Pastry

The best flour to use for this pastry is 85 per cent wholemeal (wholewheat). For sweet pies and flans, 25 g / 1 oz / 1 1/2 tablespoons Muscovado (Barbados) sugar may be added to the pastry, before mixing in the liquid.

Metric/Imperial	American
225 g / 8 oz wholemeal flour	2 cups wholewheat flour
pinch of salt	pinch of salt
100 g / 4 oz vegetable margarine	1/2 cup vegetable margarine
2 egg yolks	2 egg yolks
1 tablespoon cold water	1 tablespoon cold water

Put the flour and salt in a bowl, then rub in the margarine until the mixture resembles fine breadcrumbs. Beat the egg yolks with the water, then add to the dry mixture and mix to a dough.

As this pastry is a little difficult to handle, it is best to roll it out on a piece of foil so that it can be easily lifted.

Date and Hazelnut (Filbert) Fingers

Metric/Imperial	American
2 eggs	2 eggs
175 g / 6 oz Muscovado sugar ·	1 cup Barbados sugar
75 g / 3 oz wholemeal self-raising flour	3/4 cup wholewheat self-rising flour
pinch of salt	pinch of salt
50 g / 2 oz bran cereal	1 cup bran cereal
50 g / 2 oz hazelnuts, chopped	1/2 cup chopped filberts
100 g / 4 oz stoned dates, chopped	2/3 cup chopped, pitted dates

Put the eggs and sugar in a bowl and whisk until light and creamy. Stir in the remaining ingredients and mix thoroughly.

Spread the mixture evenly in a 28 × 18 cm / 11 × 7 inch tin lined with greased greaseproof paper or non-stick parchment.

Bake in a preheated moderate oven (180°C / 350°F, Gas Mark 4) for 30 minutes. Leave to cool in the tin. Cut into slices before serving.

Makes 12 fingers

DRINKS

A healthy body requires a considerable amount of liquid to function properly. Drinks can vary from a refreshing thirst-quenching drink, containing very few nutrients, to a complete healthy meal in a glass; they can be a slimming fruit juice or a herbal tea, or a body building milky drink.

Juices made from vegetables and fruits will provide all the nutrients of the particular food, though considerably less if diluted with water. Milk shakes, made by blending fresh fruit with milk, provide a very healthy drink; they are also very refreshing made with yogurt instead of milk.

Hot milk drinks, sometimes enriched with eggs and flavoured with liqueurs and spices, make a satisfying bedtime or winter drink. Herbal tea has long been thought to cure minor ailments. Such claims may not be true, but it is certainly a refreshing drink – especially mixed with lemon juice.

Some people find it difficult or time-consuming to eat a proper breakfast – a nourishing drink based on fruits, milk, yogurt and eggs is the perfect solution.

If you drink a lot of fruit and vegetable juice it might be worth investing in a special juice extractor, but the following juices can all be made using an electric blender.

Citrus Sparkler

Metric/Imperial	American
1 small grapefruit	1 small grapefruit
2 small oranges	2 small oranges
1 lemon	1 lemon
50 g / 2 oz soft brown sugar	1/3 cup brown sugar
600 ml / 1 pint water	2 1/2 cups water
1 small orange or lemon, sliced, to serve	1 small orange or lemon, sliced, to serve

Wash the fruit, then chop coarsely, including the peel, pith and pips (seeds). Place in an electric blender with the sugar and water. Blend for about 5 seconds until the fruit is chopped into small pieces. (Do not blend any longer or the pith will make the juice bitter.)

Strain into a bowl, then chill in the refrigerator until required. Pour into individual glasses, add ice cubes and float orange or lemon slices on the top before serving.
Makes about 750 ml / 1 1/4 pints / 3 cups juice

Peach Yogurt Shake

This refreshing, creamy drink can be served at any time of day.

Metric/Imperial	American
2 large ripe peaches, skinned, halved and stoned	2 large ripe peaches, skinned, halved and pitted
juice of 2 oranges	juice of 2 oranges
600 ml / 1 pint natural yogurt	2 1/2 cups unflavored yogurt

Put all the ingredients in an electric blender and work to a smooth purée. Transfer to a bowl, then chill in the refrigerator until required.
Makes about 900 ml / 1 1/2 pints / 3 3/4 cups juice

Rose Hip Syrup

Rose hips are rich in vitamin C. This syrup makes a refreshing drink when diluted with water, or added to milk shakes.

Metric/Imperial	American
1 kg / 2 lb ripe rose hips	2 lb ripe rose hips
2 lemons, coarsely chopped	2 lemons, coarsely chopped
2 litres / 3½ pints water	4½ pints (9 cups) water
450 g / 1 lb sugar	2 cups sugar

Mince (grind) the rose hips and lemons coarsely together, then place in a large pan. Pour over the water, bring to the boil, then simmer for 5 minutes. Strain through a jelly bag and leave to drip overnight, or for at least 2 hours.

Transfer the juice to a pan and bring to the boil. Add the sugar and heat gently until the sugar has dissolved, stirring constantly. Bring to the boil, then boil for 5 minutes.

Pour the hot syrup into warmed bottles. Seal with screw tops or corks, then store in the refrigerator for up to 2 weeks.

If longer storage is required, preserve the syrup by heat process: fill sterilized screw-topped bottles with hot syrup to within 2.5 cm / 1 inch of the top. Loosely fit the screw tops, then place the bottles in a deep pan as for bottling.

Fill the pan with cold water up to the level of the syrup in the bottles, bring to simmering point, then simmer for 20 minutes. Remove the bottles from the water and screw the tops tightly. Rose hip syrup preserved by this method will keep for up to 6 months.

Makes about 1.2 litres / 2 pints / 5 cups juice

Mulled Apple Juice

Metric/Imperial	American
450 g / 1 lb cooking apples, peeled, cored and sliced	1 lb baking apples, peeled, cored and sliced
600 ml / 1 pint water	2½ cups water
finely grated rind and juice of 2 oranges	finely grated rind and juice of 2 oranges
6 tablespoons honey	6 tablespoons honey
6 cloves, or large pinch of ground cloves	6 cloves, or large pinch of ground cloves
1 cinnamon stick, or pinch of ground cinnamon	1 cinnamon stick, or pinch of ground cinnamon
pinch of ground ginger	pinch of ground ginger
2 tablespoons rum or brandy	2 tablespoons rum or brandy

Put all the ingredients in a pan, except the rum or brandy. Bring to the boil, then lower the heat, cover and simmer for 10 minutes until the apples are reduced to a pulp.

Transfer to an electric blender and blend until the apples are smooth, but the whole spices, if used, are still in pieces.

Strain, stir in the rum or brandy and serve hot.

Makes 900 ml / 1½ pints / 3¾ cups juice

Old-Fashioned Raspberry Vinegar

This old-fashioned recipe is said to be good for sore throats. It can be drunk neat as a liqueur, or diluted with water or soda and served as a refreshing drink with ice cubes.

Metric/Imperial	American
450 g / 1 lb raspberries, washed and hulled	3 cups raspberries, washed and hulled
600 ml / 1 pint wine vinegar	2½ cups wine vinegar
450 g / 1 lb sugar	2 cups sugar

Put the raspberries in a bowl, then crush with a wooden spoon. Pour over the vinegar, cover and leave to stand for about 4 days, stirring occasionally.

Strain the vinegar into a pan without pressing the pulp through the sieve (strainer). Add the sugar and heat gently until dissolved, stirring constantly. Bring to the boil, then boil for 5 minutes until syrupy.

Leave to cool, then pour into clean, dry bottles. Seal with a cork or screw top and store in the refrigerator for up to 6 months.

Makes about 750 ml / 1½ pints / 3 cups juice

Tomato and Orange Juice

Metric/Imperial	American
450 g / 1 lb tomatoes, roughly chopped	2 cups roughly chopped tomatoes
1 small onion, peeled and chopped	1 small onion, peeled and chopped
finely grated rind and juice of 2 oranges	finely grated rind and juice of 2 oranges
300 ml / ½ pint water	1¼ cups water
1 mint sprig	1 mint sprig
1 tablespoon soft brown sugar	1 tablespoon brown sugar
1 teaspoon Worcestershire sauce	1 teaspoon Worcestershire sauce
salt	salt
freshly ground black pepper	freshly ground black pepper
few mint sprigs to garnish	few mint sprigs to garnish

Put all the ingredients, except the garnish, in a pan. Bring to the boil, then lower the heat, cover and simmer for 10 minutes until the tomatoes are reduced to a pulp.

Transfer the mixture to an electric blender. Work to a smooth purée, then rub through a sieve (strainer) into a bowl.

Chill in the refrigerator until required. Garnish with mint sprigs just before serving.

Makes about 600 ml / 1 pint / 2½ cups juice

Salad Vegetable Juice

This is similar to a gazpacho soup – a variety of vegetables are blended with yogurt, then sieved to give a thick vegetable juice.

Metric/Imperial	American
4 tomatoes, quartered	4 tomatoes, quartered
1 onion, peeled and chopped	1 onion, peeled and chopped
1 green pepper, cored, seeded and chopped	1 green pepper, cored, seeded and chopped
2 carrots, peeled and chopped	2 carrots, peeled and chopped
10 cm / 4 inch piece cucumber, chopped	4 inch piece cucumber, chopped
finely grated rind and juice of ½ lemon	finely grated rind and juice of ½ lemon
300 ml / ½ pint natural yogurt	1¼ cups unflavored yogurt
150 ml / ¼ pint water	⅔ cup water
salt	salt
freshly ground white pepper	freshly ground white pepper
TO GARNISH:	TO GARNISH:
few thin lemon slices	few thin lemon slices
few thin cucumber slices	few thin cucumber slices

Put all the ingredients, except the garnish, in an electric blender. Work to a smooth purée, then rub through a sieve (strainer) into a jug.

Chill in the refrigerator until required. Garnish with lemon and cucumber slices just before serving.

Makes about 900 ml / 1½ pints / 3¾ cups juice

Herb and Lemon Tea

Herbs and lemon make a refreshing hot drink, which is said to be good for all sorts of minor ailments such as headaches, colds, etc.

Metric/Imperial	American
1 tablespoon coarsely chopped herbs (mint, rosemary, thyme)	1 tablespoon coarsely chopped herbs (mint, rosemary, thyme)
finely grated rind and juice of ½ small lemon	finely grated rind and juice of ½ small lemon
600 ml / 1 pint boiling water	2½ cups boiling water

Put the herbs, lemon rind and juice in a bowl. Pour over the boiling water, cover and leave to infuse for 3 to 5 minutes. Strain into cups and serve hot.

Makes 600 ml / 1 pint / 2½ cups tea

Spiced Orange Tea

Tea, flavoured with orange and spices, makes a refreshing drink that can be served hot or cold.

Metric/Imperial	American
1 litre / 1¾ pints water	4¼ cups water
finely grated rind and juice of 2 large oranges	finely grated rind and juice of 2 large oranges
1 cinnamon stick	1 cinnamon stick
½ teaspoon cloves	½ teaspoon cloves
2 tablespoons tea leaves	2 tablespoons tea leaves
1 small orange, sliced, to serve	1 small orange, sliced, to serve

Put the water, orange rind, juice and spices in a pan. Bring to the boil, then pour over the tea leaves in a warmed tea pot or bowl. Cover and leave to infuse for 5 to 10 minutes. Strain and serve hot or cold with the orange slices floating on top.

Makes about 1.2 litres / 2 pints / 5 cups tea

Egg Nog

This foamy hot milk drink is best at bedtime.

Metric/Imperial	American
300 ml / ½ pint milk	1½ cups milk
1 egg, separated	1 egg, separated
1 tablespoon soft brown sugar	1 tablespoon brown sugar
1 tablespoon ground almonds	1 tablespoon ground almonds
1 tablespoon brandy, rum or sherry	1 tablespoon brandy, rum or sherry
TO SERVE:	TO SERVE:
grated nutmeg	grated nutmeg
ground cinnamon	ground cinnamon

Heat the milk in a pan to just below boiling point. Whisk the egg yolk in a bowl with the sugar and almonds, then stir in the brandy, rum or sherry. Pour on the hot milk, whisking constantly.

Beat the egg white until just stiff, then fold into the milk. Pour into mugs and sprinkle generously with nutmeg and cinnamon. Serve hot.

Serves 2

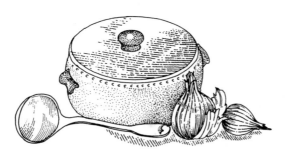

MENUS

Daily Menus for Vegetarians

Breakfast
Fruit Muesli with Yogurt

Lunch
Mixed Vegetable Curry
Brown Rice
Cucumber and Tomato Raita
Rhubarb, Orange and Ginger Fool

Supper
Broccoli Pancakes (Crêpes)
Spiced Fruit Compote

Breakfast
Morning Starter
Scrambled Eggs, Wholewheat Toast

Lunch
Cheese and Bread Salad
Blackberry and Orange Stuffed Apples

Supper
Minestrone Soup
Wholewheat Baps (Buns)
Fruit Slices

Breakfast
Breakfast in a Glass

Lunch
Herb and Nut Roast
Broccoli
Plum and Orange Cobbler

Supper
Wholewheat Pizza
Green Salad
Sunshine Fruit Salad

Breakfast
Citrus Starter
Poached Eggs and Wholewheat Toast

Lunch
Mediterranean Lentil Stew
Mixed Salad
Wholewheat Bread
Minted Apple Snow

Supper
Cauliflower Cheese Timbale
Walnut Pie

Dinner Party Menus

Starter

Guacamole, Wholewheat Toast

Main Course

Baked Trout
French Beans   Duchesse Potatoes
Green Salad

Dessert

Peach and Raspberry Cheesecake

Starter

Marinated Mushrooms with
Prawns (Shrimp)

Main Course

Roast Veal with Orange Juice
Spinach Fried with Garlic
Creamed Potatoes

Dessert

Almond and Strawberry Malakoff

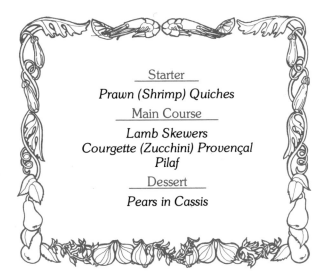

Starter

Prawn (Shrimp) Quiches

Main Course

Lamb Skewers
Courgette (Zucchini) Provençal
Pilaf

Dessert

Pears in Cassis

Starter

Sailors' Mussels
Wholewheat Bread

Main Course

Spring Beef Casserole
Celery with Orange and Nuts
Baked Potatoes in their skins

Dessert

Bramble Mousse

Starter

Avocado, Grapefruit and
Sesame Salad

Main Course

Italian Liver
Brown Rice   Spinach
Mixed Salad

Dessert

Spiced Apple and Cranberry Pie

Starter

Black Eye Fish Hors d'Oeuvres

Main Course

Chicken and Olive Bake
Broccoli   Noodles

Dessert

Strawberry and Orange Soufflé

Vegetarian Menu

Starter
Slimmers' Watercress Soup
Wholewheat Bread

Main Course
Soyabean Moussaka
Braised Cabbage   Creamed Potatoes

Dessert
Raspberry Chantilly

Summer Menus

Monday

Breakfast
Meusli

Lunch
Baked Crab
Peach Yogurt Shake

Dinner
Cucumber, Lemon and Mint Soup
Spring Beef Casserole
Hot Berry Snow

Tuesday

Breakfast
Scrambled Eggs

Lunch
Swedish Pickled Shrimp
Pineapple Sorbet (Sherbet)

Dinner
Fish Roe Stuffed Eggs
Lamb Skewers
Rhubarb, Orange and Ginger Fool

Wednesday

Breakfast
Poached Eggs on Wholewheat Toast

Lunch
Tomato and Orange Juice
Smoked Haddock Flan
Hazelnut (Filbert) and Raspberry Torte

Dinner
Chick Pea (Garbanzos) Salad
Chicken and Olive Bake
Gooseberry and Almond Crumble

Thursday

Breakfast
Baked Tomato Eggs

Lunch
Summer Fish Salad
Apricot Tart

Dinner
Chilled Pea Soup
Lamb and Vegetable Casserole
Blackcurrant and Orange Ice Cream

Friday

Breakfast
Banana Flip

Lunch
Salad Vegetable Juice
Pasta with Ratatouille Sauce
Spiced Stuffed Peaches

Dinner
Tomato Tart
Swedish Baked Fish
Strawberry and Orange Soufflé

Saturday

Breakfast
Fruit Muesli with Yogurt

Lunch
Egg Mousse
Seafood Curry
Cherry Custard Pudding

Tea
Cottage Cheese Griddlecakes
Fruit Slices

Sunday

Breakfast
Country Grill (Broil)

Lunch
Baked Stuffed Tomatoes
Roast Veal with Orange Juice
Peach and Raspberry Cheesecake

Tea
Farmhouse Scones
Muesli Flapjacks

Winter Menus

Monday

Breakfast
Prune Fluff

Lunch
Soft Roes on Toast
Spiced Fruit Compote

Dinner
Leeks à la Grècque
Meat-Stuffed Marrow (Squash)
Orange and Lemon Mousse

Tuesday

Breakfast
Wholewheat Crêpes

Lunch
Cold Lamb in Mint Aspic
Baked Grapefruit Soufflé

Dinner
Italian Bean Soup
Trout in Yogurt Sauce
Black Pear Pudding

Wednesday

Breakfast
Granola

Lunch
Spiced Fish Casserole
French Orange Flans

Dinner
Herb Pâté
Vegetable Kebabs with Pilaf
Minted Apple Snow

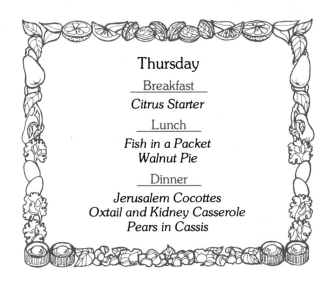

Thursday

Breakfast
Citrus Starter

Lunch
Fish in a Packet
Walnut Pie

Dinner
Jerusalem Cocottes
Oxtail and Kidney Casserole
Pears in Cassis

Friday

Breakfast
Spiced Grapefruit Refresher

Lunch
Sailors' Mussels
Apricot Syllabub

Dinner
Slimmers' Watercress Soup
Stuffed Cabbage Leaves
Bramble Mousse

Saturday

Breakfast
Poached Haddock and Eggs

Lunch
Minestrone
Baked Liver in Yogurt Sauce
Plum and Orange Cobbler

Tea
Bran Bread with honey
Parkin

Bedtime Drink
Egg Nog

Sunday

Breakfast
Farmhouse Scramble

Lunch
Chestnut Soup
Herbed Chicken
Spiced Cranberry and Apple Pie

Tea
Walnut Squares
Honey Fruit Loaf

Bedtime Drink
Mulled Apple Juice

FOOD ENERGY VALUES

The following chart provides a comprehensive list of food calorie (kcal) and kilojoule (kJ) values. Unless otherwise stated, the values refer to a quantity of 27.35 g/1 oz and this is the edible portion, i.e. without bone, skin, etc.

Food	Energy Value kcal	kJ
Almond, shelled and flaked	172	719
Anchovy fillets	40	168
Apples, raw	11-15	46-63
Apples, baked	9	38
Apples, dried	50	209
Apples, stewed	8	33
Apple purée or sauce	8	33
Apple juice	10	42
Apricot, raw	11	46
Apricot, stewed	17	71
Apricot, dried	50	209
Apricot, canned, halves	30	125
Arrowroot	93	389
Artichoke, globe	4	17
Artichoke, Jerusalem	5	21
Asparagus	5	21
Aubergine	4	17
Avocado pear	25	105
Bacon, very lean	92	385
Bacon, streaky	149	623
Bamboo shoot	9	38
Banana	22	92
Banana, 1	80-100	334-418
Barley, raw	102	426
Barley, boiled	34	142
Bass, raw	29	121
Bass, boiled or steamed	36	150
Beans, baked	26	109
Beans, broad	15	63
Beans, French, runner, raw	4	17
Beans, French, runner, boiled	2	8
Beans, French, runner, frozen	3	15
Beans, haricot, (Butter), raw	100-120	418-502
Beans, haricot, (Butter), boiled	25-30	105-125
Beans, lima, raw	96	402
Beanshoot	2-3	8-13
Beef, good quality lean only (e.g. fillet)	50	209
Beef, grilled with minimum fat	86	359
Beef, lean stewing steak (e.g. chuck)	90	376
Beef stock cube	30	125
Beef stock cube, 1	10	42

Food	Energy Value kcal	kJ
Beetroot, raw	7	29
Beetroot, boiled	14	59
Beetroot, pickled	8	33
Biscuit, plain	105	439
Biscuit, sweet	145	606
Blackberry, raw	8	33
Blackberry, stewed	6	25
Blackberry, canned	25	105
Blackcurrant, raw	10-12	42-50
Blackcurrant, stewed	8	33
Blackcurrant, canned	30	125
Black treacle	84	351
Brains	29-31	121-130
Bran	89	373
Brandy	75	315
Bread, brown	67-70	280-293
Bread, white	70	293
Bread, wholewheat	65	272
Bread, malt	71	297
Bread, currant	71	297
Bread, rye, per slice	55	230
Bread, starch reduced	71	297
Bream, raw	27	113
Bream, boiled or steamed	34	142
Broad beans, raw	30	125
Broccoli, raw	5	21
Broccoli, boiled	2-3	8-13
Brussels sprouts, raw	9	38
Brussels sprouts, boiled	5	21
Butter	205	863
Cabbage and cabbage greens, raw	5	21
Cabbage and cabbage greens, boiled	2-3	10-13
Cake, plain, made with fat	75-90	314-376
Cake, sponge, made without fat	60-67	251-280
Cake, sponge, made with fat	134	560
Candied peel	60	252
Cantaloupes	7	30
Caper	2	8
Carrot, raw	6-7	25-29
Carrot, boiled	6-7	25-29

Food	Energy Value kcal	kJ
Cashew nut	164	686
Cauliflower, raw	5	21
Cauliflower, boiled	2-3	8-13
Celeriac, raw	4	17
Celeriac, boiled	3-4	13-17
Celery, raw	3	13
Celery, canned or cooked	2-3	8-13
Cheese, Cheddar and similar	105-120	439-502
Cheese, Brie	88	368
Cheese, Camembert	88	368
Cheese, Cheshire	110	460
Cheese, Cottage, low-fat	26	110
Cheese, Danish Blue	94	393
Cheese, Edam	88	368
Cheese, Gloucester	114	476
Cheese, Leicester	110	460
Cheese, Parmesan	118	493
Cherry, fresh	11	46
Cherry, stewed	9-10	38-42
Chicken, lean, raw	40	166
Chicken, young, grilled, no coating	72	242
Chicken, young, boiled or roast	54	226
Chicken stock cube	30	125
Chicory	3	12
Chilli, fresh (See Pepper entry)		
Chilli, dried	88	369
Chives	10	42
Chocolate, milk (varies)	120-167	502-698
Chocolate, plain	155-160	648-669
Cider, dry, 600 ml/1 pint	200	836
Cocoa (unsweetened)	100	418
Coconut, fresh	100	418
Coconut, dried (desiccated/shredded)	180	752
Cod, raw	16	67
Cod, boiled or steamed	23	96
Cod, fried or grilled	40-45	167-188
Cod, smoked	22	92
Cod roe, fried	59	277
Cod roe, steamed or canned	28-30	117-125
Coffee, black, no sugar	negligible	
Coffee, with milk: 1 cup	36	150
Consommé, canned	3-6	13-25
Corn cob	15	63
Cornflour (Cornstarch)	100	418
Corn oil	255	1066
Crab, cooked	37	155
Crab, canned	32-36	134-150
Cream	100-128	418-535
Cream, sour	53	222
Crispbread (varies)	90-115	376-481
Cucumber	3	13
Currant, dried	76	318
Currant, fresh, black, red, white	8-12	38-50
Curry powder	67	280
Damson, fresh (with stone)	9	38
Damson, stewed (with stone)	8	33
Date, dried (without stone)	75	314
Date, dried (with stone)	50-60	209-251
Dill pickle	2	8
Dried breadcrumbs	101	422

Food	Energy Value kcal	kJ
Duck, raw, medium lean	47-62	196-259
Duck, roast	89	372
Eel, raw	90	376
Eel, smoked	93	392
Eel, smoked, stewed	106	443
Egg, 1 small, fried or scrambled	140	585
Egg, white, 1 small, raw or boiled	11	46
Egg, yolk, 1 small, raw or boiled	69	288
Eggplant	4	17
Endive	3	13
Fava (dried broad beans)	15	63
Fig, green, raw	12	50
Fig, dried	108	451
Fig, dried, stewed	30	125
Flounder, raw	20	84
Flounder, boiled or steamed	27	113
Flounder, fried	42	176
Flour, white	95-100	399-420
Flour, wholewheat	67-70	280-293
Frankfurter	70	293
Garlic, 1 clove	5	21
Gelatine	70	294
Gherkin	2	8
Ginger, stem	80	334
Golden syrup	84	351
Goose, raw	62-64	259-268
Goose, roast	92	385
Gooseberry, raw, dessert	10	42
Gooseberry, raw, green	4	17
Gooseberry, stewed	3	13
Gooseberry, canned	22	92
Grape	15	63
Grapefruit	6	25
Grapefruit juice, fresh	9	38
Grapefruit juice, canned, unsweetened	9	38
Ground almond	184	769
Haddock, fresh, raw	20	84
Haddock, boiled or steamed	28	117
Haddock, fried	50	209
Haddock, smoked, raw	20	84
Haddock, smoked, boiled or steamed	28	117
Hake, raw	23	96
Hake, boiled or steamed	30	125
Hake, fried	53	222
Ham, raw (cured or smoked)	142	594
Ham, boiled, lean only	62	259
Hare, stewed	55	230
Hare, roast	55	230
Heart, lambs'	45	188
Heart, ox	20	84
Heart, pig's	27	113
Herring, raw	67	280
Herring, soused	54	226
Herring, fried in oatmeal	67	280
Herring, fried or grilled without coating	73	305
Herring, canned	67	280
Herring, in tomato, canned	45	188
Herring, pickled	65	272

Food	Energy Value	
	kcal	kJ
Honey	82	344
Honeydew melon	10	40
Horseradish, fresh	36	151
Ice cream, (varies), average	31-60	130-251
Jam, average	74-80	309-334
Jelly, fruit-flavoured, made with water	18	75
Kidney	30	125
Kidney, fried or grilled with minimum fat	57	238
Kippers, raw	67	280
Kippers, baked	57	238
Kohlrabi, raw	14	59
Kohlrabi, boiled	11	46
Lamb, good quality, lean only (e.g. leg, cutlet)	40-60	167-251
Leek, raw	6	25
Leek, boiled	5	21
Lemon, juice	2	8
Lemon, whole	4	17
Lentil, dry	80	334
Lentil, boiled	27	113
Lettuce	4-5	17-21
Lime, raw	8	34
Lime, juice (fresh)	8	33
Liver	40	167
Liver, fried or grilled with minimum fat	74	309
Liver sausage, Continental	83	347
Loganberry, fresh	6	25
Loganberry, stewed	5	21
Macaroni, raw	102	426
Macaroni, boiled	32	134
Mackerel, raw	76	318
Mackerel, cooked (See Herring entry)		
Malt extract	85	356
Mango, ripe	19	78
Margarine	220	920
Marmalade, varies according to fruit	74-80	309-334
Marrow, (Squash), raw	2-3	8-13
Marrow, (Squash), boiled	1-2	4-8
Mayonnaise, average	110	460
Mayonnaise, low-calorie	50	209
Melon	4	17
Milk, fresh, whole	19	79
Milk, fresh, skimmed	10	42
Milk, dried, skimmed, powder	93	389
Milk, dried, skimmed, reconstituted	10	42
Milk, evaporated, full cream	45-47	188-196
Molasses (See Treacle entry)		
Muesli, breakfast cereal (varies according to ingredients)	100-107	418-447
Mullet	39	163
Mushroom, raw	1-2	4-8
Mushroom, fried	77	322
Mussels, cooked in water	25	105
Mustard powder	132	552

Food	Energy Value	
	kcal	kJ
Mutton, lean	75	314
Navy beans, dry	100-120	418-502
Navy beans, boiled	25-30	105-125
Nectarine	13	54
Noodle, boiled	32	134
Nuts, (without shells), almond	168	702
Nuts, (without shells), Brazil	180	752
Nuts, (without shells), cashew	164	686
Nuts, (without shells), chestnut	49	205
Nuts, (without shells), hazelnut	108	451
Nuts, (without shells), peanut	160-178	669-744
Nuts, (without shells), salted cashew	161	673
Nuts, (without shells), salted peanut	173-180	723-752
Nuts, (without shells), walnut	156	652
Oatmeal, raw	115	481
Oatmeal, as porridge	13	54
Okra, raw	10	41
Okra, steamed	9	38
Olive	30	125
Olive oil	264	1104
Olive oil, 1 tablespoon	100	418
Onion, raw	6	25
Onion, spring, raw	6	25
Onion, boiled	5	21
Onion, fried	93	389
Onion, pickled	4-6	17-25
Orange	9	38
Orange juice, fresh	10	42
Orange juice, canned, unsweetened	9	38
Oxtail	25	104
Ox tongue	84-88	351-368
Parsnip, raw	14	59
Parsnip, boiled	16	67
Pasta, raw, (varies)	95-102	399-426
Pasta, cooked	29	123
Peaches, raw	10	42
Peaches, dried	58	242
Peaches, dried, stewed	20	84
Peaches, canned	25	105
Pear, raw, dessert	11	46
Pear, raw, cooking	10	42
Pear, dried	50	209
Pear, dried, stewed	18	75
Pear, canned	20	84
Peas, fresh	23	95
Peas, fresh, cooked	20	83
Peas, dried	95	398
Peas, dried, boiled	29	122
Peas, frozen	20	84
Peas, frozen, cooked	19	80
Pepper, raw	10	42
Pineapple, raw	10	42
Pineapple juice, canned unsweetened	11	46
Plaice, raw	22	92
Plaice, boiled or steamed	29	121
Plaice, fried	66	276
Plum, raw, dessert	10	42
Plum, raw, cooking	7	29
Plum, stewed, (with stone)	5	21
Pork, lean only	67	280
Pork, fat only	112	468

Food	Energy Value kcal	kJ
Potato, raw	25	105
Potato, old, boiled	24	100
Potato, new, boiled	21	88
Potato, old, baked in skins, pulp only	30	125
Potato, old, baked in skins, with skin	24	100
Potato, old, mashed	34	142
Prawn, cooked, peeled	30	125
Prawn, cooked, with shell	11	46
Preserved ginger	80	334
Prune, with stone	37	155
Prune, without stone	46	193
Prune, stewed	19	79
Prune, canned	34	142
Pumpkin, raw	9	37
Pumpkin, baked	37	154
Pumpkin, boiled, mashed	9	37
Quince, raw	7	29
Quince, stewed	5	21
Rabbit, stewed	51	213
Radish	2	8
Raisin, seeded	70	293
Raspberry, raw	6	25
Raspberry, canned	22	92
Raspberry, frozen	18	75
Red cabbage	2	8
Redcurrant, raw	8	33
Redcurrant, stewed	7	29
Rhubarb, stewed	1	4
Rhubarb, canned	22	92
Rice, brown, raw	102	426
Rice, brown, boiled	34	142
Rice, white, raw	102	426
Rice, white, boiled	35	146
Rolled oats, raw	100-115	418-481
Salad dressing, French	115	482
Salmon, raw	50	209
Salmon, poached or steamed	57	238
Salmon, smoked	47-60	196-251
Salsify	5	21
Sauerkraut	2-3	8-13
Sausage, beef, raw	60	251
Sausage, beef, one, fried	81	339
Sausage, pork, raw	72	301
Sausage, pork, one, fried	93	389
Scallops, raw	23	95
Scallops, steamed	32	133
Semolina, raw	100	418
Sherry, dry	33	138
Sherry, sweet	36	150
Shrimp, peeled, cooked	24	99
Shrimp, canned, drained	34	144
Soya, protein	91	382
Spaghetti, raw	104	435
Spaghetti, boiled	33	138
Spice (varies)	60-100	252-420
Spinach	5-7	21-29
Sprat, smoked	91	380
Squid	14	58

Food	Energy Value kcal	kJ
Stem ginger	80	334
Stock cube	30	125
Strawberry, raw	7	29
Strawberry, canned	22	92
Strawberry, frozen in sugar	12	50
Sugar, dark brown	103	434
Sugar, icing	110	463
Sugar, light brown	112	468
Sugar, white	110	463
Sultana	76	318
Swede, raw	6	25
Swede, boiled	5	21
Sweetbread, stewed	51	213
Sweetcorn, canned or cooked	15	63
Syrup, golden or maple	84	351
Tapioca, raw	100	418
Tea, black, no sugar	negligible	
Tea, with milk: 1 cup	36	150
Tomato, raw	4-5	17-21
Tomato, fried	20	84
Tomato juice	6	25
Tomato sauce	25-32	105-134
Tomato paste	15	63
Tongue, fresh	84	355
Tongue, salted, boiled or canned	84-88	351-368
Trout, raw	31	130
Trout, boiled or steamed	38	159
Trout, smoked	36	150
Tuna, canned	76	318
Tuna, fresh	45	188
Turkey, boiled	29	121
Turkey, roast	56	234
Turnip, raw	5	21
Turnip, boiled	3	13
Veal, very lean	31	130
Veal, fried with minimum fat	61	255
Vegetable, mixed, frozen, boiled	18	77
Vegetable juice, canned	5	20
Vinegar	1	4
Walnut, shelled	156	652
Watercress	4	17
Watermelon	76	32
Wheatgerm	108	451
Whitebait, fried	152	635
Whiting, raw	19	79
Whiting, boiled or steamed	26	109
Whiting, fried	55	230
Yam, boiled	23	96
Yeast, extract (Vegemite)	46	195
Yeast and vegetable extracts	57	237
Yeast, compressed	13	55
Yogurt, low-fat	15	63
Yogurt, fat-free	10	42
Yogurt, flavoured	20-29	84-121
Zucchini (See Marrow entry)		

ACKNOWLEDGMENTS

Photography by Roger Phillips
Illustrations by Vana Haggerty, Ingrid Jacob & Isobel Balakrishnan
Food for photography prepared by Jackie Burrow & Zoë Camrass